THE HEART OF MAN; GOD'S TARGET

"For man looks at the outward appearance,
but the Lord looks at the heart."
1 Samuel 16:7b

Part One: My Life's Journey

Part Two: The Outflow of our Father's Love; a Sequel of Biblical Lessons.

By Harold Alfredo Geil

xulon PRESS

Dedication

I dedicate this book:

First and foremost to God, my heavenly Father and His Son the Lord Jesus Christ, with deep gratitude for laying the foundation of this book early in my life. Without the wisdom and the guidance of the Holy Spirit, this book would not have been written. I sincerely believe that God had His hand over me, while unfolding His plan for my life!

To my parents, Papa and Mama, for reflecting Christ's love through their lives, and for teaching me His Gospel since my earliest years.

To Martha, my faithful wife for twenty eight years, until she went home into the glorious presence of our heavenly Father, in February 1983, at age 50.

To Jeanie, whom I met after I came out of the valley of sorrow and happily married in September 1984.

To our five children: Carl, Charissa, Debbie, Gus, Lilly and their spouses, Toni, Jan, Mike, Jody, Ridgely; and to our twelve grandchildren, two great-grandchildren and to those yet to be born.

I highly treasure the congeniality, so evident among our children and their loved ones. I thank God for this unique gift.

To all our spiritual children and our many dear friends, relatives and prayer warriors across the United States, Canada, Argentina and Europe.

May this book help all of us in our relationship with Jesus Christ, the only way to our heavenly Father's heart.

Acknowledgements

I thank you Jeanie, my precious wife, for encouraging me while spending countless hours on the computer, and for editing and proofreading this book. I also thank Erin Mesday, Amy Martin and Ann Kasmer, for the tedious job of proof-reading this book.

I thank you Debbie Mesday and Amy Martin for the many ways you helped me when my computer knowledge ran out. Thank you Jan Zmuda, our family's computer expert, for promptly responding when my computer decided to become a monster.

The book review on the back cover was provided by our dear friend and spiritual daughter Amy Martin. Thank you Amy for your kind words.

Foreword

If you are not a Christian, because what you have seen and heard about Christianity has turned you off; however deep inside, you may wonder what your life is all about and how this whole universe came into being; then this book is for you. You will learn that there is a God, the Creator of all things who loves you and seeks to reveal Himself to you personally. This book is not about religion as such, but about developing a loving relationship with the God of Abraham, through Jesus Christ. God seeks your heart, that innermost part in you that will affect your whole life in order to grant you His love, joy and peace, beyond all expectations.

Karl Marx stated that "Religion is the Opium of the People." Ironically, there is a kernel of truth in this statement, in that religion without a personal relationship with Jesus Christ, will eventually lead people into a state of false security, offered by the lord of this world, whom the Bible calls the devil.

You may consider yourself a Christian, but you realize that your life is not what you really desire. There is an absence of joy and you are dragging yourself through life, wondering if this is all there is. Others seem to get it while you feel left out. This book will help you to better understand the Holy Bible and how applicable its message is for you.

You may be a born-again believer in Jesus Christ. You made a public commitment to Him and are now active in your church. Things are moving along pretty well, and you believe that when your life comes to an end you will go to heaven, to be with Jesus. Yet deep inside you are restless; you can't describe it but you are beginning to question if there is something missing in your relationship with God. You may have met Christians who seem to have an inner strength and their countenance reflects a joy that you wish you had. However, you don't dare to share your plight with anyone in your church for fear of being rejected. You may have moved from church to church trying to find the right one to the point of frustration. This book is certainly for you. I want to show you how you can enjoy intimacy with your heavenly Father and live a fulfilling life while still on this earth, and afterward enjoy what the Holy Bible describes in first Corinthians two, verse nine; "Eye has not seen, nor ear heard, nor have entered into the heart of man, the things which God has prepared for those who love Him."

O God, You have taught me from my youth;

And to this day I declare Your wondrous works.

Now also when I am old and gray headed,

O God, do not forsake me,

Until I declare Your strength to this generation,

Your power to everyone who is to come.

My lips shall greatly rejoice when I sing to You-

And my soul which You have redeemed.

My tongue also shall talk of Your righteousness,

All the day long.

Excerpts from Psalm 71

TABLE OF CONTENTS

PART ONE

PART TWO

Dear heavenly Father,

"I pray that through the reading of this book, many people will worship You from their hearts as the only true God, who created the universe and everything in it. You are Lord of heaven and earth, and You do not dwell in temples made with hands, nor are You worshipped with men's hands or lips as though You need anything, since You give to all life and breath, and all things.

You Father, made from One Man, Jesus Christ, and through His Blood, every nation of men to dwell in all the face of the earth, and determined their pre-appointed times and the boundaries of their habitation, so that they should seek You Lord in the hope that they may reach out for You and find You, though You are not far from each one of us. For in you we live and move and have our being. You have appointed a day on which You will judge the world in righteousness by the Man Jesus Christ whom You have ordained. You, Father, have given assurance of this to all men, by raising Jesus Christ from the dead.

I pray Father, that many of your hurting children will find peace and healing in body, soul, and spirit as I share my heart. I thank You Father, in Jesus' name;" Amen.

(Parts quoted from the apostle Paul as recorded in the book of Acts)

Introduction

W hat moved me to write this book when the world seems to be filled with them? People are bombarded with information from all directions; in fact, we are told that we live in an age of instant information. A period where there is a craving to know, a restlessness to get immediate answers to complex situations. The mind of men seems insatiable. Are people becoming more content, able to face and overcome hardships as a result of satisfying their intellectual cravings? On the surface it may seem so, but does it bring lasting inner peace and real joy?

I do not pretend to have answers for everyone's situation in life. But I can speak for myself by sharing my life's story. It is a journey through joy and pain, laughter and tears, victory and defeat under the watchful eyes and loving heart of my heavenly Father. Through this journey, the following Scripture verse helped me to keep moving ahead.

> "For You will light my lamp; the Lord my God will enlighten my darkness. For by You I can run against a troop. By my God I can leap over a wall" (Psalm 18: 28,29)

For months I woke up in the middle of the night with information that I believe was from God, giving me directions for what He wanted me to write. I know it was not my imagination; I felt compelled to get out of bed, record what I had received, and quickly slip back into my bed sheets. I am usually out of bed between four and five o'clock, and after my quiet time with God, I sit down at my computer. The joy in my heart, combined with a lot of energy to record what I have experienced in my life, has propelled me to write this book.

I believe that the urge to share what is deep in my heart has its roots in my early life; perhaps it was handed down from my forefathers. During the night of February 9th, 2008, I woke up after hearing these words, "What you have seen in your forefather's lives, what you have experienced in your own life, and seen in people you ministered to, must now be recorded." Deep in my heart, I knew it was my Shepherd's voice. He has fulfilled a desire that had been brewing in my heart since the end of the year 1953. I am awed of how great our God is and how perfectly He arranges the timing for the fulfillment of the desires of our heart. Little did I know that fifty-five years had to pass before this book became reality.

I have divided this book into two parts. Part one is essentially the story of my life, whereas part two is a collection of articles written over a ten year period in which I describe my spiritual growth. The reader will encounter a great variety of Bible quotations that I believe will help him in the strengthening of his faith.

God blessed me with generations of Christian believers whose faith in Jesus Christ nurtured my desire to know Jehovah, the God of Abraham. I was born in Buenos Aires, Argentina in 1931 to parents who had left their native Germany after World War I. They were instrumental in founding a Baptist Church in Buenos Aires, and for thirty-one years it remained my spiritual home. I committed my life to Jesus Christ in November 1943. Standing before a congregation of over two hundred, I gave a testimony stating that I desired to follow the Lord Jesus Christ. On November 28th, I was baptized and welcomed into the church fellowship. My pastor gave me a German hymn book with an inscription from the Apostle Paul's letter to the Ephesians 6:10, "Finally my brethren, be strong in the Lord and in the power of His might." My parents were delighted, but many of my friends were not impressed at all.

Growing up in a major metropolis, often called "Paris of the South," gave Satan ample opportunities to lead me astray. I thank God that the enemy has not gained the upper hand over my life, because I believed that the power of Christ in me is greater than he who is in the world.

In retrospect, I realize that at the beginning of every decade of my life, God led me deeper into yet undiscovered mysteries of His Kingdom. I know He wanted my heart; not just part of it, but all of it. Obviously, at that time I did not know what this entailed.

Through the years, I have learned that my obedience to God is essential for a fruitful life. In order for His love to flow through me, I had to surrender areas of my heart that I had reserved for myself. This does not mean in any way, that I had to live in solitary confinement, separated from enjoying good things in life. The joy of the Lord has always been my strength. However, I wanted my entire life to be under the direction of God's Holy Spirit. My awareness of His presence gave me the assurance of His love for me and the strength to move on in life.

"In this you will rejoice, though now for a little time, where needed, you have been saddened by various temptations, so that the genuineness of your faith, which is much more precious than gold that perishes, though it is tested by fire, may be found to praise, honor and glory when Jesus Christ will be revealed, whom having not seen you love. Though now you do not see Him, yet believing you rejoice with joy inexpressible and full of glory" (1 Peter 1:6-8).

For my ninth birthday my parents gave me a German New Testament of the Bible. For years it was my faithful companion. I have always treasured the words of Jesus Christ, and for lack of better words, I dare to say that they were inscribed into my heart. However, I was yet unable to understand God's desire to unite my heart to His. Through many years of walking on the road of hard knocks, I learned that my heart needed to be transformed to conform to the Lord's plans for my life; in other words, the old had to die in order to make room for the new. This process of sanctification will continue in all Christian believers until we appear before Him in glory.

God hates lip service. His target is our heart, because Jesus said; "These people come near Me with their mouth, and honor Me with their lips, but their heart is far from Me. In vain do they serve Me, because they are teaching their own opinions as if they were doctrines" (Matthew 15:8,9).

The most in-depth changes in my life came during periods of difficult trials and tribulations. The year 1983 became the most painful period of my life. However, in spite of great sorrow I learned many intense lessons that opened my eyes and heart to what God was keeping in store for me. It completely changed the course of my life, and my desire to be a living testimony of the power and glory of Jesus Christ intensified. My inner conviction of the veracity of God's Word, the Bible, and believing with all my heart that the bodily resurrected Lord Jesus Christ is the living Word of God, has led me into a deeper relationship with God. This experience, details of which I will share in this book, has led me into some awesome encounters with the Lord Jesus Christ, followed by overflowing love, joy and peace. The words from Acts 22:15 came to me: "You shall be a witness to all men of what you have seen and heard."

Since my childhood, I have learned to recognize the voice of my Shepherd; but obedience to Him had to be forged in the Master's school. While growing up under the care of loving German parents, I first learned their language, but soon my brain had to make room for two additional languages; Spanish and English.

I attended a private German school for seven years, followed by three years of a technical high school specializing in various trades. Upon completion, I was awarded a master electrician diploma and consequently employed by the Department of Education of the presidency of General Juan D. Peron. At the same time, I enrolled in a polytechnic institute, specializing in electrical engineering. For four years, my weekly schedule consisted of two hours a day commuting to downtown Buenos Aires to my full time job, followed by four hours evening classes. On Saturdays, I attended school for twelve hours and on Sundays I was busy in church.

In 1952, following my graduation, I was drafted into the Argentine Armed Forces. The draft was mandatory for native Argentine citizens. While in the military, I was chosen to become the interpreter for the Equestrian Olympic team headed for a seven months tour through eight European countries, including the 15th Olympic Games in Helsinki, Finland. This experience was a clear answer to my prayers. Upon my release from military duty I held management positions at Mercedes Benz and Siemens, both German international corporations.

In order to be a witness for Jesus Christ in the corporate world, I had to learn from the apostle Paul how not to be ashamed of the Gospel of Christ, for it is the power of God unto salvation for everyone who believes, (Romans 1:16) while not losing sight of the words of Jesus, to "be wise as serpents and without malice as doves" (Matthew 10:16b).

I learned early in life that I would not push my faith upon people, but wait for the direction of the Holy Spirit. I believed that since God created mankind, every human being is entitled to get to know the One who gave them life; and if the message of salvation is presented with love and conviction, it will impact the hearer.

One day, while being interviewed by a leader of an international Christian broadcasting ministry in Buenos Aires, I was asked: "Are you a mystic?" My inner reaction to this question was reflected by a smirk. In my mind I saw a man lying on a bed of nails, engulfed in a cloud of smoke, floating in mid air, while mumbling some weird sounds. I picked up a trace of sarcasm in the interviewer's voice; perhaps even a bit of contempt. But he was a friend of mine and I knew where he was coming from. I answered: "It may seem that at times I am floating in mid air, but my feet are firmly on the ground." I was convinced, even early in my life, that Jesus Christ was not a mystic, but a perfect human being, the Son of God and a friend of sinners.

I thank God that I have inherited a sound mind and a good sense of humor; two powerful characteristics to not only survive in a world of tensions and controversies, but to overcome hardships and celebrate victories afterward.

In 1962, I sensed a strong desire to immigrate to the United States. When I presented my plans to my company, I was offered an attractive opportunity to move to Germany. However, my mind and heart were set on the United States of America. My whole plan to leave Argentina, with my wife Martha and my sons Carl age 6 and Gus age 3, including the way it all became reality, can only be described as a miracle. Later I will share how God intervened, as He did many times in my life.

In July 1962, after three weeks of sailing on board the German vessel Cap Castillo, we arrived in New York City, full of hope and great excitement. It had been my wish for years that when I move to the United States, I wanted to enter through what I believed to be the "front door;" sailing past the Statue of Liberty, right into New York. In New York

City we took a Greyhound bus, first to Chicago, where we met dear friends who then drove us to our final destination in Milwaukee, Wisconsin to start a new life.

Chapter One

The Faith of My Forefathers

My Father, whom I called Papa, was a peaceful and truly loving Prussian. Contradictory as this may seem, he was my greatest mentor. He was a man of few words, but his actions spoke loudly of his heart commitment to Jesus Christ. Murmuring and complaining or using harsh language, were not characteristics of Papa's personality. He was a man who exuded love and treated people with kindness and respect.

Born in Essen, the industrial center of Germany in 1892, he was inducted into the Kaiser's Army (Emperor Wilhelm II) at Potsdam, near Berlin in 1914. During the four years of World War I, he served first as a telegraph operator and later as a medic. His relationship with Jesus Christ was as deeply spiritual as it was down to earth. His words and demeanor put people at ease when in his presence. Even in his more advanced age, and in spite of some extra body weight, he was able to march in his Prussian goose-step while bursting into hardy laughter.

My father's parents and grandparents were born in Danzig, East Prussia. After decades of political upheaval in Europe, they decided to return to Germany and settle in Essen on the Ruhr River in the 1870's. They became believers in

Jesus Christ through the Baptist movement started by Johann G. Oncken.

Born in 1800, Oncken was an orphan, adopted and taken to England by a Scottish couple where he witnessed the great revivals in Wales and Scotland. Deeply affected by the move of God's power, he gave his heart to Jesus Christ. He returned to his native Germany in 1823 and was later baptized by a friend in the Elbe River by night. Shortly after, he established the first Baptist Church in Hamburg. His famous statement was; "Every Baptist-A-Missionary."

In spite of severe persecution by the established churches, the movement spread to various European countries with great success. Oncken distributed two million Bibles throughout Europe. His zeal for Christ permeated his entire movement and was still well alive when my parents helped establish a Baptist church in Buenos Aires, Argentina in 1927.

My paternal grandfather had an education in business and was employed as a manager at the Krupp Industrial complex in Essen on the Ruhr. In 1902, my grandparents decided to immigrate to the Unites States. My Papa, the oldest of four children, was ten years old. Sailing from Hamburg on board the ocean liner Deutschland, they arrived at Ellis Island for immigration processing. From New York City they boarded a train to Elizabeth, New Jersey, where my grandfather opened a shoe store with a friend as his associate.

Two years later, his associate had to return to Germany due to the sudden death of his father. Not knowing if or when his friend would come back, coupled with other adverse circumstances, prompted my grandparents to return to Germany. My Papa told me that this was a hasty decision generated by his mother. He often mentioned that he wished his family would have stayed in the USA. One of my Papa's wise expressions that frequently helped me when faced with a difficult decision was; "My son, no matter what you are faced with; always keep a cool head and a warm heart, with a smile on your face, knowing in your heart that Jesus Christ is always with you." Obviously, "hot headed and cold hearted people" were not my Papa's favorite ones.

It boggles my mind, when I picture my grandparents leaving their hometown for the seaport of Hamburg with four children, ranging from ages one to ten, sailing across the ocean to New York and settling in Elizabeth New Jersey, only to return to the old country within two years. Did I inherit some of their wanderlust?

Back in Germany, my father pursued his education in the towns of Bielefeld and Rothenburg. I often wished I had asked Papa to share more about his life. Fortunately he decided to write his autobiography, just a couple of years before his death in 1971. Upon reading it, I was moved by my Dad's relationship with God; his trust in Jesus Christ was instrumental in my decision to follow Jesus.

The Lord manifested Himself to Papa in amazing ways. In 1914, before he left his home in Essen to report to the recruiting center near the capital city of Berlin, his parents invited him to a farewell dinner. He told his parents that the Lord revealed to him that he would return from the war unharmed. Well, in 1918, after four years of horrible experiences as a telegraph operator and a medic in the trenches of several fronts, he walked from France to his home in Essen, Germany, unharmed.

Before leaving for Berlin, a neighbor had asked Papa about his interest in a girlfriend. He responded; "my future wife is now seven years old." He was twenty-two when he was inducted. Amazingly my mother was fifteen years younger than my father. His intimacy with His heavenly Father enabled Papa to hear the voice of his Shepherd. I believe that his heart was free of major blockages that keep so many sincere Christians from communing with God. Without many words, he certainly provided the foundation for my quest for more of God.

After World War I, my grandparents decided to return to the Unites States. But since immigration for Germans was closed, they decided to follow a promotional for Europeans to come to Argentina. In 1919 the five member Geil family arrived in Buenos Aires, wondering what in this new world was waiting for them. The obvious soon became evident; they had to learn a new language and face a culture shock.

My father, age 27, found employment with a construction company as a structural engineer. Tough times were ahead. His restless parents provided enough distraction to keep their "boy's" mind from choosing a wife. Papa certainly had enough contenders ready to fill the vacuum. But it was not yet to be. Not only his parents, but also other members of his family demanded his attention, and his finances. However, in 1926, to the chagrin of his family, my mother suddenly showed up and filled the great vacuum in his life. I will share this event as I cover my mother's background.

Argentina was also affected by the Great Depression at which time my father lost his employment. In order to feed his family, he decided to raise chickens and cultivate a wonderful vegetable garden. Papa just trusted his Lord with all his heart and He never failed him.

I was only about three years old, but I remember my mother and father running their hatchery. In the company of my two brothers Luis and George, I had lots of fun feeding and chasing the hens and roosters. Cuddling tiny chicks right after they worked themselves out of the egg was a delightful treat that I cannot forget. I believe that God filled my young heart with love and tenderness toward all life.

Papa found employment with the construction division of Siemens as a structural engineer, specializing in the design of reinforced concrete high rise buildings, bridges, subway tunnels, etc. He commuted by train and subway to his office in downtown Buenos Aires.

In 1934, Paul von Hindenburg, president of Germany died and was succeeded by Adolf Hitler who declared himself Fuehrer (Leader), combining the offices of president and chancellor in one. As the head of the national socialist party, (Nazi Party) he exercised dictatorial power over the German nation. He was a very angry man. Behind his façade, profoundly embedded in his personality, there was this split inner child that would switch from strange sentimentalism into a raging despot at the snap of a finger.

I remember my father wearing a black tie in honor of Hindenburg, while taking a "wait and see" attitude toward Hitler. One day I saw Papa reading Hitler's Mein Kampf; (My Struggle) but it was not long after, that the book disappeared. On my Papa's office wall, there was a picture depicting four German leaders: Frederick the Great, King of Prussia, Otto von Bismarck the unifier of the first Reich (Empire), Kaiser William II, emperor of Germany and Adolf Hitler.

Several years later, I saw Papa cutting away the picture of Hitler, leaving the other three intact.

During one of many conversations about the war, I over-heard Papa saying, with his father and brother Eric agreeing, that the Nazis have "touched the Apple of God's Eye," meaning the persecution of the Jewish people, and that they believed that Germany would lose the war. My parents had a number of Jewish friends. My pastor who baptized me had Jewish roots. He was a loving man of God, and a frequent guest in our home. His laying on of hands, while praying over someone, deeply touched me. He was one of my spiritual mentors. He had fled Nazi Germany, and shortly after settling in Argentina, he became the Pastor of our church in 1937.

While still a boy, Mother used to share an interesting account about Frederick the Great, King of Prussia. One of his servants was a believer in Jesus Christ, who often shared his faith in the King's Palace. One day the king summoned him to his office. He asked his servant; "What makes you believe that God is real?" "The Jewish people, Your Majesty;" he answered.

My father never forced me to go to church or read the Bible. Most of the time I watched him act out what he believed, and that was really all I needed. He rose very early in the morning, and the times I saw him come out of his bedroom, he held the Bible under his arm ready for his quiet time with God, followed by physical exercise. Around seven AM he commuted to his office in downtown Buenos Aires. After his eight or nine hour work schedule, he would pick up extra work assignments from an architectural firm owned by R&K, the initials of two Jewish architects in order to supplement his income. Papa was highly appreciated during the nearly thirty years he worked for them. My parents often said that this was a special blessing from God

I cannot overstate how strongly my Papa's faithfulness to the Lord influenced my life. Without any doubt, there was enough turbulence in Argentina to disrupt the lives of the population. Whether political unrest, galloping inflation or conflict among people; my Papa's trust in Jesus Christ seemed unshaken.

The following episode was to me, one of the most powerful examples of my Papa's spiritual strength. In 1947, two years after WWII, tens of thousands of immigrants from many different countries settled in Argentina. I befriended several teenagers who had recently come from Germany. They had experienced the ravages of the war that no doubt had left them with deep emotional scars. We became friends and before long we were out camping. Sitting around the camp fire we tried to outdo each other by telling all kinds of stories. Whether fact or fiction, it was immaterial as long as it stirred up the excitement of a bunch of adventurous teenagers. One evening, while enjoying our campfire in my parent's back yard, Pete (not his real name) one of the teenagers from Germany, shared how a group of young boys roamed the streets of the heavily bombed city of Berlin, looking for hand grenades, some of which were undetonated. Then he told us that he would give us a demonstration of a flamethrower. He lit a bunch of large matches and started blowing into the flame when suddenly he fell to the ground and started to roar like a lion. This was not fiction!

As Pete's body went into convulsions; we tried to subdue him with little success. Only a few feet from our campfire was my Papa's office built with fiber-cement outer walls. He kicked against the office walls with such fury that some of these four by eight sheets broke into pieces. To make matters worse, it was past midnight when everybody was asleep; but not for long. Suddenly I saw Papa in his nightgown coming out of the house. Oh no; what is going to happen next? What followed was something to behold. Pete suddenly stopped his rampage, jumped to his feet and ran to my Papa, and while falling on his knees he held on to my dad's hands and in tears begged to be forgiven. To this day, I am amazed by Papa's peaceful and loving response to such destructive behavior. I knew without any doubt that demonic forces were at work but soon subdued by the power of Jesus Christ manifested through my Papa! My parents did not demand that I break off my friendship. They knew that their son loved to share the Gospel with his friends, even when circumstances were not really conducive. My brothers and I repaired the damaged office and the whole incident became history.

My grandparents Geil were blessed with a strong faith in God. Grandma suffered from open varicose veins which made it very difficult for her to move around and her legs needed constant attention. With her eyeglasses clamped to her nose, she spent a lot of time reading the Bible and knitting endlessly. I know she loved her grandchildren, which meant a lot to me, as she expressed her affection through lovely birthday cards.

As Grandma's health deteriorated in her advanced age, my Papa decided to sleep near his mother's bed in order to be available when she needed help. Her two sons and two daughters took turns in taking their mother into their homes. Obviously this was not a frictionless operation as the mix of personalities was not conducive to total harmony; to say the least. One early morning at five twenty, Papa heard his mother's voice; "Ludwig I am going home." After he walked to her bedside he knew that she had left her body to meet Jesus! It was the day of Pentecost, May 17th, 1958. Grandma was ninety two years old. I was standing outside the door when my Papa informed me about his mother's departure. Interestingly, in May 1959, also on the day of Pentecost, my son Gus was born.

My Mother;
whom I called Mama, was also a devout Christian, with a caring heart. She was an excellent cook, a seamstress, a gardener, a wonderful hostess, and much more. Visitors came and went, rarely disappointed. We, three brothers called our home "the bridge to the Old Country." Buenos Aires was Argentina's seaport to the world, and so, what better place was there in town than the "Geil Hotel" for friends, relatives or even strangers from different towns to stop over on their journey to Europe. I wondered how many guests were awakened by Mama's prayers, since her prayer room was not soundproof. I always knew when Mama was praying.

Born in West Prussia, Germany in 1907 (now part of Poland) she was the youngest of twelve children. Her oldest brother Johann was twenty when Mama was born. There was relatively little that was unknown to me in my mother's life. Some things that I didn't know were revealed at her deathbed, when she was ninety-two years old. She was an avid story teller, and in her son Harold she found receptive ears. I loved my mother and I knew that she loved me. She had a good sense of humor and was certainly not a legalist, because her faith in the Lord was as spiritual as it was down to earth.

My forefathers' inability to develop deep roots often reminded me of the children of Israel as recorded in the Old Testament of the Bible. However, in most cases they were displaced through circumstances not of their own making. My mother's parents were born in Galizien, Austria, after their forefathers had left Germany. Near the end of the 19th century my grandparents returned to Germany and reestablished German citizenship. Because of their frequent moves, I am unable to trace their exact itinerary.

From what my mother shared I was able to get a good description of their lives. Her forefathers were traditional Lutherans. However, Mama's parents accepted Jesus Christ as their Lord and were baptized in a Baptist church, established through the work of Johann Gerhard Oncken. My grandfather had an agricultural education and was a landowner in an area near Berlin and the burgomaster of two adjacent villages for twelve years. The story goes that when he committed his life to Christ and asked to be baptized as a believer, his wife threatened to divorce him. As Lutherans they had received infant baptism and it was inconceivable to be baptized again.

While my grandfather was on a work-related trip, my grandma accepted Jesus Christ as her Lord and Savior. Upon return from his trip on a Sunday, grandpa looked for his wife and was told that she had attended the Baptist church. As he entered the church he saw that the front pew was occupied by baptismal candidates. To his great surprise he discovered Marie, his wife, among them. This was one of the most joyful days of his life. Later, my grandpa became an ordained elder. His commitment to His heavenly Father and his faith in Jesus Christ deeply transformed his life. He truly affected the lives of his children and future generations. His was a faith forged in the furnace of hard trials and tribulations. My grandparents Hack had twelve children; seven boys and five girls of which my mother was the youngest. Five boys died before age nineteen. I often pondered upon this great tragedy that also affected many other male descendants. Many years later, the Holy Spirit began to shed light and insight into this tragedy. I told Mama that I believed that there was a death curse on my grandfather's generational line. Through much prayer and personal ministry, I know that this curse was broken over my family, by the power of the Blood and the cross of Jesus Christ.

Another awesome experience in my grandparent's lives, that I cannot forget, took place near the beginning of World War I, circa 1915. My grandpa was at a town meeting trying to resolve an embezzlement issue. The meeting went beyond midnight, and grandpa had to walk home through a wooded area along a lake. Suddenly, he had a strong urge to fall on his knees and call on the Lord for protection. When he got home, grandma opened the door and said: "George, what happened? The Lord woke me up and told me to pray for you." Miraculously it was the same time grandpa was on his knees. Not knowing what or if anything strange had happened, they went to sleep.

The next morning, while on his way to the town hall, Grandpa was approached by the nearby bartender who was very upset. "Mister Hack, do you know what happened last night? It was after midnight when this man stormed into the bar and ordered several drinks. After a while he began to share that you were walking near the lake when suddenly you knelt down to pray. He was hiding behind a bush pointing his gun at your head. Then he saw two men dressed in white shining robes walking next to you." Grandpa responded that he saw no one but quickly said; "My God sent angels to protect me." The story spread through the town and the suspect asked Grandpa for mercy. All charges were dropped.

According to my mother's account, her father was the best man in the world. As a young boy I felt proud to have such wonderful forefathers. However, later in life I often wondered why certain sinful habits began to surface as I grew in my faith in God and in my understanding of the Holy Scriptures. Where or when did I acquire them? Who taught me these strange things? Many years passed before I began to realize that, although God is the Giver of all life, there is also an "inheritance" coming down from our forefathers that is affecting our lives. The Bible cites many accounts of how God's law of sowing and reaping has strongly affected the lives of His children.

My paternal grandparents and the rest of my Papa's family lived within a short distance from our home in Buenos Aires, which gave me the opportunity to interact with them.

However, my mother was separated from her parents at age nineteen because of circumstances not of her own making. She never saw them again for the rest of her ninety two years. In my increased desire to corroborate some of Mama's stories about her parents, I had to consult her sister who lived with us for over twelve years. From what my aunt did not share with me, I tried to fill in the blanks through my own imagination. As the youngest of twelve siblings, Mama may have received preferential treatment from a father, who by then had softened his disciplinary methods. While enjoying my wonderful mother I had to wait decades before finding answers to my intriguing questions about her parents' lives.

Later in my life, as I became involved in a prayer ministry, I realized the importance of being aware of and addressing generational and personal iniquities, preferably before the onset of old age. First and foremost we need to be reminded through the Holy Scriptures, that all Christian believers will appear before the judgment of Christ, not to be condemned, but to give an account of our lives on earth and receive the

Lord's reward. Furthermore, a "clean house" will also make life a lot easier for our potential caretakers.

Mama's oldest brother Johann left Germany for Argentina in 1922 and settled in a northern province near the jungle. He had his share of miraculous experiences, first in Germany and then in a new country more were waiting for him. During WWI he was buried alive under the debris of a bombed out house for several days, before he was finally found alive. My uncle had a large scar on his face, a reminder of an accident he had as a youngster. While playing on his father's farm he was attacked by a bull that dragged him on his horns. Thank God he was rescued by his mother who had incredible control over the animal. Uncle Hans, as he was called, was an amazing man of God. In the 1920's, He established a Church in the province of Entre Rios that is still functioning today. I admired his faith in the Lord. He was a man who exuded strength and authority. Whenever he came to Buenos Aires for business, he would stay with us and I would not miss a word he spoke.

In 1926, my grandparents Hack left Germany and sailed to Argentina with their son Carl and daughters Emilie and Hildegard, my mother. My father, who had been in Argentina since 1919, learned that a ship was arriving from Germany and went to the port of Buenos Aires to "meet his bride." As passengers were disembarking, he had his eyes on the Hack family and saw Hildegard who was nineteen years old. He introduced himself, met Hildegard a few times and married her in June of 1927. It still amazes me to this day how Papa, who seemed so reticent, was able to pull this off. Without any doubt, the Lord was in it. Papa treasured his gift from God all his life. He modeled in a unique way how a man should love his wife.

After arriving in Buenos Aires, my grandparents Hack joined their son Johann, who had settled in a northern province in 1922. My uncle worked as a saddle maker and later established a car dealership and an auto repair shop. These were times of great hardship. To start a life in such a wild environment reminded me of Robinson Crusoe.

I remember my uncle Johann telling me that one day he had a conflict with a native man. One evening as he walked into a heavy wooded area, he saw this native approaching him with an ax. My uncle stopped while the man held his ax up ready to strike him. Uncle Johann, filled with godly courage, looked straight into the man's eyes and commanded: "In the name of Jesus Christ, my Lord, I command that you leave." The man's arms stopped in mid-air. He later became his friend and helper. This man was a leader of an Indian tribe who helped my uncle start his business. When my uncle needed help to harvest his crop, the chief would bring his entire tribe.

Another miraculous event that happened in my uncle's life took place when he heard an audible voice at midnight while asleep; "Johann, your shop is on fire!" Running out of his house he saw his business in flames. Thank God, most of it could be salvaged.

My parents planned their wedding to be celebrated at her parent's place, in June of 1927. My grandpa, who was an ordained elder, was to officiate at the ceremony. My uncle Johann, his wife and their four sons were due to arrive a few days before the wedding in their model 1923 Ford truck. It had been raining for days which made the dirt roads very treacherous. As the day of their arrival drew close, my grandpa walked out of the house, when he was approached by a neighbor who heard about an accident on the road from La Paz, my uncle's town. Soon he heard that my uncle and his family were involved in that accident. When they finally arrived, the shock of what had happened struck everyone around. The truck spun around on the muddy road and landed on its side. Their son Harald fell out of the truck and was pinned under the vehicle. Badly injured and wrapped in a blanket he was carried into the house. Harald so much wanted to be at the wedding and recite a long poem He had memorized. Although his wish was fulfilled, shortly there-after he went home to be with his Lord. Four years later, when I was born, Mama named me Harald. Later when I became an American citizen I changed my name to Harold.

My parents wedding became a town event that lasted for several days; people just came whether invited or properly dressed or not. That somehow became a practice in the Geil home. I believe that the home I grew up in was "inhabited" by the Spirit of God. They were blessed with the gift of hospitality and God always took care of them.

Not long after the wedding, my grandmother Hack was bitten by a Yarara, a venomous snake with a deadly bite. Grandpa, never slow to act, saw two blisters on his wife's leg. With a sharp object he cut them open, sucked out the venom, and spit it out. He saved grandmas' life. However, in a rela-tively short time grandma's hair began to turn white. This determined the end of my grandparent's stay in Argentina. In 1928, shortly after my brother Luis was born, they returned to Germany. My mother never saw them again. It is sad that I never knew my grandparents Hack.

My parents moved back from northern Argentina to Buenos Aires to start their new life. Mama, who "dared" to marry Papa, soon became the black sheep in the family. Her mother-in-law and her two sisters-in-law were not in any way ready to welcome Mama, because they were losing my Papa's support. Thank God, Mama was an overcomer. In 1928 my parents had their first son, Luis.

After Papa married his bride, his brother Eric thought it would be nice to marry Mama's sister Emily, who agreed with the idea. They married and lived with my parents for twelve years. Their only child, Elizabeth (Lissy), was born nineteen days before I saw the light of the world in 1931. I loved them as wonderful mentors in my relationship with the Lord. My brother George was born in 1932. I was only sixteen months "older" than George and our relationship was always a close one, even to this day. Lissy had no idea of what she would have to put up with, living with three cousins in the same house. Perhaps it was during those twelve formative years that I learned to stick up for the "underdog."

Chapter Two

Growing Up in Buenos Aires, Argentina

The Republic of Argentina is the southernmost country of South America. It is a federation of twenty-three provinces and the autonomous capital city of Buenos Aires. It is bordered by the countries of Paraguay and Bolivia in the North, Brazil and Uruguay in the northeast and Chile in the west. The Andes Mountains run all along Western Argentina, dividing it from Chile. Argentina's highest mountain peak is the Aconcagua with an altitude of 22,830 feet, the highest point in the Western and Southern hemisphere. The name means "The Sentinel Stone" in the Quechua language. The climate of Buenos Aires is classified as moderate, with temperatures ranging from 45 to the eighties (Fahrenheit).

At times we had early morning frosts with temperatures in the upper twenties. However, extremes of below zero in the Patagonia region all the way south to Tierra del Fuego, to above 100 degrees in the tropical north, offer the adventurous traveler limitless opportunities for recreation.

Argentina declared independence from Spain on July 9th, 1816. Its present population numbers approximately forty million, more than double than what it was when I grew up. The highest percentage of Argentina's population is of European origin, mostly from Spain and Italy. Other ethnic groups include Britons, Germans, and many others.

The capital city of Buenos Aires is located within the province of Buenos Aires. Including the suburbs it has a population of about twelve million inhabitants. Often called the "Paris of the South," Buenos Aires is a wonderful cosmopolitan city. People are friendly and easy to engage in conversations. The "abrazo criollo," (bear hug) is a common way for men to greet each other. Women kiss each other on both cheeks, even when only meeting casually. Generally, people engage in friendly conversations; however at times I had to accelerate my pace in order to distance myself from displays of hot tempered conflict.

With my roots in the German culture, known for their "Gemuetlichkeit," strengthened my ability to open up to people. The word "gemuetlich" is defined as agreeable, cheerful, cozy, etc. This warmth and openness is very obvious in church circles. I am aware that I am taking the risk of touching on human characteristics that may be frowned upon as too emotional. Be this as it may, I appreciate a healthy cultural blend because it served me well.

Argentina experienced a great deal of turmoil, mainly from 1946 through 1955 during General Juan D. Peron's presidency. He was deposed by the military after a bloody revolution and left the country for Paraguay and later was exiled in Spain. In 1973, after years of political violence against the military government, Peron returned from exile to resume the presidency and after one year he died. He was succeeded by his third wife Isabel, who was his vice-president. A military coup removed her from office on March 24, 1976.

I was born during the Great Depression in April 1931 in the town of Villa Ballester, a suburb bordering the city of Buenos Aires. When the time of my birth approached, my father notified the mid-wife Mrs. Estrella. When the most critical time had arrived, Mrs. Estrella was nowhere to be seen. This was the moment when Papa, my dear father, had to put into practice what he had learned as a medic during World War I, namely to bring me into this world. My mother told me that when she was in danger of bleeding to death, the mid-wife walked in. Apparently her horse and buggy got caught in a traffic jam. She admired Papa's courageous intervention.

As I previously mentioned, I was named after my cousin who had died in a truck accident. My middle name was to be the name of the first male visitor. It was our church elder, a dear man of God, who became one of my mentors in the faith. His name was Alfred. Consequently, Alfredo became my name for my Argentinean friends, who were afraid of breaking their tongues trying to pronounce, Harald.

Though my parents were kind and very encouraging, there were consequences for bad behavior. Sometimes, after my Papa came home from his office, he had to complete what Mama was not able to achieve in her naughty boy's behavior. A mother's bare hand was often not enough to convince me to obey my Mama's instructions, when I thought I was right. It required the help of a little willow twig that Papa kept in a secret place, securely hidden from his three curious boys... so he thought. At times, while Papa unsuccessfully searched for his "disciplinary aid," I noticed that his determination to punish his boy' began to fizzle out. Adding to this my cry for mercy mixed with "crocodile tears," moved my Papa's tender heart and his hand often stopped in mid-air, or right after the first landing.

Behind our house was an elevated water tank with a fire ladder. One day, I believe it was in 1934, neighbors rushed to the streets with great excitement, while looking to the sky. My uncle climbed up on the ladder of the water tank to get a better view of what was moving across the sky. I was only allowed to climb up three steps. People were shouting; "Look, look, the German airship (blimp) Graf Zeppelin." It was an awesome sight. No wonder, this thing was 776 feet long, 100 feet in diameter, and 110 feet high, and moving at a speed of 80 miles an hour. We were used to watching biplanes and gliders on an airfield not too far from our house, but they looked like grasshoppers by comparison.

Since my early childhood I had an endless fascination for just about anything. There was something in me that was larger than me; I had to find out for myself what made people tick. Why are there restrictions like; "You can't do this or that." Even when I started to read in the Bible; "Thou shall not..." why not? Somehow, I had to know in order to satisfy my curiosity, often with painful consequences. Soon after wiping away my tears, I continued to investigate, asking endless questions; I just had to know. Deep inside me was an insatiable hunger for God, mixed with deep inner contentment. The word eternity fascinated me to no end! The Bible begins with the words "in the beginning God created the heavens and the earth." Well, if there was a beginning, who then created God? I was only in second or third grade when our teacher gave us an "answer" to what eternity means. He wanted us to picture a mountain the size of Mt. Everest made totally of solid diamond. Then he proceeded to explain to us that every hundred years, a little bird would come and sharpen its beak on the mountain; and when the mountain is totally worn off, he said, one second of eternity has passed. I looked around wondering what my friends were thinking and I felt like I was the only one in class who didn't discard this description as ridiculous. Although fascinated by this story for years to come, it did not satisfy my curiosity about eternity until my faith in God was grounded in His word, the Holy Scriptures.

As the Nazi propaganda machine worked its way into Argentina, our lives changed dramatically.

My two brothers and I attended a German school. The traditional German flag on our school was replaced by the Nazi swastika flag. This new trend began to affect our curriculum. I heard people saluting each other with "Heil Hitler," while holding up their right arm. Nazi rallies were held in clubs and special camaraderie meals were served in schools. Fortunately, the Nazi flag was removed from our school not long after it had been displayed. Street riots broke out to the point of making it dangerous for us to walk to and from school. The government was forced to keep a lid on Nazi propaganda, specifically after WWII broke out.

I remember my Papa taking me to some of these events related to our school activities. As we approached the admission ticket office, Papa was greeted with Heil Hitler. Obviously he raised some eyebrows when calmly responding with, "good morning." His employer expected him to join the Nazi party; all to no avail. Papa had a strong faith and profound assurance that Jesus Christ was directing his ways through the power of the Holy Spirit. I admired Papa for his inner peace revealed on his countenance; he just refused to get involved in arguments. He knew when and how to be truthful to his inner convictions; a trait that was admired by his observant son.

I had a great time during the seven years I attended this private school. One of my favorite teachers, Miss Anita, in agreement with the principal, asked me to teach a calligraphy class after school hours. I guess she liked my writing style and my ability to relate to people, a gift that I was not yet aware I possessed. One day, after I made an audible smart remark in response to what the teacher had said, the class exploded into hearty laughter, except Miss Anita who looked at her "favorite student" with fulminating eyes, while slowly moving to my side. I didn't look up to her but I felt her fingers affixed to my right ear and while gently pulling in the upward direction, the rest of my body followed closely behind, thus lessening the pain. I looked into her face and could see that she was trying to hide a smile.

This was not the only time that I was reminded of my parent's wisdom; "Remember son, God will not allow a tree to grow into heaven; He will clip off the top before it grows too tall." I think this saying has its roots in the Old Testament's account of the Tower of Babel. The reality of right and wrong began to sink deeper into my mind along with the realization that I was not always right, which was hard to admit.

My dear Mama loved to take shopping trips to the fashion center in the city of Buenos Aires. Two streets, Florida and Santa Fe, were closed to vehicular traffic at certain hours for the benefit of shoppers. She would wake me just before sunrise and ask me to accompany her. I jumped out of bed and in a few minutes I was walking next to Mama to board the train. This was excitement at its best. Sitting in the train and watching the sunrise were unforgettable experiences.

At the Grand Terminal Station Retiro, we boarded the subway with destination Albion House or Gath & Chaves, the multistory, British shopping centers. Usually we would get off at Diagonal Norte, the Metro System's three level underground station located at the intersection of Corrientes and Nueve de Julio Avenues; the latter being 350 feet wide. After surfacing from deep underground we were looking up the Obelisk, similar to the one in Washington, DC. Crossing this twelve lane Boulevard was an experience all in itself. I was always fascinated by this specific spot where three subway lines crossed on top of each other, because my father was involved in the design of this German project, completed in 1936. Our next stop was to visit Papa in his office on the 8th floor on Avenida de Mayo. Invariably, the next two stops landed us at the Cinema, followed by a delightful lunch at Café Kessler, as the "grand finale."

As was the practice at that time, Papa had his suits made by a professional tailor who came to our home. Though friendly, he was a man of many loud words. Whenever he came to our home he couldn't wait to start an argument. I could hear the subject of their conversation from an adjacent room. I could hardly hear Papa, but from what I did hear, he was joyfully speaking about his faith in Jesus Christ, quickly followed by the tailor's strong argument that there are other ways to Jehovah God beside Jesus Christ. No matter how hard the tailor tried, he was unsuccessful in his attempt to persuade Papa to accept his religious belief. What amazed me was not only that my father treated him with kindness, but that he asked the tailor back for his next suit.

As a young boy, I enjoyed the Boy Scouts camps and the interscholastic sport events, organized by the association of German schools. I loved sports and I performed fairly well. It gave me the opportunity to interact with people from all walks of life, no matter what their background; God created them all and I concluded that they are entitled to get to know the One who gave them life. I believed in my heart that Jesus Christ did not only speak the truth, but that He is the truth as He testified personally; "I am the way, the truth and the life. No one comes to the Father except through Me" (John 14:6).

My parents were inclusive in their selection of friends. They believed that there are believers in Jesus Christ in every Christian denomination; and if they were not Christians, Papa and Mama would share their love of God in a way that would bring glory to the Lord.

All kinds of ball games, wrestling, swimming competitions, singing contests, and other wholesome activities filled my life. I was a "happy camper," in the world and in the church. One thing that really excited me was that I was chosen to sing in my school's choir of about hundred-fifty voices. Soon thereafter, I was honored to take part in a select choir and drama group of about seventy students, performing in a number of theaters around the city of Buenos Aires.

Living only a few miles from the La Plata River, gave us an excellent opportunity to enjoy the great beaches and all kinds of fun places. My Papa was a good swimmer and when the water got too deep for me, he would help me climb up on his back. One time Papa went out by himself and somehow lost control as undercurrents took him beyond the safe limit. Fortunately, a lifeguard noticed his frustration to regain control and went out to rescue him. While struggling in the water my Papa lost his denture. Incredibly, when he returned to the beach the next day, his denture was laying in the sand waiting for him. This incident turned into an unending subject of conversation as friends and relatives poked fun at Papa who responded with his familiar smile. No amount of jesting could lure Papa into an argument. Usually, when everyone ran out of teasing remarks, he would outsmart them with some wise yet funny words.

As time moved on, I felt the need for more of God, something that I did not notice in my Christian friends. They seemed to move along without any thoughts about their inner longings. I truly enjoyed reading my Bible, while my peers couldn't care less. I began to share my joy in the Lord and His word with some of my friends, but they seemed unimpressed. Some of them had made a commitment to Jesus Christ, but their whole lifestyle seemed to be unaffected.

Together with my growing faith came an awareness of evil tendencies in my heart. Deep within me I sensed uneasiness and the need for hiding evil deeds and then lying about it. My aunt Emily, who was much stricter than Mama, had an interesting can opener. One day I took it out of the kitchen drawer and while playing with it in the yard I lost it. I believe it got buried under the excavated dirt while building a playhouse. "I can't find my can opener; does anyone know where it is?" My aunt would ask. Of course, no one else knew anything about it. My heart rate increased, but my mouth was sealed shut. I never confessed this to Aunt Emily. I did not forget about this misdeed, not even to this day, but it surely taught me how evil and good can live together in my heart. It also helped me to understand the need to confess and be forgiven in order to find peace. Aunt Emily had been in Paradise for a long time when this sin was confessed to the Lord. I might share this with her in glory.

In my seemingly insatiable curiosity I had to find out what smoking was all about. In the company of my good friends we had to venture into some areas that were described as sinful in our church. So, the way around "prohibition" was to go into hiding. While puffing a cigarette I had to be watchful not to be caught by fellow Christians who would certainly report me to the church "vigilantes;" our deacons. Some of them seemed so "mean" for not letting children have some fun in church, that I dreaded falling into their hands.

One day, while riding the train to school, I walked toward the first car, as I usually did, in order to get out before the crowd and run for the subway. As my eyes scanned the passengers, I saw one of our church leaders deeply concentrated in his reading. I really liked that brother and decided to sit down next to him. As we started to talk, I saw cigarette smoke coming out from under his hat that was lying on his lap. I quickly understood his hesitancy in getting involved in a lengthy conversation and I got up and left. What happened in my mind I can only describe as an awakening of my inner "Pharisee." I thought; if more mature Christians can smoke, so can I. However, my reasoning did not satisfy my heart.

Not too long after this interesting experience, I was again on my daily train ride cozily leaning on a slightly open window, while puffing a cigarette. The train came to a stop at the next station and to my dismay I saw our pastor on the platform ready to board the train. I was absolutely sure that he saw me and by his smile I had the terrible suspicion that he would head for the vacant seat in front of me. My suspicion was confirmed and I dropped the cigarette, but I knew that my breath was an awful giveaway. I loved my pastor. He was so much like my Papa. Under his preaching I had dedicated my life to Jesus Christ and soon thereafter I was baptized by this fine man of God. He carried on a very friendly conversation but I wondered what he was thinking while lovingly looking into my red face. There was no Pharisee in this godly man that I could see; I just saw Jesus in his countenance. Years passed, and I continued to feed the "Pharisee" in me.

Finally, I began to understand the necessity of a deep healing of my heart in order to live a triumphant life. Even in my teens I noticed that God's Word teaches a lot about the heart of man. "Man's heart is deceitful and more stubborn than anything else and very wicked; who can know it? I, the Lord, search the heart. I test the mind in order to give every man according to his doings, and according to the fruit of his works" (Jeremiah 17:9,10).

One of the casualties of my battle against evil was my habit of puffing cigarette smoke. I didn't have to ask the Lord what His opinion was regarding smoking. I just kicked the habit.

As a little child my parents taught me a bedtime prayer that I prayed while kneeling in my crib: Ich bin klein, mein Herz mach rein; soll niemand drin wohnen als Jesus allein; Amen. I am little, please clean my heart; no one shall live in it, but Jesus alone; Amen. At about seven I "graduated" from my first to my second prayer, which my brother Luis had already been praying for three years; "Christ's blood and righteousness, are my adornment and garment of honor, with these I will stand before God when I enter into heaven," Amen. Obviously, translated into English it loses its rhyme.

Then as a teenager, the prayer that Jesus Christ taught us to pray, combined with whatever else was on my heart, became part of my daily devotions, even to this day. (Matthew 6:9)

As a small boy, I often suffered painful middle ear ache. I vividly remember sobbing in my crib and soon my Papa would walk in, equipped with a box of matches, almond oil and a teaspoon. He would carefully put a few drops of almond oil into the spoon, warm it with a match and before putting it into my ear, he would test the temperature with his tongue. Obviously, this is not a practice followed by the medical profession today; but it surely soothed my earache.

I can imagine my Papa, tender and caring as he was how carefully he must have carried countless wounded soldiers from the trenches to the field hospital during World War I. As I grew up my right ear became very susceptible to infection and eventually I lost most of my hearing in that ear. Thank God that my introspection was fine tuned to the voice of my Shepherd.

In 1939 my parents planned to return to Germany, since my mother's parents and her three sisters still lived in the old country. September 7th was scheduled for departure via the ocean liner Monte Olivia. It was the time when Adolf Hitler called on Germans living in foreign countries to return to the Reich, the fatherland. My Papa was not in favor of the idea but agreed with Mama. The contents of our home were sold and farewell parties organized. However, things changed drastically. On September 1st, Germany invaded Poland, marking the beginning of World War II. The trip to Germany was cancelled, and the ship returned without passengers. As a child I often wondered why Papa, whose full name was Adolf Ludwig Geil, never used his first name. When asked for the reason of this omission he would simply respond; "I don't like it."

It amazes me, even while typing these lines, how God so often intervened in the lives of my forefathers. Our heavenly

Father's love and kindness is way beyond our human understanding. Several relatives and friends had left in May of the same year. Most of them survived the ravages of the six year war. Fortunately, my parents were reimbursed for their tickets; but everything else was gone, except their piano. They had to start over from practically nothing. I do not remember any murmuring or complaining. They just trusted the Lord in everything; and it included their failed trip. So, life went on with Papa playing their surviving piano and Mama singing with her soprano voice.

Soon after, another adventure was planned for the end of December 1939, a vacation trip to Uruguay across the La Plata River. However, before that day arrived, something drastic happened that affected Uruguay and Argentina. It was called the battle of the La Plata. This temporarily put our trip on hold. The German battleship Admiral Graf Spee was involved in a battle with a British flotilla in the waters of Montevideo, the capital of Uruguay. As a result of heavy damage to their ship, the German Captain Hans Langsdorf gave orders to enter the Port of Montevideo for repairs. However, under international pressure, the government of Uruguay ordered the Graf Spee out of the harbor within seventy two hours, allowing enough time to bury their dead sailors. As they moved out, the captain anticipated British reinforcement of their flotilla and decided to sink the ship.

Some of the British ships had also suffered heavy damage which forced the evacuation of their sailors. The billowing smoke could be seen from Buenos Aires; I was only eight years old but these events are still vivid in my mind. Argentinean ships brought thousands of British and German sailors to Buenos Aires. Many were accommodated at the immigration hotel, including Captain Hans Langsdorf.

My parents learned that some of the German sailors were Christian believers, and after clearance from the Argentinean authorities, they were allowed to spend some time with my family. However, their movement was restricted, as they were considered prisoners of war. Watching British and German sailors on Argentinean soil was certainly big news. It only grew in intensity as newspaper headlines reported that the captain of the Graf Spee had wrapped himself in the traditional German flag and shot himself. This triggered the greatest burial event in Argentina's history.

Fortunately, our vacation trip to Uruguay took place as planned. As our paddle ship approached the site of the sinking of the Graf Spee, I saw the tower of the ship sticking out of the shallow waters of the La Plata River.

As a teenager I liked to spend my lunchtime visiting various sites in the city of Buenos Aires. One of these was the German cemetery where some friends were buried. I would also stop at the tomb of Captain Hans Langsdorf and the gravesides of some of his crew members who had died as a result of the battle of the La Plata River. With his anti-Nazi mind set, I wondered if or how long Captain Langsdorf would have survived, had he returned to Nazi Germany.

Years later, I met the officer in charge of the ship's blasting operation. He also helped remove the captain, who was determined to remain on board his sinking ship, according to an old navy tradition.

My exposure to evil and injustice, beginning in my early life, helped me in my reflection on the condition of man's heart, and how hatred and love dwell together in the same place. The ugliness of anti-Semitism and deadly acts of terrorism, perpetrated on the streets of Buenos Aires left deep impressions on my heart. Add to that the demonstrations against the Peron government with the police using tear gas to disperse the crowds, and you have a real mess. Too often the military had to intervene with bloody consequences. Frankly, it often felt like walking across a minefield while living in Argentina. What really shocked me was that some of the street gangs began to attack Jewish people and desecrate their places of worship. I was glad when the association of Evangelical churches expressed their solidarity with the Jewish community in deploring these acts of violence. Undoubtedly, my faith in God was severely tested, but I came through it all by trusting Him with all my heart.

After completing my primary education at a private German school in 1944, I attended a trade school eight hours a day six days a week for three years. Saturdays were mostly dedicated to work shops in several trades. This school was operated by the government and as such included a Catholic education class. I liked church history and wanted to befriend people from all walks of life, so I decided to attend this class. After completing this phase of my education, the school administration offered me a job position as the school's draftsman.

One day, while sitting at my drafting table, Father Jose, my religion teacher, walked into my office. I liked him because he was a pleasant man. "How did you like my classes?" he asked me. And after he continued with his questions he stopped at one of my answers and asked me; "Are you not a Catholic?" "No, I am an Evangelical Christian," I replied. There was deep silence while his face became serious and I wondered if he regretted having given me top grades. But his face changed while he uttered some friendly words. Before he left I asked the priest if we will someday meet in heaven; to which he replied, "Yes, I believe so."

The years following my elementary education were very difficult in the sense that I was now totally immersed in a different culture from my German upbringing. My schoolmates were for the most part Lutherans, whereas during my secondary and higher education I was practically the only exception among Latin-Catholics. However, what seemed a culture shock at first soon became bearable and slowly many of my classmates, who at first showed disdain, became wonderful friends. Most of the harassment was created by the war and my German background. In my heart I wanted them to get at least a glimpse of how much God cares about every individual.

I believed that the government's allegiance to the Roman Catholic Church could not prevent the downslide of the social fiber of the country. The widespread corruption mixed with witchcraft, pervaded society to such a point, that I was grateful for God's mighty touch from heaven, manifested through great revivals in the 1950's. In my perception, I saw God's redemptive power descending upon a spiritually starving society that sparked all kinds of strange manifestations. I concentrated on the redemptive power of the Holy Spirit, whereas some of my Christian friends focused their attention on what did not line up with their theology, and walked away from it. What really saddened me was that their light for Christ was hardly flickering. They also ignored Satan's attempts to keep people in his bondage, away from truly experiencing the transforming power of the Holy Spirit.

For the most part, the revivals in Argentina helped me in my own understanding of God's work on earth. It also intensified my belief that if a Christian's heart is not healed and open to the Holy Spirit's sanctification process, not much good fruit will come forth.

In 1947, after I was awarded a master electrician's diploma, I applied for a job. Our next door neighbor, who was a professor in a polytechnic institute, secured me a job at the Department of Education under the presidency of General Juan D. Peron. While holding this eight hour job, I also enrolled in the polytechnic institute where my next door neighbor was teaching. He prepared me and two other friends for the entrance exams. I remember the hardships of being fully immersed not only in a second language but in a different cultural atmosphere. Furthermore, my neighbor was very careful and strict in not showing any preference for his frightened kid next door. In spite of initial hardships, I was able to adjust to my new environment and establish meaningful relationships soon after school started. I was now on the road to pursue a career in the electrical power distribution field.

The political landscape of Argentina was rapidly changing under the presidency of General Peron. His aspirations for the highest office had a long history. In 1941, Juan D. Peron, joined by a group of politicians, staged a coup d'état and took over the Department of Labor. He proceeded to transform the labor movement, creating new unions. Peron was made vice president and Minister of War in 1944. This created a strong opposition within the Armed Forces. As this opposition became more widespread, Peron was forced to resign all his assignments and in October 1945, he was imprisoned in Patagonia, the southern area of Argentina. His resignation sparked a government crisis that was resolved on October 17th. His labor supporters rescued Peron from prison and while carrying him on their shoulders, shouted; "Viva Peron." October 17th became a national holiday. Four days later, Peron, a widower, married his mistress Maria Eva Duarte, who became fondly known as "Evita." The group that freed Peron from prison formed a new political party known as the "Descamisados," (the shirtless ones); implying that they were not of the middle class-wearing suits.

As time progressed, the political situation in Buenos Aires worsened to the point of confrontation between factions of the Armed Forces. Often my sleep was disrupted by the noise of Army tanks rolling through our town, heading for downtown. Too many political parties were vying for power. Bloody street riots and gangs of hoodlums made life very disruptive. My hair and skin color gave me away as a gringo, and although the war had ended, the worst was still to come for Argentina. More than once I had to run for my life to escape the rage of those who called me Nazi, just because of my appearance. In retrospect, I believe that all those painful experiences helped forge my character.

The apostle Paul knew something I had to learn on my road of hard knocks. "Now, He who searches the hearts knows what the mind of the Spirit is, because He makes intercession for the saints according to the will of God and we know that all things work together for good to those who love God, to those who are called according to His purpose" (Romans 8:27,28).

One time a gang of about five saw me riding my bike and while I tried to ride past them one of them stuck a fishing pole into my front wheel. My bike came to a sudden stop and I flew head over to the ground. To my dismay, these guys landed on top of me and let me have it; I mean they just worked me over. I guess I became the lightning rod for all their long accumulated rage and frustration. I will never forget the name of the gang leader; I will call him Mr. Ocho.

I was well aware of the Bible injunction; "Love your neighbor as yourself" and "vengeance is Mine says the Lord, I will repay;" but "my better judgment" dictated that I must do something to stop this nonsense. I do not remember how long thereafter; all I remember is that I was on my way to the train station when my eyes caught that gang leader. This was my great moment. I just had to seize the golden opportunity and act. I walked up to him and looked him right in the eyes; he instantly recognized me. I was about a head taller than he. The color of his face changed as I moved my fist close to his face. I knew he got my message. I did not see him again until several years later, while working as a supervisor at a paint manufacturing company. One day, while touring the plant, I walked into another department to speak to the supervisor. To my great surprise it was Mr. Ocho. "Do you remember me?" I asked. "Yes, I do," he replied with trepidation. I reached out to shake his hand, and we became friends.

I enjoyed working for this company, owned by two Jewish families. Most of the managers were Jewish, and so was my boss, the manager of the engineering department. There was a climate of camaraderie and the company was very employee minded. Free meals were provided for all employees and a great vacation resort was available "free of charge" to all who asked.

After several months of employment I began to notice that my boss did not like me. I never found out the reason for his attitude. More and more I felt that I was being harassed. His double standard in his treatment of many employees in my department became very irritating. One day, while sitting at my desk, busy with my daily assignments, he asked me a question loaded with sarcasm. I decided not to utter a single word. All I did was close the drawers of my desk, (actually I slammed them shut) and went straight to the personnel department.

The Argentine labor laws for the termination of employment were as follows: If you are fired without prior notice and asked to leave immediately, the employer is required to compensate with two months of severance pay, plus one month for every year of employment, in addition to vacation pay and a percentage of the Christmas bonus. However, if the employee leaves on the spot he will forfeit all monetary claims, and this was my situation. On my way to the personnel department I met the personnel manager, Mister K. I was very brief and to the point in my request to leave on the spot. I did not say a word about my manager. All I asked for was that he would allow me to leave without having to return to my desk. Before he said a word he filled out a form and handed it to me and said; "Mister Geil, anytime you choose to come back, please know that you are always welcome." I walked only a few steps before I decided to read the form. I could hardly finish reading as tears blurred my vision. The form "entitled" me to leave with full compensation as if I was fired on the spot; except without being fired—another gift from my Father.

Several months later I decided to visit my former employer to enjoy the wonderful friendships I had established. No sooner had I approached the guard station I heard someone shout; "Did you hear Mr. Geil, that the manager of the engineering department was fired not long after you left?" I was shocked, howbeit not surprised. Little did I know that many more interesting experiences were waiting for me. At that time I was twenty-four years old. I perceived a voice speaking to my heart. "I am your protector and your defender, your helper and your provider."

Was the Lord gradually preparing my heart for what He planned for my future? In retrospect, I know that He was carefully weaving the tapestry of my life. The sifting process becomes most effective in the heat of adversity. I began to learn by personal experience, that as followers of Jesus Christ it is not sin in itself that prevents us from growing closer to God, our Father; we have the precious Blood of Christ, the Lamb of God to wash away all our confessed sins. The real problems are flaws in our character; identified in the Holy Scriptures as iniquities of our forefathers. This word appears over two hundred times in the Bible. It is one slice of the "sin-pie" as I heard a Christian teacher explain. The other two slices are sins and transgressions. The roots of these iniquities are often very deep and can frequently be traced back and found in the lives of our ancestors. Spending many hours in intimate devotion with the Lord, He has helped me to unearth and eradicate many character weaknesses by the power of the cross of Christ.

The freedom from habits, compulsions and addiction that used to drive me to sin, followed by deep-seated joy and greater fruit bearing is immeasurable. Blaming Satan, our enemy, and other people in my life was greatly reduced. I will share more regarding our insidious sin nature that prevents us from enjoying our Father's love and the freedom that awaits us on the other side of overcoming, in Part II of this book.

Chapter Three

New Exciting Adventures

One of my mother's best friends was the daughter of a wealthy family. They owned a gold jewelry manufacturing company in Buenos Aires. In the 1930's they purchased an island in the Delta of the Parana River. This delta system covers an area of 14,000 square kilometers with thousands of islands. The gigantic Parana River, with its source in the jungle of Brazil joins the Uruguay River, flowing into the La Plata River and finally into the Atlantic Ocean. It is a funnel-shaped indentation on the South-Eastern coastline of South America, extending 180 miles from the rivers' confluence to the Atlantic Ocean. Where the two rivers join the water is 30 miles wide and running to the southeast it widens to 137 miles before flowing into the ocean. This is the widest estuary in the world.

The city of Buenos Aires is only a few miles from this beautiful vacation dreamland. Unfortunately, after years of neglect this whole area became incredibly polluted. I believe that with all the emphasis on environmental safety this area has now been restored to its original beauty. However, for a period of about thirteen years, it was an unpolluted vacation paradise for our family. My mother would take us boys for one to three weeks at a time, to enjoy what I can only describe as a taste of Paradise.

In the 1940's this wealthy family built a castle-like house for the members of their family, a guest house, and a house for laborers and servants. Endless pathways across fruit orchards, with refreshment stops along the way, offered the weary wanderer a delightful time of relaxation. Specific fishing stations were provided at strategic spots, for fishermen's delight.

Before I miss anything, I need to share what was in the boat house. Would you believe a beautiful yacht and several boats of various sizes? The smallest ones were used to traverse the narrow canals. Then there were the larger ones for the transportation of fruit to the wholesale market, plus a number of rowboats for the less daring. On top of the boathouse there was a wood carving shop, where one of the family members carved the most artistic pieces of furniture. This was one of my favorite hangouts. I could spend hours watching this artist patiently carving a table leg in the shape of a standing lion, or creating a statue of a blacksmith from a block of red "quebracho," one of the hardest woods found in the jungle of northern Argentina and Paraguay.

One day in 1946, after I came home from school, my mother told me that her friend, the daughter of this wealthy family, had purchased a piece of land on a mountainside in the picturesque province of Cordoba with plans to build a hotel. I thought, "so what?" Then Mama said, "She wants you to come along and help her during your summer vacation." This was more than a fifteen year old boy could safely digest. Of course, I was delighted about this treat. Even to this day I am awed by God's unmerited favor shown in my life. As the wealth of this family increased, they began to get involved in all kinds of business adventures.

After a sixteen hour train ride with accommodations in first class cabins, we arrived at the beautiful town of

Calamuchita, nestled in a valley beside a crystal clear brook. I had the most phenomenal time of my teenage years. Many fun-filled experiences such as horseback riding, mountain climbing, swimming and, of course, helping with all kinds of chores, filled my days.

The hotel administrator's wife was a sickly woman and on various occasions I had to walk down the long hillside path to the pharmacy in town; sometimes late at night. I knew that there were mountain lions in the area and with a kerosene lantern I was not able to see much except the rocky path ahead of me. What I could do was pray for God's protection. I knew He was always with me, giving His angels charge to protect me. In conversations with friends I met at this hotel, I was delighted to share my faith; specifically with my benefactor and her daughter.

In retrospect, I knew that God loved me and that He was preparing me for specific assignments in life. I guess I could liken my journey through early adulthood to a germinating seed pushing its way through the soil. However, while moving through my teenage-years, I was troubled by the awareness that mixed with the inner desire to please God; there were tendencies that pulled me in another direction. The apostle Paul writes in his letter to the Romans, in chapter seven that he discovered that there were two laws at work in him; namely, the law of sin in the old nature, and the law of God in his new, redeemed creation. Through confession and repentance, I always found my way back to intimacy with God. When others murmured and complained that their glass was "half empty" I tended to see mine at least "half full" and soon running over.

However, in my adventurous teenage spirit, and my eagerness to achieve higher and better things in life, I often sought to satisfy my curiosity by venturing into unchartered territory. Obviously, wisdom is by no means a high ranking virtue found among teenagers, as I learned through often foolish experiences. In spite of my Christian foundation and my knowledge of the Holy Scriptures, the devil had plans that were diametrically opposed to those of the Lord. I thank God for His mercy and unending love in not allowing the enemy to keep the upper hand in my life.

If I were to take an inventory of the mixed bag of adventures during my youth, I would come up with one very important fact that helped me throughout my walk with Jesus Christ; namely, the ability to distinguish between light and darkness. I know beyond any doubt that the devil, our enemy, is not only real, but that he will spare no efforts to deceive mankind, specifically those who believe in Jesus Christ. Consequently, it is essential to perceive the voice of our Shepherd while being aware of Satan's deceptive devices, in order to live victoriously.

Several years after my return from this wonderful trip to Cordoba, my mother's friend came for a visit. I happened to be home when I overheard a conversation between them that deeply affected me. I heard my mother speaking about her faith in Jesus Christ, to which her friend responded: "Hildegard, I used to believe in Jesus Christ, but now I have chosen a different religion; Jesus was only a carpenter." Then I heard her speaking about reincarnation and Hinduism. I was stunned, because I thought she was a believer in Christ. Not many years after, she died of a rare disease, which gave me a lot of food for thought.

Shortly after my return from Cordoba (February 1946), Juan D, Peron, who had been promoted to the rank of General, was elected president of Argentina for a one six year term, as determined by the Constitution. This event marked the beginning of many years of political unrest. As a result of a substantial victory, Peron pursued a pro labor, pro nationalist political agenda, helped by Evita, his wife, who became a powerful and influential, although informal member of his administration. This situation agitated not only members of

Peron's cabinet, but it snowballed into a large segment of the population and the Armed Forces.

I was grateful that, in spite of political uncertainty, I enjoyed peace in my heart. Teaching the Bible in the German and Spanish languages had been an exciting assignment. My uncle Eric, Papa's brother, who lived with us, was an excellent Bible teacher, and one of my favorite mentors. With the Word of God planted into my heart since early age, it certainly equipped me to teach, first children and later youths and adults.

As I advanced in my teenage years, the combination of a full time job and my studies, in addition to my Sunday assignments, began to take its toll on my health. Medical examinations revealed that, as a result of persistent stress, I was developing ulcers in my duodenum. The pain became so severe that it affected my lifestyle. I needed to prevent stressful situations, specifically in my employment. This was not easy with such a busy schedule. Through a strict regimen and lots of prayers I was able to function. Through this stressful period, I learned quite a bit about conflict resolution which served me well throughout my entire life, specifically in the corporate business world.

Our church was beginning to move through a transition from German to Spanish; which helped me to become more proficient in both languages. I truly enjoyed working with our youth. Frequent picnics, loaded with fun and laughter, Bible studies, games and a lot of singing kept our group together. My mother, being a wonderful hostess, gladly opened our home to anyone looking for attention and love as well as good food. So, that gave me the freedom to socialize with people either in church or at home.

Chapter Four

My Eyes Land on a "Flower"

In 1949 I became the youth leader of my church. I loved people and sensed that God has given me a gift of leadership. Conflict among people bothered me and I felt that I needed to do my part to establish peace. Obviously, there were situations when my help was not welcomed and I had to retreat for my own safety.

One Sunday in 1949, I discovered a newcomer with a familiar face among our youth group. I could not get my eyes off this pretty girl. Then, I remembered I had first seen her about five years earlier in our Sunday school; her name was Martha. As she came under my close scrutiny, I noticed some raised eyebrows among guys that apparently had picked her out of the crowd before me.

Back in 1944, I first saw her at a Sunday school outing. I remembered that we stood in a circle playing a ball game that required very quick responses. The ball was quickly tossed to another person across the circle. I was amused when I heard shouts of protest, accompanied with some whistling as the ball went from her to me, too many times. In my mind I called her; "the pretty girl with beautiful wide open eyes." However, she suddenly disappeared and I did not see her for five years when she suddenly showed up at our youth meeting.

On January 8th, 1950, while leaving our youth meeting with a group of friends, I "happened" to walk close to Martha. "Are you walking home by yourself?" I asked. Aware of the dangers posed by street gangs and the dismal street lighting in our suburb, I was concerned about her safety. I also became aware that a few other guys were contending for Martha's attention. They were buzzing around her on their bicycles, attempting to beat me. With a little skill and a smile, I waved at them and took off with Martha at my side. On our walk to her house, I found out that her parents had moved to downtown Buenos Aires, to be closer to the hospital where both worked as medical aids.

Martha took me by my arm and said: "You are the boy I was looking for since 1944." We were both attending the same school; she was in fifth, while I was in seventh grade. After that evening we knew the Lord had brought us together for life. Later she showed me a page in a 1944 school workbook where she had drawn two hearts with the initials H-M. Martha was born in 1932 to Latvian-German parents, on a cotton farm near the town of Villa Angela, in the Argentinean province of Chaco. Life on the farm, not far from the jungle, was very hard. To make matters even worse for Martha, her father, although a born-again believer, was a harsh man. Ironically, his name was Adolf. Contrary to my Papa, he had only one name, so he was stuck with it. Her mother Berta was a loving and joyful woman.

When Martha was a small girl, she was bitten by a pig while holding on to the fence. Several fingers of her right hand were severely damaged and half of one thumb was bitten off. Later when she was six years old, Martha watched her little sister Inge, age eighteen months, as one of their horses kicked her on the head. She touched the horse's rear leg with a little twig and it reacted as any tame horse would.

Watching her only sibling bleeding profusely, Martha went into shock. Unable to save her life, Inge died a few days later. Martha's whole life was traumatized by this tragic event. Shortly thereafter the family moved to Buenos Aires.

Our homes were about two miles apart and my robust Swedish bicycle was our means of transportation. My days were extremely busy and Martha worked long hours as a sales clerk at a department store. I was amazed how we were able to cram our busy schedule into twenty-four hours. Sleeping for me became a side job that was mostly managed by snoozing during my train rides. Nevertheless, it was a sweet time with lots of excitement.

Chapter Five

Inducted into the Argentine Army

A s the year 1951 progressed, I found out that in June
I would receive my first military conscription notice.
I had finished school and I was ready to be sent anywhere
from the Iguazu waterfalls near the jungle, to Tierra del
Fuego, the southernmost province of Argentina or anywhere
in between, except Buenos Aires. Of course, this idea of
escaping from my home town was conceived before I discovered my "Flower!"

On one of my frequent walks to the Port of Buenos Aires,
during lunch time, I stood near an ocean liner and dreamed
about a trip to Europe. I looked up to the sky and said:
"Heavenly Father, I would love to visit the land of my forefathers." After my short prayer I thought; come on Alfredo,
be realistic, Argentina does not have any military outposts
anywhere in the world. I did not have the money; neither
could my parents afford to spend it on their son's dream.
The following week, while on the train, I met my best friend
Enrique (Henry). While browsing through the newspaper
my attention was directed to a small article that said: "Some
soldiers of the incoming draft may have an opportunity to

travel to Helsinki, Finland." I showed the article to Henry and he replied; "Sure, do you think for a moment that they would pick you and me from tens of thousands of soldiers?"

In September 1951 I received my induction notice from the Argentine Army and had to report to the Army Base, near Campo de Mayo, only a few miles from home. This, I thought, was the end of my wish to be far away from home.

After receiving general instructions and with my head shorn, I was instructed to report to the Escuela Militar de Equitacion, (Military School of Equitation) in February 6th of 1952. Needless to say from that day on my life changed drastically. While milling around the barrack grounds in the company of over two hundred conscripts from several provinces, we were "kindly informed" that from now on instructions were given through shouts, whistle blows and salutes.

The head of the school, a Captain, gave orders to line up for medical screening. I observed that two lines were formed; one very long, the other short. After my medical check-up I was told to join the short line. To my dismay, I learned that I was in the line of the "unfit for duty." I took one look at these guys and felt more rejected than ever in my life. I do not know what my face looked like but, while reflecting on my potential future, someone pointed his finger at me. "Hey, you soldier, what are you doing in that line? Come here." He was a doctor and after a check-up said: "You are more fit than anyone here; go to that line." Endless questioning followed. Asked about foreign languages, I responded; "I am fluent in German and knowledgeable in Basic English and, of course, Spanish." Several of the clerks looked at me; this time with a friendly face, rarely seen in that environment. They mumbled something among themselves, but all I could hear was "Olympics," and told to move on.

Next, we were stripped of our personal clothing which landed in white bags marked with our names and tossed on a huge pile in a specific storage area. Equipped with casual uniforms for basic training, we lined up in front of our sleeping quarters for further instructions. Wake up time was 5:20 AM followed by a shower and outdoor exercises. No opportunity for questions or comments was given. The mess-hall was our next scheduled stop. As we walked in we were hit by this unpleasant smell that did not stimulate anybody's appetite. Since there was no other place to eat I followed the beeline and sat down on one of the long tables.

Big soup pots were moved around on crude looking carts and every soldier got his plate filled. I was starved and slurped my meal while fantasizing about mother's deli-cious menus and ignoring my compatriots' complaints about strange objects in the soup. The spectacle that followed our "meal" was something to behold. Over two hundred guys were chased by Sergeant Pinto into the sleeping quarters through one door. The sergeant screamed from the top of his voice while swinging a short whip.

I found my place of rest on the lower level of one of the many triple bunk beds and quickly fell asleep. What a way to wake up; at exactly 5:20 AM, the shrill sound of the now familiar whistle blew and two hundred guys jumped out of their beds ready to storm into the shower room. This was indeed not my customary way to take a shower. The size of the room was supposed to accommodate over two hundred human bodies that were now chased like animals into their corral. This was indeed a spectacle without equal. Dozens of shower heads, the size of small sunflowers, filled the ceiling. The screams of the sergeant were meant to silence the herd; but it did not accomplish its purposed objective. Hot water was not available for recruits and the metal water tanks were on the roof exposed to the outside temperature of about 32 degrees Fahrenheit. There was only one water shutoff valve and it was under the control of the sergeant. When the chatter seemed to quiet down, a deluge of ice cold water suddenly discharged upon the crowd, with deafening screams. In order to get our attention the sergeant opened and closed the valve several times until he accomplished his objective.

After the shower we got dressed in a few minutes, and while still wet we had to run outside onto the frozen grass for basic training. This was the next activity that did not come naturally. Obviously, to crawl on our bellies that early in the morning was not something that most of us were used to. At this time, the commanding officer appeared—which only increased the sergeant's zeal. I wondered how long I would be able to endure this new lifestyle without given the opportunity to "voice my opinion."

Several hours later, I was handed a machine gun and while crawling on my belly under the strict orders of "el Sargento," I heard my name over the paging system. I dared to lift my head, only to fall back down again under the shrill whistle blow followed by a shout; "keep moving, soldier." I noticed I had lost my civil rights. Soon I heard my name again. This time I dared to stand up to tell the sergeant that I was the one being paged to show up at the officer's headquarters. His face changed into one of unbelief. Since I had no clue where to go, someone had to escort me.

I slowly entered the building and before me I saw several high ranking officers sitting around a table. It was a very solemn environment. I had learned that the Argentine military had been trained under the Prussian drill. At that moment, I was moved with compassion for my Papa who had to endure four years of this lifestyle while serving the German Kaiser in World War I.

I was handed a sheet of paper by the highest ranking officer, who said with a somber voice; "Read this letter back to me in Spanish." I learned that someone had translated his letter into German. With my knees shaking, I looked at the letter, while asking the Lord to guide me. I thought it went well, but the scrutinizing faces of the group of officers seemed to indicate something else. "Go back to your troop," I was told.

Chapter Six

Chosen among Thousands

Soon after I had rejoined my "comrades in misery," I heard my name again. The sergeant's face changed from anger to bewilderment. On my second walk to the headquarters I saw more relaxed faces. In fact, I noticed something like a smile on some of the officers faces. What a relief. They were leaning back in their plush seats, ready to deal with me; I had no clue what would follow. Did the sergeant report me for insubordination?

"Soldier Geil, we have chosen you to become our equestrian team's interpreter on our trip through at least eight countries in Europe, to compete in the Spring/Summer equestrian tournaments. We will depart from Buenos Aires, on March 19th 1952, with an open return sometime in November. Our main focus will be on the Olympic Games to be held in Helsinki, Finland. That gives us less than three weeks of preparation. In order to properly represent our nation, you will be given special training and tailored uniforms. We need you to help us in various trip related matters."

I left the room with the feeling like I was walking on clouds. In a matter of hours the news spread across the compound, and I became "El Olimpico," the Olympian.

I was instantly out from under the sergeant as well as his commanding lieutenant's domain. My heart was not only beating faster, but also overflowing with great joy and gratitude for God's hand in all that was happening to me. This was indeed a "heavenly rescue operation" for someone who was determined to believe in the unfailing promises of God; "Delight yourself in the Lord, and He will give you the desires of your heart. Commit your way to the Lord, trust also in Him and He will bring it to pass" (Psalm 37:4,5).

As preparations began, I found myself bombarded with personal questions regarding details of the trip. Fifteen horses, selected for various competitions, would be taken on the trip. The riders, a total of seven officers and one attorney, had been trained for months. One of the officers was also a professional veterinarian. Two sergeants, one an assistant veterinarian, the other a blacksmith were taken along for the care of the horses. Additionally, five soldiers were chosen as horse grooms. I heard that the team needed another interpreter. Well, I thought, how about my good friend Henry? I knew he was stationed at the barracks of El Palomar, a few miles away. I passed the information to the officer in charge of administration. This man, Captain Vee, was the strictest and non-communicative of the entire team. He remained absolutely mute to any of my questions. In fact, he would not even look at me.

It was only a matter of hours when Captain Vee had me paged to meet him in his Jeep. "I give you ten minutes to change into civilian clothes;" I knew he was not kidding me. I was horrified when I looked at the pile of over two hundred clothes bags, figuring out how in the world I was going to find my bag and be changed in less than ten minutes, unless by some miracle this officer would have an ounce of grace? Thank God, through "angels" sent by Him, I was able to find my bag, change and show up at the jeep ten minutes later.

The ride started in total silence. All I could think was that the officer must have been mortified by sharing his ride with a plain recruit. The silence was suddenly broken when he asked me if I knew my friend's unit at the base in El Palomar. Upon arrival and after shouting to the guards, he was informed about Henry's whereabouts. Henry was a watch repairman, and according to "good Argentinean tradition," the head of the base had sent my friend home for a week on a personal watch repair mission. Captain Vee, requested that Henry be transferred to Campo de Mayo and meet me for instructions. Fortunately, the trip back was more pleasant.

In order to prepare myself for the trip, I was sent home for a week. Mama, I said, as I walked into the house; "I'm traveling to Europe for seven to eight months with the Olympic Equestrian team, leaving on March 19th." "Harold, my son, your suntan tells me that you must have been in the hot sun too long. Sit down and rest." But my mouth was like a waterfall, I could not hold anything back. By now Mama was in tears. "And, you know what else, Mama; my friend is coming along. I am going to his home right now to tell him the good news." My bicycle pedals couldn't turn any faster.

His mom, who noticed that I was out of breath, told me that her son was not home. When I told her that I was chosen for the Olympics she responded; "You are always so fortunate;" to which I responded; "Wouldn't it be nice if Henry came along?" "Well, that's a pipe dream," Henry's mother said. At this time my friend walked in. After his mother told him the story, I said; "My friend, you are coming with me." To which he responded; "Sure, it would be nice if it were true." It took me a while to convince Henry before his excitement erupted.

In addition to becoming the team's interpreter, I was assigned two horses, Rexy and Mineral. Their personalities were as different as their color. I had acquired some experience with horses on my uncle's farm, but had no clue what was ahead of me. Mineral became like a friend whereas Rexy was more aloof. As the date of our departure approached, we were told that a group of dignitaries were scheduled to visit our barracks to review the team and that everything had to be in tip-top shape.

In order to prevent restlessness among the horses we were told to take them for a walk across a large field. The weather was hot and a brewing thunderstorm was approaching. I mounted Rexy and pulled Mineral on his leash. The sergeant, who was born to scream and shout out orders, directed us first to walk the horses, but as I was securing myself into the saddle, we were accelerating from trot to gallop.

Rexy followed obediently while Mineral had different plans. At the sound of a loud thunder clap, Mineral, after pulling himself free, took off in a different direction. To my dismay, and shaking in my boots, I saw Mineral not only running across the field, but heading toward a big muddy puddle. For a second I wished I were a little boy and could cry. But at age twenty, dressed in military attire; this was certainly not the right thing to do. As Mineral rolled in the mud with a perfectly polished saddle and all the necessary gear for the parade, I had to endure the rage of "el Turco," the nickname of one of our team's sergeants. In addition, I had to put up with a bleeding hand inflicted by the rough leash slipping through my hand as Mineral went on his escapade.

What followed is difficult to put on paper. I was barraged by the sergeant with every harsh word known in our Argentinean street language. Mineral was recaptured and towed in for a shower. While I knew in my heart that God was with me; I am still amazed how quickly Mineral was back in perfect shape, with a "grin on his face," ready to be reviewed by the dignitaries. To my great surprise, and I thank God for this, none of the team's officers was upset about the whole incident. They were as friendly as can be.

In a meeting with Argentinean's President General Peron, our Team's leader, a Colonel, was asked how he would handle the language barriers in Europe. "I have this German soldier on the team; he will take care of it," he answered. When I heard about this meeting and the president's response, my thanksgiving to God went into a crescendo.

Although Martha was excited for me, the thought of being separated for such a long time was hard to bear. We wondered how the mail would reach me with so many different towns and countries on our itinerary. But with our faith in Jesus Christ and our sincere love for each other, we knew that all things would work out. That confidence, anchored deep in my heart, has taken me through any difficulty in my life.

On the day of our departure March 19th, 1952 we were taken to the ship Buenos Aires. We learned that it was a Victory ship acquired from the United States and used in World War II for the transport of troops and supplies. Under Argentinean flag, the Buenos Aires was used to transport thousands of immigrants to Argentina, mainly from Italy.

This was indeed a high point in my life as many friends and relatives came for the farewell. As my Papa hugged me he whispered into my ear; "Harold, my son, when you meet girls, remember your mother was also a girl." When it was Mama's turn for our last hug she said: "Think about who you are, my son; you are a disciple of Jesus Christ, and there is nothing that you think, speak or do that your Father in heaven doesn't know."

This was a tall order for a twenty year old soldier who was ready to enjoy a trip across Europe, with all kinds of dreams. I cannot say that I fulfilled my loving parent's counsel with flying colors. They did not see me, but God's watchful eyes did. The devil tried to accuse me but my heavenly Father did not; and in His grace led me to repentance, and I quickly accepted His forgiveness.

Our fifteen horses were housed in proper padded boxes built on the top deck. Ample food supplies as well as hay and straw bales were provided. While a military band filled the air with music, hugs and kisses were exchanged mingled with tears, while the vessel was loosed from its moor.

Chapter Seven

"Hasta la Vista", Buenos Aires

Slowly, the skyline of Buenos Aires disappeared in the distance. Before long we passed the site of the sinking of the battleship Admiral Graf Spee. Much less remained visible from the time I saw it in 1940 on our family trip to Uruguay. The trip across the ocean from Buenos Aires to Genoa, Italy was scheduled to take sixteen days, with one stop at the Canary Islands for refueling. The first of a series of European tournaments would begin at the Piazza di Siena, in Rome, on April 19th, 1952. This allowed sufficient time for our officers to prepare the horses for the International competitions.

On March 25th after almost a week of travel, we had developed a good working system. The horses were well cared for inside their confined boxes in spite of the monotonous rocking of the vessel, when all of a sudden everything came to a stop. "Hey, what happened," everybody asked? The loud sound of the exhaust fans on deck stopped, lights went out; fresh water rationing was announced and torch like objects were raised to the top of the main mast indicating; "Ship in distress." The ship's turbines came to a standstill. This was the beginning of several candle light dinners. Our ship became a toy of the ocean waves, which severely affected the well being of the horses, not to mention the condition of the few passengers.

The horses' joints started to swell. Rubbing them with a special ointment and bandaging their legs brought some relief, but the worst was still ahead of us. Our veterinarian officer did his best to keep things calm. Captain Ed, was a good man. Besides his medical assignments he was also in charge of the team's finances. Throughout the entire tour he made sure that I always had enough cash for my personal expenses.

On my night watches, looking after fifteen horses while keeping my balance on a slippery deck, I would have my "inner dialogue" with God. Looking at the starry sky, I prayed for everything that came to my mind. I had the assurance that He was with us and that in His time the answers to my prayers would come. I thought of my parents with deep gratitude for their loving input into my life. They were my powerful faith builders, passing on to me what they had received from their parents, namely; a vibrant faith in Jesus Christ.

One night I was shocked to my core by a violent noise that sounded like the ship was breaking apart. After a little while, the same horrible sound again. I began to notice, that as the ship was rocking in a forward-back motion, following the crests and the valleys of the waves, there came a time when the next wave would hit the ship on her way down. (The loss of power made the ship vulnerable to the churning sea.) But even knowing what was happening was not sufficient to put me at ease. I had the greatest respect for the ship's captain.

On the second day of our ordeal, a vessel stopped near us and communicated a message to our captain and to the maintenance crew. Soon the ship's crew came up with an interesting way of entertaining us. The ship was surrounded by sharks. Standing at the railing I was able to see a good number of them anxious to be fed. Our combined ingenuity resulted in the building of an interesting fishing mechanism. Before long, the first victim was hooked and what followed was a wild scene as everybody around wanted to have a part in this adventure.

With too many hands pulling on the rope, the hook bent and was unable to hold the weight of the shark, and to our dismay he plummeted back into the ocean. A larger hook was then used to bring several sharks up onto the deck. They were cut up into pieces and prepared for the freezer. Like everybody else, I wanted a souvenir; and I ended up getting a piece of a shark's spinal column.

While our attention was diverted to our exciting fishing adventure, the ship regained partial power and very slowly moved 30 miles west toward the Brazilian port city of Pernambuco (Recife). With three days delay we anchored in the harbor of Recife. Mechanics had been flown in from Buenos Aires for repairs. Several letters from my sweetheart Martha came into my possession. Bedtime was the ideal letter reading time. These precious moments were savored to its maximum.

While anchored, I was busy grooming my horses when I watched the sergeant speak to a man in a white suit. It sounded to me like he was negotiating with him. The man left and the sergeant approached me and said; "I brought with me fifty leather wallets and this man offered to buy them. I want you and four other guys to come with me to town to deliver the wallets." We were happy to get away from the ship. And with each of us carrying ten wallets we took off. Sergeant Dem had agreed to come along.

We arrived to the agreed upon corner in town and met that guy in the white suit. "Give me some time; I am waiting for my friend who stopped at the bank to get the money," the stranger said. I learned that the sergeant was going to get a pretty hefty amount of cash. Instead of the guy's friend, a large police car stopped and we were "invited" to take a seat. The other sergeant, when asked to get into the car responded; "I have nothing to do with this." In fact, when that supposed friend was delayed he had urged his colleague to let us soldiers go. At this point I knew that this was a setup by the man in the white suit.

As the cop car sped off, under the loud sound of sirens, the sergeant whispered to me asking to negotiate our release with the Brazilian officer in charge. Why would he ask me, when Portuguese is close enough to Spanish? I guess I was overcome with compassion by his whining voice. My attempts were fruitless. If anything, the race only increased. The two cops were absolutely tight lipped—period. Escorted by the two officers we walked up the seemingly unending stairway into the city's stately police headquarters. By now I began to suspect that leather products were considered contraband in Brazil. It was late in the evening and by the presence of the dignified chief of police, I knew this case was going to hit the newspapers.

We were sitting around the chief's desk when I saw the sergeant smoking one cigarette after the other. I had never seen him smoke before. He saw me chatting with the Brazilian authorities and expected me to negotiate his release. There was nothing that I could do to persuade the authorities; they just looked at the chief and followed protocol. Sergeant Dem, who had managed to take off in time, reported the incident to our commanding officer on board the ship. It was after midnight when Major J. showed up to settle what had become an international incident. They were joined by the Consul of Argentina and other authorities. I still wonder why I was drawn into the negotiations. We finally learned that Brazil had very strict laws and severe punishment for smuggling illegal goods; among them leather products. There is a saying among the populace in Buenos Aires; that for every law there is a way around it. I wondered if things were any different across the border.

At some point in the negotiations the police chief demanded that fifty wallets be placed on his desk. We emptied our pockets and began to stack ten wallets on five piles. As an officer counted them he found that one stack had only eight. In a deep, but firm voice the chief said: "Dois mais carteiras," two more wallets. Slowly, and red faced, one of our soldiers surrendered the two missing wallets.

At the end of the negotiations, the police chief tore up all recorded evidence and everybody shook hands. When the group started to break up, the sergeant whispered into my ear: "Ask them about the wallets." The Police chief overheard him and said; "Oh no, no; the wallets remain here." When we walked out, I noticed an officer storing the wallets in what seemed to be a contraband storage cabinet. This was the end of the wallet story for the local Brazilian authorities; but not for the Argentinean team. In addition to losing his wallets, the sergeant had to endure a lot of scorn and endless laughter from the team, even beyond the tour.

I noticed that after this incident, the sergeant turned against me and whenever he thought he had an opportunity he would use his authority to harass me. However, it was futile since I was under the authority of the leading officers.

On March 31st, after reparations were completed, the vessel pulled out of Recife, seemingly at normal speed; but not for long. For the next week, while crossing the Atlantic, the alternating stop and go of our Ark, as we called her, began to wear on the patience of us all. The horses were in poor shape and losing weight. Thank God; the delightful aroma emanating from the kitchen kept the crew in good spirits.

One day, while inside the horse boxes, feeding and cleaning them, one of our colleagues was bitten by the horse he was grooming; fortunately it was not serious. It was obvious that the animals were getting very irritated. I was cleaning Rexy's hoof when he was bitten by the horse next to him. Rexy reacted by kicking me above my knee, while I was holding his rear leg. For days I was limping around trying not to neglect my assignments.

The ongoing failure of the turbines resulted in other inconveniencies that made our trip less enjoyable. Our sleeping conditions, which were not the best to begin with, began to worsen as the pump systems failed to keep the seeping water out of the bottom of the ship. While trying to sleep on our three or four high stacked bunk beds, we were kept awake by the constant sloshing sound of the water which seemed to increase day by day.

We had to walk on wooden planks to the bathroom facilities, while realizing that our "hotel room" was actually immersed who knows how deep under the ocean level. It is my nature not to get stuck on negatives; so I need to move on to something absolutely great. I was convinced that by trusting God, negative things will be counteracted by His blessings, enabling me to overcome. This is God's nature; and those who obediently follow Jesus Christ, His Son, will never succumb to circumstances, but live above them.

Every morning, at about four o'clock, we woke up to this irresistible fragrance emanating from the baker's quarters who was baking "pan Frances;" French bread. There's hardly anything more delicious to the Argentine palate, than freshly baked bread and pastries. When it was my turn for the night watch, I would go to the baker and give him a pat on the back for his excellent job, while a few freshly baked rolls landed in my pocket.

I knew that my dear parents meant well when they insisted that rye, full grain, and other dark breads were the healthier choice. But every now and then I had to break with tradition and sneak out to our corner bakery from where this absolutely tempting fragrance issued from.

In Argentina, French bread was baked three times a day; just before every meal. Often I had to stand in line, but the prize was worth the effort.

Finally, the Canary Islands appeared on the horizon on April 8th. This was intended to be a refueling stop, but we had enough time for a tour of Las Palmas, the capital city.

When we returned from our walk we could not believe what we saw. The ship was leaning at an incredible angle. As we climbed up the boarding plank, we could hardly walk on deck without holding on to the railing. The ship's captain saw us coming and gave an announcement explaining the situation. He said that the fuel oil was first pumped into a large tank on one side of the ship and then slowly distributed into several other compartments to attain the proper balance. We assumed that this would be accomplished while in the harbor. Wrong; minutes later we were moving out. What an ordeal trying to get our job done while sliding across the deck. Our poor horses were in a state of utter confusion; not that we were any better off.

The coast of France appeared and soon afterward we entered the Mediterranean Sea through the Strait of Gibraltar. It was getting very cold and windy, accompanied by ice rain and snow flakes which required that the horses be covered with heavy winter blankets. To make things worse, the ship was stopping again while not yet balanced. This is getting too much for all of us. Darkness was setting in while on my night watch and babysitting fifteen horses, when the announcement came through that a storm was approaching the Golf of Leon. That's all we needed on top of everything else. Not being able to walk the horses on deck for several days increased the restlessness of our four-legged friends. We all wondered how in the world they would be able to perform during the upcoming equestrian events in Rome, when there was hardly any time for warm-up before the start of the competitions.

The order was given to pack the horses in straw to prevent them from being tossed around in their boxes. The entire team was up and while the ship's lights were turning off and fortunately soon back on again, we were told to cover the entire horse boxes with huge tarps. I was lying on my belly on top of the boxes helping my buddies with this incredible job, while the intensity of the waves increased. With the ship rocking sideways, while not yet totally balanced, the ocean came too close for comfort. Besides, we were getting soaked as huge waves landed on top of us. I was convinced that an invisible hand kept me from sliding into the dark ocean. In spite of this whole mess, I was assured in my heart that we were going to be all right. However, patience was wearing pretty thin. Fortunately, the storm did not reach the predicted intensity.

To the South of us we saw the lights of the city of Tangier, the Capital of Morocco in North Africa, built on the slope of a mountain. On the opposite side is Gibraltar, a self governing British colony located south of Spain, visited by thousands of tourists.

Chapter Eight

Europe, Here I Come

Good Friday, April 10th, I attended a Catholic worship service; a welcomed time of spiritual refreshment. The next day we began to prepare for our arrival in Genoa, Italy. With an encouraging speech and good Champagne, the captain of the Buenos Aires bid us farewell. At three AM, on Easter morning, we finally stepped onto firm ground. Our horses were carefully walked into special cages and lowered onto the pier. This was something to behold. Our four-legged friends were absolutely perplexed by what was going on. They let out the most intense sound we had ever heard; it was without any doubt an expression of relief to finally stand on firm ground again.

We had to hang on to their leashes with all our strength while they kicked and stood on their hind legs. In spite of the early morning hours, people stopped to watch this strange spectacle. Seeing us in our uniform some shouted; "Tedescos?" Others asked; "Ruskis?" (Germans, Russians) When we said that we were Argentineans, they were relieved.

Next, we had to walk to the train station for our trip to Rome. We were assigned two freight cars that had to be equipped with padded dividers; another challenge to test our skills. Sooner than we expected, our cars were hooked to a high speed electric train. Our officers were assigned first class sleeping accommodation, while we recruits enjoyed a little less comfort; namely, sleeping with our horses on hard cots. We felt like happy campers. The scenery in Italy was breathtaking. More than once I had to pinch myself to make sure I wasn't dreaming. We passed through many tunnels and saw a lot of bomb craters and destroyed buildings; vivid reminders of WWII.

We reached our destination at the majestic Stazione Termini, in Rome; (Terminal Station) the largest in the world. Our cars were unhooked and taken to the freight station from where we had to walk the horses to the Caserma Pastrengo; the barracks of the National Guard, for our accommodation. This walk took us through downtown Rome with all its traffic and people walking everywhere. Here I was, walking on cobble stone streets, along streetcar tracks, leading two horses that had not yet recuperated from an incredible ordeal, while not losing sight of our leader. Holding on to the leashes of two horses who were beginning to get horrified by an oncoming streetcar, I found myself getting severely squeezed between Rexy and Mineral. There was absolutely not enough space between us three and the approaching trolley on one side and the tree-lined sidewalk on the other.

With only seconds left, I pushed Mineral onto the side-walk which sent people running in all directions. To my dismay, Mineral pulled himself free to enjoy his own sight-seeing trip through Rome. In a matter of seconds, chaos hit the streets of Rome as I watched Mineral galloping down the street while picturing the sergeant on top of me. "Oh, Mineral, another mess you got me in," I thought. He had an incredible personality that kept me flying from panic to excitement. On one hand he would ever so gently take a candy out of my mouth, and moments later he could pull an incredible trick that threw me into a spin. He was the kind of horse that kept spectators on their feet while stunned by his incredible equestrian skills. I was proud of this dear creature and grateful to the officer who put me in charge of him.

Back to reality; at this moment Mineral was getting all the attention on the streets of Rome. One particular feature of his personality was that when he was enjoying his freedom he would let me approach him, waiting until I was about a yard from him, before escaping. How in the world are we going to get him back under control? I thought. People tried to close in on him from four directions with no immediate success. Mineral had to have his way first before capitulating. The end of the whole ordeal was bearable and I survived. I had to; it was only the beginning of a seven month trip.

Our horses were housed at the Caserma Pastrengo, a barrack for Carabinieri, a kind of National Guard. We got acquainted quickly, and before long I had a lot of friends.

On my birthday, I walked across town to the Coliseum. On my way I stopped at various historical sites, including the Vatican. By the time I arrived at the Coliseum it was dark. Sitting on a bench, I reflected on the history of this famous building. I envisioned the many thousands of spectators watching the Gladiators' competitions. But, what really saddened me was that many Christians lost their lives as they were thrown to hungry lions. The cages and passage ways for the beasts were right in front of me. Christians became the scapegoats of an irrational Roman emperor who found no better outlet for his own blunders. Christians were falsely blamed for setting Rome ablaze.

This ellipse shaped amphitheater was built around 70 AD and inaugurated by Titus in 80 AD. Its size is 615 feet long, 510 feet wide and 158 feet tall, with a seating capacity of 50,000 people.

The international competitions, to be held at the Piazza di Siena in Rome, were scheduled for April the 19th through the 27th, and after that, our team would participate in other equestrian competitions. We wondered how our horses would be able to compete with so little warm-up time after the long drawn-out journey across the Atlantic.

As the day for the Parade of the Nations approached, people from many nations were milling around. My services as the team's interpreter began. It was interesting that I was asked to help Northern Italians communicate with their Southern compatriots with my knowledge of Argentinean Spanish. I began to see my pictures in several magazines. The succession of exciting experiences overwhelmed me. Other nations began to seek me out. I began to wonder how well I would be able to handle this instant popularity without bursting out of my uniform. It was truly a high privilege.

Dressed in their traditional attire, the Mexican team headed the Parade of the Nations proudly displaying their professional horsemanship. In spite of our horses' condition, our team performed excellently. In fact, we won the Cup of the Nation of Italy, a valuable trophy.

One day we received an invitation from the Argentine Ambassador for a tour of the city of Rome, followed by a trip to the St. Callisto Catacomb, near Monte Albano, the residence of the Pope. During our month long stay in Rome, we were able to get acquainted with the city, but this tour was unforgettable. Picked up by a 1950 Packard limo in the company of the Consul, we felt like floating in the air. Visiting cathedrals, parks, the Coliseum, and endless other historical sites, we found ourselves moving along the Via Appia, (Apian Road), the oldest highway in the world, built during the early period of the Roman Empire. This road is lined with incredible historical buildings and beautiful parks. Built with granite pavers it is just wide enough for one vehicle.

Our next stop was the Catacomb of St. Calixtus along-side the Via Appian road. Our tour guide took us into this underground burial ground used by Jews and Christians to hold their meetings and bury their dead, two thousand years ago. Holding up a torch, we had to follow him closely as the passage ways became very cavernous. To stay too far behind was dangerous as there were no other lights. We were told that not long before a group of tourists separated from their guide and a number of them perished.

Needless to say, the account of this tragedy helped us to stay glued to our guide. I believe that lighting has been installed since then. I learned that there are nearly seventeen kilometers of accessible underground passage ways. Alongside both walls are openings containing the nearly two thousand year old bones of Christians who died during that period of persecution. At times, these narrow paths widen into what were meeting areas with granite benches. It amazed me how much history is preserved in Italy. Our tour was crowned with a lavish banquet sponsored by the Argentinean Consul and his staff.

On May 9th we left our place in Rome for our two freight cars that were assigned to us for the entire European trip. The journey from Rome to Bern, Switzerland, through the scenic Alps was absolutely breathtaking. We stopped briefly in Milan and Domodossola, Italy, at which point we entered a fifteen kilometer long tunnel, right into Switzerland. Bern, the capital city of Switzerland, is a neat place with friendly people. It is the seat of the federal authorities whereas Geneva, Basel and Zurich are the country's economic centers.

Switzerland is a federal republic consisting of 26 states called Cantons. The establishment of Switzerland is traditionally dated to August 1st, 1291.

Compared to our activities in Italy, this stop was a welcomed vacation. I believe our horses agreed with this assessment. They were housed in a military stable, close to our delightful Bed & Breakfast Inn, surrounded by snow covered mountains. On Mother's Day, May 11th, after a few competitions and several trophies, including the Cup of Switzerland, we moved on to the beautiful city of Lucerne at the Four Canton Lake.

Argentina was becoming a household name across Europe and, as a result, I was haunted by an increased number of reporters. Our team's leader asked me to help Mexico and Chile with their language barriers. All this in addition to organizing our frequent trips, dealing with Olympic committees, listening to competition schedules called out over loudspeakers, plus many personal requests, more than filled my days. In addition, Rexy and Mineral needed love and care. Often they had to be cared for by others while I was busy signing autographs and tending to many other assignments.

The excitement of watching our team winning so many competitions increased from country to country. My interpreting skills were often severely tested when called to mediate disagreements. Our Team's leader, a Colonel, was not a man of indefinite patience. When displeased with the judges' decision, he confronted them using his Buenos Aires street language. When not satisfied with his opponent's facial expressions, he would look at me saying; "You did not tell him what I meant." I had to come up with a more applicable word in order to satisfy my boss while carefully avoiding a conflagration. This was a tall order for someone whose personality was one of a peacemaker.

Preparing our horses for a competition was a tedious job. Depending on ground and weather conditions, the horses' shoes had to have the right size of pegs to prevent slippage. We had to make sure to carry with us a proper assortment of them for every competition. This required that the holes in the horseshoes where these pegs were screwed in are always kept clean.

I often found myself in difficult predicaments, only moments before the riders name was called out over the sound system. Standing next to the officer, he would let me know what pegs he wanted on his horse's shoes. After searching my pockets for the right size I would lift the horse's leg and sometimes, to my dismay, I would discover that the holes were filled, not with cotton as they should be, but with dirt and gravel. With a special tool I proceeded to clean the holes hoping that the eight pegs will make their way into the holes with the help of a wrench, before the rider's name echoed through the loudspeakers. While perspiring profusely, I saluted the officer wishing him success.

When I thought I had a moment of free time, I was suddenly approached by reporters, who would not go away no matter what I told them. Obsessed with an insatiable hunger for news, they would not be satisfied with a little bait. However, in spite of all my activities, I was hardly ever stressed. The excruciating pain I suffered back home from the ulcers had left me. The Lord confirmed to me His promise that He will never leave nor forsake me, no matter what the circumstances; and I believed Him. Thank God, that fun and laughter are part of my faith in Him. Without keeping up with my journal it would have been impossible to record the multiple events that crowded my schedule.

During our stay in Switzerland I established some good friendships. One of these came about through an invitation to the home of a Swiss army officer who shared many interesting stories. He lived with his family in a beautiful country home, located on a mountainside. It was surrounded by a breathtaking panorama. Through this very friendly family I got a lot of information about their country. He had trained a cow to jump over steeples; this was hilarious, to say the least. After a month in Switzerland, we prepared for our trip to Germany, where we planned to spend the longest time of our entire trip.

After we crossed the border into Germany, I thanked God for His answer to my prayers to be able to visit the country of my ancestors. Traveling along the Rhein River and through the Black Forest was an awesome sight. We stopped for a couple of days at the historical city of Cologne, on the Rhein River. Founded by the Romans in 38 BC, it was granted the status of a Roman City in 50 AD.

I was shocked by what I saw; destroyed buildings as far as I could see. Block after block, nothing but piles of debris and weeds that looked like crippled trees. I walked and walked, and here and there I met some people; some of them coming home from their shopping trip. As a result of my conversations with those passing by, I learned that some of the stores had been precariously rebuilt and stacked with limited merchandise. I took many pictures, but my heart was heavy, trying to remember what my Papa told me about Germany. His native city of Essen was not too far from Cologne. It was also in ruins.

During my seven years of attending a private school in Buenos Aires I had learned German literature, history, culture; and now I found myself in one of the largest cities in ruin. It was a shocking experience. I learned that, during WWII, the city of Cologne had endured 262 air raids which caused approximately 20,000 civilian casualties and completely wiped out the center of the city. In 1945, architect and urban planner Rudolf Schwarz called Cologne the "world's greatest heap of debris." He designed the master plan of reconstruction in 1947. The majestic Cathedral of Cologne, initially started in 1248 and abandoned in 1560, was finally finished in 1880. I saw construction crews repairing the heavy damage inflicted during the war.

The Hohenzollern Bridge that crossed the Rhein River was broken in half. While sitting on a heap of debris, I had time to gather my thoughts and reflect on the desolation all around me and what I had learned about Germany years earlier.

Since the beginning of WWII on September 1st, 1939, I was exposed to conversations and general information about the rise of Nazism and its penetration into Argentinean life. Though a native of Argentina, the color of my hair and my complexion, gave me away as one of German descent. This exposed me to mocking and ridicule by street gangs; some of them venting their frustration by shouting profanities at me, while throwing stones and calling me Nazi. At times I would get upset, but usually I managed to shake off the frustration, thanks to my love for God and His Word.

Even as a boy, I loved the Bible. I believed in my heart that its content is the Truth. Then, later in my teens, I began to understand God's infallible Laws of the Universe and that if I try to break them, they will break me. I learned that God, the Creator of the universe is just and righteous, but also loving and merciful. That means, if I break God's laws I will reap what I have sown, unless I confess my sins knowing that their effect will be cancelled out by the cross of Jesus. The apostle Paul states in Galatians 6:7; "Do not be deceived, God is not mocked; for whatever man sows, that he will also reap."

I meditated upon God's laws of sowing and reaping and the laws of increase as well as blessings and curses. Of course, it took many years for my faith to grow and get where I am today. But applying what I knew from the Bible during my trip in 1952, I understood that much of what had been sown under the destructive leadership of Adolf Hitler was reaped during WWII.

Our trip continued to our next stop in Warendorf, located in the picturesque state of Westphalia. This was the place our team had chosen to warm-up the horses for the Olympics in Helsinki, Finland. In a nearby forest, owned by a royal family, we erected a steeple circuit, resembling the one at the Olympic site. The head of the estate, a Baron, was the person to whom our team's chief had written the letter that was used to test my interpreting skill. We, the service team and our horses, were accommodated at a horse breeding estate, also owned by the Baron. There were great horse stables and lodging and eating facilities that reminded me of a neat Bed and Breakfast Inn. The Big Wigs, of course, picked the best hotel in town. I was granted a lot of free time, visiting relatives and inviting them to our place. I was picked up by people who were drawn to our equestrian competitions and taken to various places across Germany. Many people in Europe were amazed at my command of the German language, when they found out that I was a native of Argentina.

Contingents of our team competed in several cities such as Cologne, Düsseldorf, Lippe, and others. The number of trophies increased rapidly. My role as the team's liaison man for visiting dignitaries from various countries was an exciting job. Everybody around admired our team, and there was a sense of camaraderie between the various nations.

One day, one of the team's officers told me to get ready for a day trip to the city of Bielefeld, where my father went to school. On our ship we had met a university professor who invited us to visit him in Bielefeld. I was relieved that the Argentine officer was very friendly to me which was contrary to his usual mood. While he was driving I plotted the map and soon we arrived at our destination. The road conditions and the beauty of the scenery were incredible. Practically every home was surrounded with colorful flowerbeds and trees. Everything looked immaculate in spite of what had happened to the country only a few years before.

From the distance, on top of a hill, we saw this huge monument. My father had talked about the Hermann the Cherusker monument and now I had the opportunity to visit it. Built in the 1870's it is 356 meters high (1,100 feet) it was erected in honor of a hero who defeated the Romans in the forest of Teutoburg at the beginning of the first millennium. This monument is a favorite tourist attraction. As I stepped into the building I noticed it was crowded with American,

British and French soldiers from the Allied occupation forces in Germany.

When the time came to prepare for our trip to Helsinki, Finland, I was involved in discussions whether to travel by train through Soviet territory or sail across the North Sea via Hamburg, Germany. Because of restrictions in the Communist Soviet Union, it was decided to take the sea route. On July 1st, with newly won trophies, our team headed for the Warendorf train station.

We were surprised by a group of people, mainly children, who were waiting for us at the station. As we moved out of Warendorf, we were touched by the enthusiastic group waving their handkerchiefs and singing one of Elvis Presley's favorite songs; "Muss I denn, muss I denn, zum Staedtele hinaus, Staedtele hinaus; und du mein Schatz bleibst hier." (Must I then, must I then leave this place far behind, place far behind, and you my love stay here?) The sliding doors on our freight cars were kept open during the day so we would not miss any detail of our trip.

Again, I was awed by the beautiful landscape and the friendly people greeting us at every stop. There was so much to take in on this trip, now in its fourth month. My heart was filled with thanksgiving for this unique privilege. I had been shocked at the bombed out city of Cologne; however, what I saw in Hamburg was beyond what I had seen anywhere in Germany. Living in Argentina and hearing about the war and now seeing the consequences of it with my own eyes, were totally different stories. City block after city block lay in ruins. I had nearly a whole day to walk around and take pictures. The city returned to basic life after seven years since the end of WWII; that was an amazing demonstration of determination and industriousness. The heaviest bombings were executed in 1943 by what was called "Operation Gomorrah." It was said of the Germans; "They have sowed the wind and so shall reap the whirlwind." Someone quoted

Hitler as having said in regard to the destruction of Hamburg; "further attacks of this nature might force Germany out of the war." Unbelievably, the war continued for another two years.

Chapter Nine

Helsinki, Finland, Site of the 15th Olympic Games

At the Port of Hamburg we boarded the Finnish ocean liner Sirius, headed for a three day trip to Helsinki. Again, boxes had to be constructed to accommodate our fifteen horses. We were treated royally by the crew. This trip was very different from our past experiences. We sailed from the North Sea into the Baltic Sea through the Kiel Canal; also called Kaiser Wilhelm Canal. This is an artificial waterway, 61 miles long, in Schleswig-Holstein, North Central Germany. At sea level the canal extends from the city of Kiel on the Baltic Sea to the mouth of the Elbe River. Locks at each end of the canal, minimize tidal changes. Built in 1887 to 1895 it was widened and deepened from 1905 to1914 to enable pass-through of large ocean vessels.

After we entered the Baltic Sea, we were given strict instructions for activities on deck, given the fact that we entered areas under Soviet surveillance. Cameras and any other suspicious activities were prohibited. This became a challenge for us who had to spend much of our time on deck caring for our horses. The temptation to snap pictures was hard to overcome, but the airplanes flying over kept these daring Argentineans in check.

The approaching coastline of Helsinki was an impressive sight. Everything was clean and the people who helped us unload were very friendly. We were one of the first teams to arrive in Helsinki and with the Olympic Games scheduled from July 19th through August 3rd, we had plenty of time to get settled.

Finland seemed like a different culture from what we had experienced thus far in Europe. I gained great affection for the Finish people. I was glad to have been able to communicate in German and English. Their language has practically no similarity to any European language, except that it is slightly related to the Estonian and Hungarian languages. During the very short time I had before leaving Argentina, I had studied all I could about Finland, including some basic knowledge of their Suomi language. The 1940 Olympic Games which had been awarded to Finland had been postponed due to WWII.

Finland is known as the country of many lakes, islands and forests. It is full of interesting contrasts, such as four seasons, the midnight sun, the long winter nights, and the different cultural heritage of the eastern and western regions.

Our officers were given accommodations at the Olympic village, while we were housed at a home for invalid children of the Russian-Finish war. It was a nice place and I enjoyed my interaction with their precious children. The more my interaction with the people of Finland increased, the stronger I felt that they were somehow unspoiled by Western culture. Their sincerity and readiness to help was genuine. Most of the buildings on the Olympic compound had been built for the Games planned for 1940. Each of the horse stables was designed to accommodate four countries. Mexico, Chile and Brazil became our neighbors. Day after day, as teams arrived, the whole area became more and more crowded. This required increased vigilance to prevent sabotage to our horses.

After the Olympic Flame was lit by Paavo Nurmi, everybody prepared for the Opening Ceremony at which time 69 Nations lined up for the official welcome. The stadium looked very crowded as 4,955 athletes, (4,436 men and 519 women) lined up to salute their national flag. With 149 sport events scheduled, we had a large assortment to choose from for our entertainment. But, sitting at the stadium day after day soon became too boring, which led us to plan more personal activities around the city of Helsinki.

The office of the Argentine Embassy issued special passes for us to enjoy all kinds of free entertainment and use of all public means of transportation. I was usually in charge of night watch schedules and all kinds of daytime assignments. My colleagues, except those on duty with the horses, were free to roam the city.

It was difficult to adjust to the fact that the sun never completely disappeared on the horizon for our entire stay in Finland. Nightfall had to be closely monitored by our watches or public clocks, because it never got dark. At times we would walk without specific directions, unaware of the time. Without the Olympic Tower in sight, we were able to find our way home by instinct or intuition. Obviously, there was not much time to sleep.

The horse stables on either side of ours were occupied by the Soviet team and other communist countries. This was the first time that Russia participated in the Olympics since 1912, when they were held in Stockholm, Sweden. It was reported that some horses had been singled out for possible sabotage. In order to prevent injury we were instructed to stay inside the boxes of our horses, scheduled for competition, for a period of at least twenty-four hours prior to the event. It amazed me how careful these dear animals are in their interaction with humans. There was not enough space for both horse and groom to lie down at the same time. My usual companion was Mineral, my old buddy. When he went to sleep, I had to stand.

Interestingly, when he stretched out, it took only a few minutes before he started snoring. Shortly thereafter he was up again and now it was my turn to sleep, assuming the officer on duty was busy elsewhere. When Mineral thought it was his time to sleep, he would bump his head against me several times until I got out of his way.

Our meals were served in a large mess hall. The food was basically very good, but too sweet for us. Even all kinds of salads were prepared with plenty of sugar. One day, one of us came up with the idea to purchase a young goat and cook it outside on a grill. This was one of the greatest mistakes of the whole trip. Only moments after starting the fire, we heard shouts and even screams, ordering us to immediately stop the cooking. Police officers, followed by fire trucks and reporters, literally piled on top of our cooking equipment. We stood there horrified, watching helplessly how everything got blasted away under the powerful stream of water. As the interpreter, I got the brunt of the authorities' onslaught, because it is a crime to build fires in a forest. These trees are pines on a highly combustible forest floor, as the police officer in charge explained to me, in a more civil voice. Our officers learned about the incident through the newspapers. There was no way around the laws of the land; consequently, we had to forego many of our Argentinean practices. Fortunately, one of the cooks offered to broil our goat in his oven, but not before the ashes had been washed off. What a delicious meal that was and, needless to say, we had plenty of helpers.

Obviously, our team's interest was focused on equestrian competitions, such as steeple chasing, as well as long and high jumping, as these were the most common events of our tour through Europe. However, there was an equestrian event that was unique to the Olympic Games; it was the three day event. This event tests the all-round ability of horse and rider; and consists of dressage, endurance tests and show jumping. It is, as I have witnessed, a make or break competition.

Horse and rider are stretched to their maximum strength and ability. I was extremely busy during those three days. Specific horses had been kept for this event. We soldiers were posted in specific stations around the neighboring forest. When our respective horses arrived at these stations, we had to be prepared to provide refreshments, plenty of water and replacement gear for horse and rider in case of wear and tear. This was not all fun. More than once I saw horses and riders tossed into the air, and hopefully landing in the water, when the horse tripped on one of these fixed steeples. I don't remember if any of our team members received any trophy.

This was the first Olympic Games that women were admitted to the equestrian competitions.

It was interesting to watch the Russian, as well as other communist teams, separate themselves from others and stick together as a team. We learned that they had to follow strict orders not to mingle; it was obvious that they were closely watched by undercover agents. They even requested that entire floors in the living quarters be assigned for the Soviet teams.

The Olympic marathon was one event I did not want to miss. Sitting on a strategically located seat, I watched the runners take off. As they were about to complete their run around the stadium, I quickly ran to the exit to take a few pictures until I saw them disappear into the forest. Going back to my seat I followed the marathon on the scoreboard, while watching other sport events. I watched the name of one of the competitors who began to separate from the group. It was Emil Zatopek from Czechoslovakia. After running 40 Km, 26.2 miles, the runners were about to enter the stadium.

Everything came to a halt as Emil Zatopek, all alone, appeared first. Zatopek, though having won the 10,000 meter race, had never run a marathon before Helsinki. The crowd of nearly 70,000 shouted: "Zatopek, Zatopek!"

He crossed the finish line and, while a couple people unsuccessfully tried to throw a blanket around him, he kept running, wildly cheered by the spectators. He finally stopped after completing another round, when the Jamaican relay team carried him to his wife Dana. She was also an athlete who had won a gold medal for the "throw," a few days before. Zatopec, nicknamed "the Check locomotive," continued to dominate the Olympics. An Argentinean runner finished second.

On July 26th, upon arriving at the stadium, we saw the Argentinean flag at half mast. We were informed that Eva Maria Duarte de Peron, the First Lady of Argentina had died on that day, of cancer, at the young age of 33. We were ordered to wear a black armband on our uniform. Earlier during our trip we overheard rumors that our team had been invited for a month each, to Mexico, the USA, and Canada. However, after Evita's death we were notified to return home to Buenos Aires, after the end of the initially scheduled tour of eight countries. Even though I would have loved to visit those three countries, I was getting anxious to return home to Buenos Aires, for very obvious reasons. My lengthy separation from Martha was taking its toll on me.

The United States ranked first in medal count with a total of 40 gold, 19 silver, and 17 bronze medals. After the closing ceremony on August 3rd, we prepared to move on to what was called the Post-Olympics to be held in Stockholm, Sweden. It was decided to split our team by sending five team members and five horses back to Argentina, while the remaining group was chosen to continue the trip to five additional countries for another two months. I had mixed feelings about this decision; on one hand I wanted to return home, but on the other, I felt privileged to continue with our team. Besides, I was not yet ready to rejoin the old barrack environment.

After our ten horses were safely accommodated on deck of the Swedish ship Svanesund, I was surprised with a package and letters from home. Martha and I developed a wonderful relationship by mail. At times it was a bit embarrassing when my letters far outnumbered my colleagues'. I thanked God for my girlfriend, who also loved the Lord Jesus Christ; and that sealed our unity.

This trip from Helsinki to Stockholm across the Baltic Sea afforded me an opportunity to enjoy premium time with God and dream about my future with Martha. Although the ship was teaming with people from many nations and there was a lot to share about the Olympics, I was able to find an isolated spot on deck. I was twenty-one years old and Martha nineteen. We knew that God had brought us together and now it was up to us to obediently follow the Holy Spirit's guidance.

Some readers may wonder what in the world makes me think so much about God. I am aware that I may annoy some people, which is not my intention. Frankly, I cannot explain in mere words what it really is other than to believe it comes from God through that inner Shepherd's voice. As I respond to the Lord's prompting, my heart is filled with unspeakable joy! I have no doubt that this is available to anyone who sincerely seeks God because His word declares it: "But without faith it is impossible to please Him, for he who comes to God must believe that He is, and that He is a rewarder of those who diligently seek Him" (Hebrews 11:6).

Sweden's coast line is truly something to behold. Lined with endless Fjords and islands, they offer the country a strategic defense system. Fjords are long narrow arms of the sea bordered by steep cliffs, usually formed by glacial erosion. The city of Stockholm is nestled deep inside one of these bays. My camera was clicking at high speed. The ship was really crowded with teams from many nations that had been asked to participate in the Stockholm sport events. I noticed that a number of refugees from several communist countries were hiding on board.

Sweden, like Finland, is a very clean and well organized country. Military personnel helped us to disembark. The sport events were held at the Olympic stadium built for the 1912 Games. Like in England, the traffic moved on the left side of the road. Our brave horses performed wonderfully while our trophy count, including the Cup of Sweden, totaled nearly 150.

It was easy for me to communicate in Sweden because of the similarity to the German language. With so many currencies to deal with, my souvenir coin bag was getting pretty heavy. The Krona, Sweden's currency, became the seventh one for us to deal with.

After a two week stay in Sweden, the tedious job of getting our fifteen, four legged friends back into the train was our next assignment. Fortunately we were able to keep our two freight cars for the rest of our stops in Denmark, Germany, Belgium and Holland. The teams of six other countries boarded the same train. I was asleep when I suddenly woke up and felt as if the train was rocking. I looked out and saw nothing but water. In Malmo, Sweden, the train had rolled onto a ferry that brought us across the Baltic Sea to Copenhagen and later to Flensburg, Germany. There was a lot to enjoy on this trip that had Aachen, Germany as the site of our next international equestrian competitions. I soaked in as much as I could. Every major train stop became an opportunity for sightseeing and shopping.

Aachen is located in West Central Germany, near the borders of Belgium and the Netherlands. King Charlemagne (Charles the Great) died here at age 72 and was buried under the Dome of the Cathedral, in the year 814 AD. He reigned over most of Europe for 47 years.

Our horses were housed in two of several old stables that survived the heavy bombing of WWII. On October 1944, Aachen was the first major city defeated by the Allied Forces after their landing in France. Much of the city was still in ruins. Many people still lived in bunkers. I learned that the battle for Aachen changed hands six times until it fell and came under Allied Forces' control.

Like before every competition, our veterinarian doctor gave strict feeding guidelines for the horses. Food, such as hay and oats was stored in an area at the end of the stable. The individual boxes were built of heavy steel with secure gates. We soldiers were given the choice to lodge in a nearby Bed and Breakfast "pension," as they are called in Germany, or pocket the money and sleep on our cots in the stable. Well, the latter prevailed.

One night, I woke up to the sound of strange noises. My first reaction was to look at Mineral's box only to find out that it was empty. His box door was open; but how in the world did he get out? I ran to the feed storage area and to my horror I discovered that he had torn open a sack of oats and with his head inside, Mineral was having a banquet. We could not figure out how this smart horse opened his box door, walked over nine guys spread out on the floor and soundly asleep, all the way to the storage room without touching any of us! I thought I had learned everything about horses; not yet, there was more to come.

Even though feeding orders for the horses were to be strictly followed, three of our soldiers were farmer boys and they "knew better" what the horses really needed to be in top notch condition. So, rules were secretly broken and more lenient diets were dished out. Another of our champion horses was Canguro, a totally clumsy, unstylish horse. He was a Percheron, one of a French breed of draft horses with a black coat. Compared to the many competing Arabian horses he looked more like a steam locomotive. He was our champion in high steeple jumping.

Preparations were under way when Canguro was lined up for one of his high jump competitions. He was no stranger to the thousands of spectators from many nations. Tension began to build as the officer led Canguro to the main stand to salute the judges. Instantly after the rider's hand came down, Canguro took off like a canon ball. With no style except his own, he approached the hurdles with both front legs stretched forward as if applying the brakes, came to a stop and then jumped like a kangaroo. The crowd roared, and while waving their handkerchiefs they shouted his name. Reporters pressed in on me, curious to know where this funny horse came from. Canguro jumped so well that he beat the Olympic record. I believe it was 1.8 meter. No doubt, he became the darling of the crowd. Canguro seemed unmoved by all the publicity, as long as he had enough to eat. These, and so many others, were proud moments for our team. I felt so blessed to be a member of this successful team.

It was absolutely amazing how well our horses performed and their shiny appearance testified to their excellent health. Of course, the real secret of our team's success was not revealed until our return to Buenos Aires. It was during a party organized by the military to celebrate Argentina's success, that one of us publicly disclosed our long held secrets. Of course, not before our honorable discharge certificates were signed by the top brass and securely in our possession. Fortunately it was followed by roaring laughter and wild applause. Thanks to the farmer boys of our team, our horses were spoiled during times when they were supposed to receive very strict diets.

More trophies were awarded to our team, including the Cup of Germany. On August 19th we left Germany for a four week stay in Belgium and Holland. Our first stop was

Brussels, Belgium and from there we travelled to Oostende and Knokke for international competitions. These cities were different than all our past stops in that they were located on the ocean front. We were able to enjoy the beaches for swimming and horse training. Oostende, the largest population center on the Belgian coast, is protected from the North Sea by a network of dikes. It received a city charter in the 13th century. The consequences of WWII attacks on Belgium were still very visible.

It was during a competition in Oostende that Canguro was scheduled for a steeple chase. I watched every move of this brave horse. All of a sudden, I could not believe my eyes; while clearing hurdle after hurdle, blood began to stream out of his mouth and nostrils. He was still competing, when I saw the rider's uniform heavily blood stained. Canguro came to a stop and was led out of the stadium for immediate medical attention. The public was stunned. People began streaming down from the stands; there was an atmosphere of unbelief.

Immediately, our team's leader put me in charge of Canguro to assure that he would get absolute rest and no food whatsoever. I was instructed to tie him on a very short leash with no straw under him. With that, the officer left the stable informing me that he would be back by five or six in the morning. After properly securing Canguro according to strict instructions, I put my arm around his neck to express my affection for his brave accomplishments.

Suddenly, around four thirty, I woke up from a "forbidden nap." I looked for my four-legged friend, but all I saw was his leash hanging on the wall. Where in the world, or in the stable is he? I was dumbfounded, and while hoping that my worst suspicion would not become reality, I discovered him with his head inside a bag of oats with no intention of being disturbed. In a matter of minutes I thoroughly washed his mouth and teeth and put him on an even shorter leash. I had just regained my normal breath when I heard the officer's voice; "Good morning soldier, how is Canguro?" "All is well my captain," I responded. In my mind I thought; well, another incident to be added to our top secret list. Medical tests revealed that he had a torn lung. Special treatment was prescribed with absolute rest. I was very grateful for his gradual recovery. I believed that God would heal Canguro.

Soon our "gypsy caravan" got ready for the next adventure, namely in the Netherlands. We were getting pretty homesick; but as I reflected on Israel's wandering across the wilderness I quickly stopped murmuring. On September 2nd we arrived at the train station in Rotterdam, Holland, where more trophies were added, including the Cup of Belgium.

Again, as so often before, I was sad to see so much destruction to what was truly a great city. The center of the city was practically gone; its beautiful Cathedral heavily damaged and many people were killed and countless lost their homes.

On May 14, 1940, Hitler's air force attacked Rotterdam, first with what were to be precision attacks with JU-87 (Stukas), and later followed by carpet attacks with Heinkel He 111 bombers.

While riding across Rotterdam in a taxi cab, dressed in my Argentine uniform and speaking fluent German, I had the driver convinced that I was born in Germany. His face reflected deep resentment, but he quickly calmed down when I identified myself as an Argentinean. The many horrible scars of the war deeply shocked me; but it again taught me how good and evil are lodged in the minds and hearts of men.

The Dutch people are very friendly and generous, which made it easy to establish friendships. I was grateful that I had been blessed with a natural ability to befriend people of all walks of life.

I was impressed by the gigantic windmills that decorated the Dutch landscape. Its real name is the Netherlands.

Holland is merely the name of two of a total of twelve provinces comprising the country. A fairly large area of this picturesque country is located under sea level. A great portion of land has been reclaimed from the ocean and by traversing the country one can see the many dikes that are holding back the ocean. There was so much to absorb on this great trip that it would require books to describe it all.

Prince Bernhard of the Netherlands, who is an excellent rider, had befriended some of our officers while on a visit to Argentina, years ago. He came to visit our team several times and on two occasions competed for our team, riding Mineral. This was truly an honor for me. He was also instrumental in securing a place on a Dutch Ship for our return trip to Buenos Aires. We added a few more trophies to our collection and on September 12th, we boarded the cargo ship Albireo, and left Rotterdam late afternoon.

Again, special boxes had to be built for our ten friends, who so wonderfully represented our country. I pictured a triumphant welcome upon our return home. Our living quarters on board were excellent. A locomotive and several train cars destined for Buenos Aires were part of the freight. From what I learned about the travel schedule, this trip could take nearly a month. Cargo stops were scheduled for the Canary Islands, Spain, then across the Atlantic to several stops in Brazil.

In front of the horse boxes, five on either side of the deck, we built wooden platforms to walk the horses. The weather was very hot. Fortunately, there was a pool on deck which helped keep tempers cool. As we sailed through the English Channel I was impressed by the shining white cliffs of the coast of England. The coast of France was visible on the opposite side. Two days later we entered the Bay of Biscay with beautiful weather and incredibly calm water, which is unusual for this area. It made it easy to walk our horses. On September 18th we anchored in Las Palmas for refueling. We were familiar with this Island from our trip to Italy. Every opportunity for sightseeing had to be enjoyed. So far this trip was like being on a vacation cruise. We slept an average of twelve hours a day. This was not hard to take. After a twelve hour stop we headed for the open sea.

At midnight, September 22nd, I was deeply asleep, when one of the ship's sailors stormed into my cabin. In his Dutch language, which was easy for me to understand, he shouted; "A horse is walking on deck." I jumped out of bed and ran up the stairs, and at the rear of the ship I saw the silhouette of our dear Canguro. There he was, the horse that was able to jump over a 1.8 meter hurdle, standing against the railing that was not much higher than one meter. Slowly approaching my dear friend, while praying that he knew that he was not on the competition track, I gently spoke to him. I was glad it was not Mineral who was unpredictable. Once I had him on the leash, I walked him back to his box. Incredibly, Canguro had removed a couple of 12" wide boards from the front of his box and stepped into freedom. The soldier on night watch had fallen asleep.

Chapter Ten

Back Home at Last

After five more stops and with great anticipation, the skyline of Buenos Aires appeared on the horizon; it was on October 17th, 1952, an important holiday during the Peron administration.

Ocean liners had to be towed along a dredged channel into the harbor of Buenos Aires because of the shallow waters of the La Plata River. After enduring agonizing hours of anticipation, I began to recognize the faces of those who were waiting for our arrival. My eyes were fixed on my dear Martha; I couldn't wait to take her into my arms but I had to follow protocol. My family, friends and military dignitaries were all lined up for a great reception, at which time medals were handed out.

It took me a long time to mentally and emotionally process the immensity of this experience. Back in the barracks, my heart sunk under the thought of returning to military life. Sergeant Punta as well as the officer in charge of our troop were still there, probably rubbing their hands ready to get me under their control. They did, but fortunately only for a brief time. Before long I was called to the officers' headquarters and given an assignment that would keep me busy until my discharge in 1953. I was handed a German book on horse training and asked to translate it into Spanish. In addition, I was given a permanent pass to come and go as I pleased.

One unfortunate day, I had to return to the barracks to discuss some matters regarding my book assignment. After clearing my way through the guard station, I was heading toward the officers' headquarters when totally unexpected I came under the "radar" of sergeant Punta and the lieutenant. To their obvious delight, they ordered me to follow them. Moments later, the Director of the Military Equestrian School saw me and called me into his office. I was again a free man, and a lot smarter.

President General Juan D. Peron, who had been elected in 1946 for a six year constitutional term, decided to amend the constitution and shut down the Congress, before the end of his six year term expired. He thought it was better to have one boss running the country rather than many. As was to be expected, not everyone agreed with his decision. Needless to say, Argentina was plunged into a long period of civil unrest.

After my discharge, I returned to my employer in order to resume my engineering position. Not long after my discharge from the military, the ulcer pain returned. Trusting in the Lord, I moved ahead with all my commitments. God's Word became my daily food and I found great comfort in the book of Acts where the power of Jesus Christ was manifested in the lives of His followers.

I had several medical check-ups in hopes of finding relief for this excruciating pain. Three doctors had predicted that there was not much that could be done, other than surgery. They cautioned me to watch for internal bleeding.

Chapter Eleven

No Longer One, but Two

Martha and I decided to get married, and this meant that I had to formally request her hand. The fact that her father was not the friendliest man on earth did not make matters easy for me. I had to carefully rehearse my speech before meeting him face to face. As was the custom in most Christian homes, I was welcomed with a glass of fine wine. Anticipating the reason for my visit, he actually laid the groundwork for my speech, by sharing his own experience with his father-in-law. The meeting was successful and Martha and I were free to plan for our future. On December 25th, 1953, we celebrated our engagement. We had a wonderful time, with my paternal grandmother taking charge as the master of ceremony. At age ninety, with her natural sense of humor, mixed with a spirit of control, she had everybody doubling over in laughter

On November 6th of 1954 Martha and I were happily married. Later our Lord blessed us with two wonderful boys; Carl born on February 13th, 1956 in San Martin, Buenos Aires, and Gus on May 17th, 1959 in Boulogne, Buenos Aires. Raising these precious gifts in a way we understood the Holy Scriptures, became an awesome responsibility for

Martha and me. We both believed that praying together in agreement was pleasing to the Lord and would help our children in their lives. There was nothing more important for us than to seek God's blessings in every life's situation. We saw the fruit of our obedience in our lives and later in the lives of our children. Before going to sleep, Martha and I would pray over our children, imparting God's blessings upon them. Right from the beginning of our marriage, we made it a practice not to fall asleep unless we first settled any hurtful disagreements. At times this was not easy, but our willingness to sacrifice an hour of sleep, was greatly rewarded, not only the next day but in years to come.

Not only did we pray over our children while they were peacefully sleeping, but even while in their mother's womb; I would lay my hands on Martha's body and bless God's wonderful creation from conception all throughout the entire gestation period.

After we were married, we lived in an apartment that my parents had added to their house. However, as so often in my life, my aspirations led me to envision a place that would afford more space. I presented a plan to my in-laws, and they were in favor. The idea was to convert their single story home into a three story building. My Papa offered to draw the plans for a re-enforced concrete structure. The electrical installation was my project. This was quite an undertaking; but it worked out well and I know that this building will still be there long after we all left for our eternal home.

Chapter Twelve

Political Upheaval

O ne very early morning in 1955, I woke up to the sound of military tanks driving to downtown Buenos Aires. It was not surprising as political tensions were building up. President Peron had been excommunicated by the Roman Catholic Church as a result of implementing political changes that upset the Vatican. Additionally, he alienated a major sector of the military which brought about a coup that eventually unseated Peron. He sought political asylum in Paraguay. Not long afterward, I learned that he moved from Paraguay to Panama, then to Venezuela, and later to the Dominican Republic, ending up in Spain where Peron spent seventeen years in exile.

Upon his return to Argentina in the 1970's, he married Isabel who eventually became his vice-president. The revolution of 1955 claimed many dead and injured. The Navy, the strongest power behind the coup, bombarded the city of Buenos Aires from ships anchored in the La Plata River, causing many casualties and damaged buildings. Several times I found myself in the crossfire.

After the Liberation Forces took over the reins of government, I hoped that things would improve, but it was not to be. The military governments that succeeded Peron were unable to stamp out Peronism. The memories of Peron were engraved in the hearts and minds of what seemed to be the majority of the population, which fueled several attempts by the Peronists to regain power. As these attempts failed, the level of unrest increased.

Many foreign enterprises that had been expropriated during WWII were gradually returned to their former owners. However, new contracts with European corporations, signed during the Peron administration, were now in jeopardy, which meant that existing contracts had to be re-negotiated. One of these companies was Mercedes Benz, owned by Daimler Benz in Stuttgart, Germany. A five phased contract for the manufacture of pick-up trucks, trolley buses and other vehicles had been signed, requiring the construction of a huge plant in the outskirts of Buenos Aires. The contract also included living quarters for thousands of employees.

While still employed at the paint manufacturing company in 1955, I heard about the huge Mercedes Benz project in the outskirts of Buenos Aires. Without much delay I contacted the human relations office and applied for an engineering position. I learned that due to strict hiring procedures imposed by the Argentine government, my name was added to the two months waiting list. Surprisingly, much sooner than expected, I was notified that my application was evaluated and consequently asked to show up for work. I was very pleased with the offer of an engineering position in a company that was employee-minded. The excellent benefits package made this job hard to turn down.

Soon after, I found out that a good friend of mine had been working behind the scene, paving the way for me. Of course, I knew that "Someone," much more powerful had His hand over me. Martha and I had an opportunity to visit some of the model homes at this huge project and we were eager to live in one these nice houses. The company had a fleet of large Mercedes Benz buses for the transportation of all employees from their homes to the plant, located approximately fifty miles from my home. The excellent working climate made this job a pleasant experience.

The political climate continued to worsen. After some incredible maneuvering, a Peronist Labor friendly government had managed to assume power, which again brought conflict within the branches of the military establishment. Rumors had it, that a coup was in the making. Mercedes Benz had hired a good number of retired Navy officers to fill management positions.

One day in 1957, while in my office, I overheard rumors that the factory workers affiliated with the Peronist Labor party, had planned to take over the plant the following day. As we found out the next morning, the company's management had gotten wind of the worker's plans. After we arrived at the plant, we discovered that a military contingent had occupied the entire plant, and the workers were ordered to resume their activities.

While operations seemed to proceed as usual, we learned that the city was in turmoil. On our return trip home that day, it felt like we were driving through a battle field. Our bus literally drove through flying bullets fired by pro-and anti-government factions. Amazingly, I had learned to survive in a climate of military and civil unrest.

Prior to my employment with Mercedes Benz, I had to commute by train to downtown. I had made it a practice to check the area around my seat for suspicious packages. More than once, I sat in a train for an incredible length of time, only to find out that terrorists had blown up a rail switch. What else was there to do but to abandon the train and find a bus connection?

While my company's contract negotiations with the Argentine and German governments were under way, orders came from headquarters in Stuttgart, Germany to reduce the number of employees to a skeleton crew of two hundred; until such time when operations would hopefully normalize. Over a thousand people received generous severance packages. I was among the two hundred chosen to wait out the storm. The stipulation for this remnant of two hundred was that they would agree to stay with the company until normal activities would resume. If someone decided to leave before, he would not receive the severance compensation.

Sincerely trusting God, I was assured that He would continue to provide all my needs according to His divine plan for my life. However, even then in my twenties, I knew that in order to deepen my relationship with Jesus Christ and hear His voice, my heart required additional fine-tuning. As I asked God for wisdom, He made me aware that certain things in my life had to change. The dying to self is a slow and arduous process and there are no shortcuts. The excuse that other Christians seemed free to do what they thought was right, did not work for me. The directions from my Shepherd would only come from within my heart.

"It is not till sinful self is slain; that Christ can fully reign." This became one of my slogans.

The obedient surrender of my heart, that most profound area within me where the Holy Spirit united me with Christ's Kingdom, brought about the most satisfying experiences in my life. Of course, today I have a much better understanding of what was happening. Over the years of my walk with the Lord, I gave Him access into areas of my heart that were still under my own jurisdiction. As a result of my willingness to relinquish these secret areas, I was beginning to enjoy an inner dialogue with Jesus; something that may sound weird to some, but it is so real that I wouldn't change it for anything in this world; precisely because it is not of this world. I believed Jesus' words, that as a believer in Him I would hear his voice. "My sheep hear my voice, and I know them, and they follow Me" (John 10:27).

Surprisingly, I was not becoming some loony that people would stay away from. Apparently, my colleagues felt that I was still an earthling that they could relate to. I was grateful that I was respectfully accepted by my German managers and colleagues who are known to shun those who act "religious." In fact, I was consulted not only in technical but also in managerial and personal matters. Jesus wants us to be "salt on the earth and light to the world."

Back to the situation at Mercedes Benz; just waiting without at least a silver lining on the horizon was not one of my strengths. After several weeks of diminished activities, I decided to put out my feelers into the job market. I learned that Siemens, another German enterprise, had started operations under a new set of agreements with the new government. This place was close enough to my home. I could ride my bicycle and later my motor scooter; and still later, my 1946 "Morris Eight" car.

Without much vacillation, I reported to the personnel department at Siemens. After a few minutes chat with the receptionist, the personnel manager showed up. He instructed the secretary to notify the company's director, who also joined us. I had to pinch myself to make sure I was not dreaming. During the interview I began to realize that I had two important factors working for me; I was employed by Mercedes Benz and was bilingual.

They offered me an incredible job package. I would be trained by a manager for a year, after which time I would take over the relay and transformer manufacturing department. The acting manager would return to Germany at the end of his contract. The department had about 150 employees. "By the way Mr. Geil, you will be the youngest manager in the entire world-wide corporation, ever to hold this position." With that I was released with a handshake, while slowly "descending back to earth." You may wonder what I am trying to prove. Frankly, I want to testify about the goodness of the Lord and that He is ready to bless all who sincerely trust Him, far beyond their expectations. These blessings or what may be called "luck" by some who are strangers to the goodness of God, were totally orchestrated by the Lord!

But now, what story would I have to conjure up in order to face the head of Mercedes Benz, who had personally asked me to stay? I decided to simply trust God and leave everything in His care. Surprisingly, I was informed that all the directors of German corporations would meet regularly for their Bavarian beer parties. When I met the head of my company to share my predicament, he literally interrupted me to inform the personnel manager to hand me the severance package. Before I left his office, he said: "I lend you to Siemens; and when our operations resume, you are coming back."

I truly enjoyed my job at Siemens. This was another company that strongly encouraged wholesome employee relationships. After my managers' job contract expired, and he returned to Germany, I took over the leadership of the department. With the Golden Rule in mind and heart; (do unto others as you want others do unto you) I embarked in developing an atmosphere of camaraderie that resulted in a substantial increase in productivity, with workers taking home larger paychecks.

One day, during a meeting with my boss, he informed me that the company had decided to employ several blind people. I agreed to take two into my department. One of them was legally blind, whereas the other had no eyeballs. As a small child, Alex (not his real name) was diagnosed with an eye disease that required the removal of his eyes. While meeting with my supervisors to prepare workplaces for these new workers, I felt that I wanted to train Alex myself. It was amazing to observe the change in my department's working climate as these two blind men found their way into our hearts. Later, Martha and I purchased a small portable radio and a Braille wrist watch and surprised Alex on his birthday.

In a short period, I learned from Alex what would have taken me years. I began to understand the importance of the fruit of the Spirit that the apostle Paul mentioned in Galatians chapter five. Even though there are nine listed; fruit is singular, as opposed to works of the flesh listed in verses 19-21. I believe that the fruit of the Spirit is an excellent foundation for the gifts of the Holy Spirit. When Paul speaks of the power gifts in 1 Corinthians chapter twelve, he states something that I always took to heart; "but earnestly desire the best gifts. And yet, let me show you a more excellent way," and the apostle goes right into listing the characteristics of godly love, which is paramount for a fruitful Christian life (1 Corinthians 13).

In my simple understanding, I like to compare the fruit of the Spirit and the power gifts of the Holy Spirit with the fruit on a tree and the ornaments on a Christmas tree. The fruit on the tree is the result of everything the tree is; from the seed in the earth to the enjoyment of its final delicious fruit. The ornaments on the Christmas tree will be hung onto the tree just for a season on this earth. Consequently, our fruit will last forever, whereas the power gifts will cease when Christ returns.

Jesus said; "By this everyone will know that you are My disciples, if you have love for one another" (John 13:35). Through Alex I had a marvelous opportunity to practice what the Bible teaches.

My new friend's appreciation of countless things that I took for granted, touched me so deeply, that my life took on a new perspective. My faith in God and my interaction with people moved into a new dimension. Alex became such an important part of my life that I treated him like a son. His daily commute to work took him over two hours, just one way. He lived with his mother in a suburb northwest of the city of Buenos Aires. He had to take two bus rides, two train rides, and one subway ride, plus walking in between. I rode with him one time to get a taste of his ordeal.

What amazed me most in Alex was his wonderful disposition in just about any situation; even during his very long commute. He did not join in with the complainers, but tried to defuse unnecessary tension by responding with a friendly attitude, ready to please. After I trained him on a job that was safe for him, he gradually increased his productivity to the maximum established standard. I believe that this experience was God-sent as part of the transformation of my heart and the renewing of my mind, making me aware that He said: "My sheep will hear My voice, and I know them, and they follow Me. And I give them eternal life, and they shall never perish; neither shall anyone snatch them out of My hand. My Father who has given them to Me, is greater than all; and no one is able to snatch them out of My Father's hand" (John 10:27,28).

How can I not pursue Him who loves me so much and has included me in His eternal plans? I am aware that some, who read my book, may think that such life style is available to only a few select; not so. It is available to all who diligently seek Him. (Hebrews 11:6) Granted, that God's calling and gifting varies from one Christian to another, but our heavenly Father, the Creator of all things, wants every child of His to truly rejoice in Him.

His promise to never ever abandon me was too deeply engraved into my heart for me to fall into despair. It is a glorious experience to come through the darkest night and see His light shining onto my path again. This is only possible with Jesus, our Shepherd who is always at our side. My faith in God became very real and practical; I truly enjoyed life.

Even though I was grateful for my employment at Siemens and for everything the Lord had provided for me and my family in my native Argentina, my mind and heart began to move beyond the borders of Argentina. Upon my return from my Olympic trip in 1953, I had considered moving to the United States. My Papa's words to me, that he had regretted that his parents returned to Germany after they had come to the US in 1904, still resonated in my mind. But the thoughts fizzled out after the attractive job offer mentioned earlier. However, as my boys were growing up, I dreaded the thought of raising them in such a restless society.

However, I could not imagine how I would be able to tackle this move for four people. Well, as many times before, I had some in-depth consultations with my heavenly Father. "Lord, I know that You are not only aware of my desires; but You know my thoughts even from afar off; Your Holy Word tells me so. There is absolutely nothing impossible for You, my Father." Since early childhood, I had learned to earnestly trust my earthly father and now as an adult, this heartfelt trust was extended to my heavenly Father. His response to my obedience was loaded with amazing blessings. I was sold on my God. However, the time was not right for this gigantic move.

In the mid 1950's Argentina experienced a period of spiritual revivals. American Pentecostal evangelists were invited to bring the Gospel of Jesus Christ to the Argentine people. The huge Atlanta soccer stadium was filled to capacity, night after night. A number of members of our Baptist Church attended these rallies, witnessing signs and wonders. As a member of our church board I would join those who expressed criticism of what was claimed to be an outpouring of the Holy Spirit.

One day Martha and I decided to attend one of those revival rallies. I wanted to keep an open mind, lest I judge something that was really from God. Unfortunately, the Christians that most strongly promoted this revival did not reflect, in words and deeds, what should have brought glory to Jesus Christ. This came at a time when I was diligently seeking a deeper relationship with Jesus Christ. When Argentina's president, General Domingo Peron, found out about the many miracles, he asked the evangelist to pray for him. He had a very strange disfiguring skin disease; I remember standing in front of him at a meeting while working for the Department of Education, wondering what had caused his skin to deteriorate. The evangelist prayed over him and he was healed.

Whenever the subject about the power gifts was discussed, either in our church or in Christians' homes, I would always state that I was convinced that the absence of more supernatural manifestations of the Holy Spirit was the product of the hardness of our hearts, and not that they had ceased. Thank God I was to learn much more about this very important subject.

At the end of 1959, at age twenty-eight, I had an amazing experience with the Lord. I was overwhelmed by His presence and I felt as though I was engulfed with warmth and light. In other words, it felt glorious. Something like this is hard to express in words; but be that as it may, I came out of this "cloud" not only totally healed of my nine year battle with stomach ulcers, but filled with joy unspeakable. Bottom line is that after almost fifty years, I am still healed and as joyful as one can be on this side of heaven. Free from this nine year long agony and filled with the joy of the Lord, I committed myself more fully to my God, my family, and my job.

Chapter Thirteen

An Adventurous Vacation Trip

The "love affair" with my Swedish bicycle that had served me well as my personal means of transportation for many years, gradually began to fade into the background, as my mind entertained loftier dreams. But how in the world would I be able to replace my two-wheeler for one with four wheels, when car prices were sky high, way out of reach for the average Joe? Since I was getting used to reaching for the sky, it would not be much different for the acquisition of a car; I reasoned. Aware of the reality that God cannot run out of resources of any kind, I began to search the newspapers for a used car.

My attention was directed to a Morris Eight 1946 and minutes later I hopped onto my bicycle and showed up at the owner's home. We agreed on a price and full of excitement I whispered into Martha's ear that we became owners of an automobile. I gave her only two choices; either agree, or say yes. Of course, this was not a Mercedes or a Maserati; it had a 28 British horsepower, four cylinder engine, and in my excitement I didn't care about anything else as long as it ran. What was a little odd on this British car was that the steering wheel was on the right, for left lane traffic. It was nice when parking it, but it was surely difficult to pass slow drivers. After enjoying this toy for a while, we fantasized about a trip to Rumipal, an idyllic town in the mountains of Cordoba, at a distance of about 350 to 400 miles from Buenos Aires.

I modified the back seat into a bed for our two boys who were now two and five years old, and off we went on a road system that had much to be desired, specifically in the mountains. The entire trip took twenty-four hours. The mountain roads were not paved; just gravel that felt like driving over washboards. The ridges on the gravel roads were the product of torrential rains cascading down the mountainsides. The almost constant vibration of our car made me wonder how this little thing, with hardly any suspension, would be able to take us to our destination. But with God all things are possible, we believed.

Suddenly, with no prior warning, we were shocked by this awful noise that I surmised came from the rear end of the car. I carefully pulled the car over to the side and stuck my head under it. To my dismay I discovered that the rear axle was broken. What is there to do when all one can see are mountains and more mountains and a beautiful sky? There could not be a more applicable verse from God's Word than Psalm 121 verse 1; "I will lift up my eyes to the hills- From whence comes my help? My help comes from the Lord, who made heaven and earth."

After I walked only a short distance, I found myself standing in front of a car repair shop. At first sight, it looked as if it was in the middle of nowhere. A very kind man stuck his head under the car and told us that he could weld the axle. Thanking God for His help we went to a nearby little restaurant, and a couple of hours later we were on our way again. The trip across the mountains was breathtaking in more ways than one. The road was not only curvy and steep, but at times it was so close to the precipice that I had to stay fully concentrated without totally disregarding the many questions echoing from the back seat. Add to this the oncoming cars and the heavy vibration from the rough road it was not hard to understand why I had to keep my hands glued to the steering wheel. What followed next was too difficult to safely process while keeping a cool mind. I needed immediate supernatural intervention. I saw before me a steep descent, followed by a sharp curve and a bridge. As any normal driver would, I applied the brakes to slow down the vehicle; except this time the pedal hit the floor; simply put, I had no brakes. After pumping repeatedly I regained some breaking power but—not for long. By now I was downshifting and when I tried to activate the emergency brakes; they didn't work either. Obviously, something was wrong with the brake system. After a relatively short time I was able to develop a system that brought us safely all the way to our final destination. I wondered how many angels were put in charge of our trip. Our heavenly Father sends His angels to protect those who trust Him;

"For He shall give His angels charge over you, to keep you in all your ways" (Psalm 91:11).

We firmly believed God's Word. Strangely, I was more upset while writing this account into the book, than I was nearly fifty years ago while rolling down those beautiful mountains. As one who was able to "see" the good, even in bad situations; I just trusted the Lord.

We were delighted when we saw this great resort surrounded by beautiful flower beds and impeccable grass. It was funded by the German Embassy and made available to those who requested it. There were certain requirements, including a modest fee, but somehow we qualified and enjoyed the ride. One specific experience that really touched us was that Jewish people, who had survived the Nazi concentration camps, were offered free lodging. For whatever reason, this particular Jewish gentleman became a good friend and we spent many hours in his company. He was very friendly and soft-spoken. In response to our questions, he shared some of the horror stories during his encampment in Europe. What truly amazed me was that his countenance reflected no bitterness or resentment. Martha and I knew that there was a purpose in God's plan for this experience. After enjoying our gorgeous vacation, we packed our semi-disabled four-wheeler and trusting the Lord with all our hearts, we embarked on our return trip.

One nice sunny day, we decided to take a ride through downtown Buenos Aires, and invited Grandma to accompany us. Many of the large street crossings were still manned by traffic police. While we were slowly crossing this eight lane boulevard, our Morris came to a sudden halt. My feverish attempt to get this thing restarted failed miserably. While surrounded by tooting horns and deafening police whistles we disembarked; Grandma, our two boys, Martha and the driver. There was not much else left to do, other than push the car toward the curb. By the way, we all wore comfortable house slippers. Since I was very familiar with the area I decided to walk to a nearby auto repair shop. Not thinking that it was Sunday, I had to devise a plan to move the car to the garage. With plenty of help and a fairly leveled road our Morris ended up in the "hospital" where it spent the next couple of months.

The totally unexpected diagnosis revealed that the engine block had to be replaced. A broken piston had worked its way through the cylinder wall and—who knows what else was damaged. Anyway, the mechanics were really nice guys and did what was necessary to get my "toy" back onto the road. The reason for the delay was that every major part had to be ordered from England. What was not amusing was that I had been "taken to the cleaners" by the seller. He assured me that the car was in good condition. Did I have any options besides swallowing the bitter pill and try to smile? What was there for me to do in order to get compensated for the damage after I perceived the following words of Scripture?

"Beloved, do not avenge yourselves, but rather give place to wrath; for it is written, Vengeance is Mine, I will repay, says the Lord" (Romans 12:19). From experience, I learned not to argue with directions coming from heavenly headquarters.

Peace pervaded my heart and after about two months of being demoted to my faithful bicycle, the Morris left the shop with a "fair" bill of health. Like He had many times before, the Lord ordered ways to turn bitterness into sweetness. It always amazes me how many experiences God uses to refine our character. How often do we run out of patience or get angry at people without realizing that Satan is involved, more than we are willing to believe; and when he is done with his evil deeds, the Lord takes over and turns it into something good. I was happy to be able to drive to work protected from the weather conditions. Sometimes, when the engine failed to start I used the crank and only one single turn did the job.

Even though I enjoyed my management position at Siemens and the potential of advancing into greater responsibilities, I was concerned about the socio-political situation in my country. Faced with an exorbitant rate of inflation and a shaky political situation, my plans to leave Argentina began to accelerate. But how in the world could I move to the USA, since I had no one to direct me, and Germany was out of question? Jesus said; "With men this is impossible, but with God all things are possible" (Matthew 19:26). Wow, this is awesome; if Jesus said so, I have absolutely no problem believing His promises; I heard the voice of my Shepherd many times before. Consequently, I decided to set my mind on the United States.

Near the end of 1961, a copy of a German Christian magazine landed in my hands. On the back cover was a small article addressing German speaking Christians in Europe, who were considering immigrating to the United States. The ad was posted by the pastor of a German Baptist church in Milwaukee, Wisconsin. I carefully kept this magazine in a safe place. One day, in early 1962, I came home from work and for the first time I disclosed my plans to Martha.

"Honey, what do you think about leaving for the USA?" "You must be kidding," she responded; "sit down and rest, you will not get me out of Argentina." But I was confident that I would be able to persuade my sweetheart. It did not take long before Martha agreed. I proceeded to write a letter to Pastor John in Milwaukee, Wisconsin, asking three basic questions regarding housing, school schedules, and weather conditions. When I shared with my friends that I was considering moving to Milwaukee, Wisconsin, they gave me a strange look and said: "Why are you moving so close to the North Pole?" The apostle Paul said regarding hardships: "None of these things move me...." (Acts 20:24a), and like the apostle, I wanted my life to count for the cause of the Gospel of Jesus Christ.

Within a short time I received a reply from the Pastor that absolutely overwhelmed me. "I am reserving an apartment in a duplex building owned by a Christian lady. I will mail you a work contract, and an Affidavit of Support, plus a weather chart and school schedules." I was awed by the Pastor's letter; "can this be real?" The next letter followed soon after with a question concerning our arrival date. I had not yet taken the first step of countless items that needed my attention. My first step was to appear at the American Embassy. I was delighted by the Consul's friendly reception and by his expedient processing of all immigration formalities. My visits to the American embassy were nothing short of pleasant experiences; I felt like I was in a different world.

The big problem ahead of me was to request a variety of documents for my family of four. We were all born in different locations. Martha was born on a farm in the province of Chaco, near the jungle. Fortunately, through a relative of hers who was willing to get a certified copy of her original birth certificate, I was spared a lot of trouble. Though bureaucracy in Argentina functioned like a lame turtle; miraculously, within a few weeks I had everything required by the Embassy, securely in my hands.

Next, I had to present my plans to my employer. They tried to persuade me to accept a position in Germany instead of moving to the USA with what they thought, was an uncertain future. However, my heart was set on America. The word uncertainty was not part of my vocabulary. I was absolutely sure God can do everything and anything. Nothing is impossible for Him, because He says so in His book, the Bible. I gave the company six months notice, enough time to train my successor.

Chapter Fourteen

"Don't Cry Argentina."

We decided to travel by ship which allowed us to take most of our belongings with us; which included three large crates and several suit cases. We were booked with the Cap Castillo, a German freighter with first class accommodations for six passengers, scheduled to leave Buenos Aires on the 20th of July 1962. The trip would take approximately three weeks with several cargo stops in South America. Dear friends and relatives helped us with the many preparations, including the transportation of our luggage to the Port of Buenos Aires. Fortunately, we were able to sell our home on time to an acquaintance. Our two boys, Carl six and Gus three years old were excited and ready for this grand adventure. A number of our friends and relatives were also busy planning to leave Argentina as well, with various destinations.

The situation in Argentina deteriorated to such a level that a large segment of the middle class left the country. Of course, my native country was dear to me, and I hoped and continued to pray that overall conditions would improve.

It was not an easy departure from so much that was dear to us. Our parents and my brothers with their loved ones, plus other family members and lots of friends were gathered at the dockside wildly waving as the ship slowly moved away. Buckets of tears flowed while we wondered if or when we would ever see them on this earth again.

It was the third time that I saw what was still visible of the sunken German battleship in the La Plata River. Only the top of the antenna was sticking out of the shallow river that must be constantly dredged to keep the ocean liner traffic moving.

The frequent stops along the coast of Brazil for loading and unloading of cargo, was an exciting experience for all of us. Martha was the only female on board, among over thirty male crew members. We were treated royally in every respect and enjoyed our meals in the company of the captain and the first officer. Although the vessel was relatively small, it was impeccably clean and well equipped for the comfort of six passengers. We were assigned two first class cabins with a connecting door.

Chapter Fifteen

United States of America, Here We Come

Several days after we had left the last city in South America, the radio operator announced that a severe storm was moving into our path. It was evening and we were eating supper. I finished my meal and went to the upper deck. It was very dark as heavy clouds covered the sky. It started to rain, but it did not distract me from speaking with my heavenly Father. My heart was in such intimacy with the Lord that I felt engulfed in His love. "Father, You have opened the door to the United States for us, and I know deep in my heart that You will never leave nor forsake us. I commit this ship, and all the people on board to You for Your protection. I love You and trust You with all my heart. In Jesus' name;" and I went back to our table.

This trip gave me plenty of time to further my knowledge of the English language. My brain had to make room for a third language in a much broader dimension than I had possessed before. This knowledge had to extend into all aspects of life; literature, history, geography, science, the Holy Scriptures, and so much more. But concerning the

Bible; which English translation was really the "inspired one?"- I wondered.

Memorizing Scripture was always of highest priority for me, I grew up in Martin Luther's translation, originally published in 1534 and Casiodoro de Reina's Spanish translation, first published in 1509. Add to this the many modern versions in both languages and I found myself in a dilemma, to say the least. But I wasn't in America yet and I wondered what of my basic British English that I learned in school was to survive in my new home country. I could not have anticipated that, not too long after our arrival, I would be told that the King James Bible was, is, and always will be the only trustworthy Bible. Bless them Lord, they are my brothers and sisters.

The first visible sign of America was a patrolling ship of the Coast Guard. Combined with the switch into English on all the radio stations accelerated my excitement for what was ahead. As the Statue of Liberty appeared my heart went into a tail spin. This was the fulfillment of my dream, namely to enter the USA through the "front door." The first officer knocked on our cabin door all excited shouting; "Mr. and Mrs. Geil, we must have angels on board." I opened the door and asked him why he said this. "This is the first of twenty-one trips from Buenos Aires to New York without encountering a storm." We just smiled and thanked God for his protection and for the opportunity to shine for Him.

After transporting our cargo to the train station in Brooklyn, with destination to Milwaukee, Wisconsin, we headed for Manhattan for a few days of sightseeing. I instructed the taxi driver to take us to a motel on Fifth Avenue. He recommended a hotel near the Empire State building and I agreed. It was about 8 PM as we walked toward the reception counter. Martha and I were impressed by the stately looks of the lobby. We agreed to check in first and then enjoy a nice dinner.

Unfortunately, our first impressions were quickly dashed as we were led to our room on the fifth floor. The attendant tried to unlock the door, but even after trying several keys he was unable to do so. After uttering some unintelligible words he disappeared and when he reappeared he had a crowbar in his hand. To our consternation he started to break away part of the frame and finally the door sprung open. After leaving the scene again, he returned with a broom and a dust pan.

Again he said something that, by his facial expression, I assumed he was apologizing for the inconvenience. We entered the room and pushed a sofa against the door in order to keep out any uninvited guests. Lighting was extremely dim. Needless to say, Martha was not too happy by what she saw. I entered the bathroom and, after my futile attempt to find the light switch, I felt something on my forehead that I assumed was a heavy cob web. As I proceeded to remove the cobweb from my face, I noticed that I was pulling on a string and to my great surprise a light fixture lit up. This was not in line with the plush lobby we had walked into; I thought. Martha's face spoke louder than any words that I anticipated would soon issue from her mouth. After a few more unpleasant surprises, I knew that we were not going to spend the night in this hotel and I told my loved ones that we would discuss our plans over a nice dinner.

It was past midnight when we boarded a Greyhound bus from New York City to Chicago, where we met dear friends from Argentina. They had left a couple of years earlier. From here we called Pastor John in Milwaukee, Wisconsin to announce our imminent arrival. He was beside himself wondering where we were. He had been waiting for weeks unaware that we were traveling by ship. With all the pressure and excitement during our preparation for our trip, I totally forgot to inform our new pastor in Milwaukee of our travel plans.

Our friends took us to Milwaukee where Pastor John and his dear wife welcomed us in their home. He showed us the upper flat of a house that he had reserved for us on 34th Street and helped us in the purchase of our basic necessities. "Brother Geil, you will start your job in two days, so get ready quickly," he said sternly. For a moment I had forgotten that pastor John served in the German army as a chaplain, which didn't allow me much room for negotiating. He was the Pastor of the Baptist Church that became our spiritual home for the next fifteen years. I began to practice what I had thought long before our arrival in America; "Keep your ears and eyes wide open, your brain properly engaged and your mouth shut."

We loved our new church friends. It reminded Martha and me of our church in Buenos Aires. These were mostly German speaking refugees from different countries in Europe; naturally bringing with them all their local idiosyncrasies, to which we added our own mix from Argentina.

One evening, while unpacking our belongings, we heard this absolutely loud noise that shook the two story building. We were shocked. "What in the world was this?" We ran out of the house and found absolutely nobody out there. If this would have happened in Buenos Aires, the entire neighborhood would have been packed with curious people. We walked to the nearest food store, not meeting a single soul on our way. In my funny English I asked about that explosion. The answer came; "Oh, that was a sonic boom." I had no clue what that meant. We saw no fire trucks, no police cars and the owners of the building were out on their bee farm where they lived during the summer months. Since we had no telephone yet, we had to wait until Sunday. In church we learned about the Cuban crisis and that the scary "explosion" was the sound of a jet plane flying faster than the speed of sound. I needed to get with it and carefully disguise my ignorance.

Two days later I stood on the corner of our street, waiting for someone who had been instructed to pick me up for my job at a construction site, who knows where. Close to an hour later we arrived at our destination. Practically at a snap of a finger I was shoveling gravel through a basement window. With the temperature rapidly moving into the nineties, I was drenched in perspiration. While fantasizing about our three week vacation cruise, I failed to notice the blisters that began to appear on my hands. After the pile of gravel disappeared, I found myself in the basement tamping the gravel and getting it ready for the pouring of cement.

Suddenly I heard: "Hey, brother, slow down, you are working too hard." Is this the voice of an angel? I thought. Who else would bring a reprieve to my predicament, I wondered? This "savior" introduced himself as a relative of the owner of the construction company and we became good friends. The sun had set, and when I could hardly see anymore, car headlights provided the necessary illumination. I wondered what Martha thought had happened to her man. She had called the owner's wife and was told that I was doing fine. When I finally walked through the door she wondered whether I regretted coming to the USA. Did I reflect on my management positions in Buenos Aires? Perhaps; but in no way did I think that I had made a mistake. We thanked God every day for bringing us to this great country; and for those dear people who helped us in the process.

After having been picked up several times by one of my fellow workers, I thought it was time to buy a car. I quickly got my driver's license and without any delay, the Geil family landed on this dealer's used car lot to look for "our automobile." The dealer, who was a friend of many members of our church, walked us through the car lot, when suddenly my loved ones stopped and pointing to this enormous station wagon said: "Daddy, let's get this one." It was a 1959 Chevy Parkwood, which the dealer said we could buy for $1,200. This was the exact amount we received for our 1946 Morris Eight before we left Argentina. The difference between the two cars was mind boggling; one with a 28 horse power engine and this one, twice as long, with a 350 horsepower engine. Our children were ecstatic. Finally, they were able to make their bed for our long trips. With this powerful vehicle we were able to rent any trailer for our frequent camping trips. God must have smiled seeing His kids filled with excitement.

Though I was grateful for my first job in the US, I did not plan to accumulate a lot of seniority. After several weeks I landed a job as a maintenance electrician with a well known small gas engine manufacturing company. My knowledge of the English language increased day by day as I was very eager to become proficient in my third language. Consequently, Martha and I attended evening courses and later citizenship classes.

Upon my arrival at the personnel department, I joined a number of applicants for a briefing session. I picked up about 20 to 30% of what was said. I thought I would learn as time moved on. Yes I did, but not without some painful pitfalls along the way. Everybody was handed some literature and a pair of eyeglasses and I was then escorted to the electrical department. No great welcome or shaking of hands. Strange words bounced off my brain without registering. I was taught Basic English in school, not anticipating that I would be exposed to American English and not British. To assure that I would not make a fool of myself, I always carried a Spanish - German pocket dictionary with me. There were hundreds of machine tools and die cast furnaces in the plant.

Every machine had a number assigned and, for a few times, I was escorted to a machine that needed repair by one of the old time electricians. The operator would explain what was functionally wrong, and with the electrical print before me I was to trouble shoot the multifaceted machine. I wished I could understand the girls who frantically tried to explain their trouble. With lots of smiles and hand motions I had to analyze the problem and fix it. I was on my way back to the shop when this angry man approached me shouting; "where did you come from?" "From Argentina," I responded. I wondered what he really wanted; grabbing my arm he walked me across the plant in the direction of the electrical department, with all eyes upon me.

He must have known by my tools that I was an electrician. Here I stood, absolutely puzzled, while this man is speaking with my supervisor. What in the world have I done wrong? Half in German and half in English, my boss explained that I was stopped by the safety engineer, because I had not worn my safety glasses. It was absolutely forbidden to walk near die cast machines without safety glasses. It was now etched into my brain—never to be forgotten. My own words immediately popped into my mind; "keep your eyes and ears open, your brain engaged, and your mouth shut."

This was only the beginning of my Americanization process. There was much more to come. My next assignment was to follow Bill, one of the senior electricians, to a large warehouse building. Bill stopped, and while chewing his tobacco said; "get the scaffold." He was a man of very few words and I was not ready to give away my ignorance. Walking a few steps, acting as if I knew where I was going, I hid behind a huge pile of storage pallets, and carefully consulted my English-Spanish dictionary. Now, one word that I had already heard endless times was "get." I opened my little dictionary and found a whole page of definitions of the word "get;" but which one would apply to "scaffold?" At first I was so grateful that I found the word scaffold with only one definition; "A place where a person is hanged." Oh no, Bill was pulling my leg. I am puzzled, but I cannot show it.

On the streets of Buenos Aires you do not give away your ignorance; lest you are taken advantage of. Now, here in the great United States of America, I felt like a "dog in a bowling alley." Thank God, Charlie, a fellow electrician, who was on his way to a trouble call, saw my puzzled face and in his basic knowledge of German asked; "What do you need Harold?" I explained, and he showed me a cart full of pipes and clamps. Of course, I thought, we needed this structure to hang lighting fixtures on this twenty plus feet high ceiling. Thank God for another angel. A few days later Charlie said to me; "Harold, in two years you will be out of here and get a job in a different company." I was puzzled, but it encouraged me to move on.

In a matter of days I became known around the plant. When my boss thought I had enough training, he sent me out to a trouble call with a helper. On our way to the broken machine, my helper stopped me and said; "I am in charge, you are my helper." Well, I was puzzled, but perhaps I had misunderstood my boss and I obliged. Later, back in the shop, I heard through the grapevine that my boss straightened things out. It had something to do with Union regulations. The boss shared the outcome with me, and I moved up a notch in his mind and heart, while my former helper became another friend of mine.

Our first winter in the USA made its debut with a big bang. With temperatures dipping to minus twenty seven degrees Fahrenheit, the city of Milwaukee drastically changed its landscape into a winter dreamland or a nightmare, depending on who we spoke to. With the incredibly powerful engine under the hood of my car, I had no clue how to handle this vehicle through what I saw on the other side of my windshield. Smiling at my new friends while listening to their well meaning advice, I was convinced that this risk taker from Buenos Aires had learned to survive any imaginable traffic situation. However, this was absolutely beyond anything I could have imagined. A particular early morning, after entering the huge parking lot of my workplace, I quickly turned my steering wheel while aiming at a specific parking spot. To my horror I found myself "disconnected" from my vehicle, the moment I put my foot on the brake pedal; it just wildly spun around. Instantly, the words of the State Motor Vehicle examiner flashed into my mind to turn the steering wheel in the opposite direction and, praise God, it worked. However, there was much more to come; after I had my first experience driving on icy roads.

Surprised to see my buddies go out to their cars with their lunch bags, I learned that they warmed up their engines for an easier start at quitting time. I decided that I would be better off inside the heated plant and take care of my car at the end of my shift. Obviously, this was not a smart decision as I soon found out. With the temperature at almost thirty below zero, and my car parked against the wind, I learned one of my hardest lessons ever. I turned the ignition key and all I heard was a very brief sound, indicating that the engine was not even moving. With my head under the open hood, I inadvertently touched the hearts of some co-workers, who called the nearest service station for help. While waiting for their response, I briefly reminisced about the subtropical climate that I had left behind. After a few attempts to start my car, the mechanic decided to tow my car into the garage for a quick battery charge and, minutes later, I was on my way home. This was only a taste of many more new things that were to come.

So here I was thirty one years old in a new country, and even though I had learned much about the Bible, I needed to become more acquainted with God's laws of the universe and how they operate in our lives. We cannot break them; they will break us through the cycle of sowing and reaping or cause and effect, unless cancelled by the cross of Jesus Christ, through repentance and forgiveness. So, what is my point, you may ask. Back in the 1950's, millions of Europeans immigrated to Argentina. Many settled in Buenos Aires, the capital city and had a hard time adjusting to the life pattern of a thriving metropolis. I was sure that, as a native, I had judged many for acting strangely and now I found myself on the reaping end. All these many and various experiences became character building blocks for my walk with the Lord, granted that I would keep my sense of humor alive and well.

It amazed me that I had started my employment with this company on September 28th, 1962 and on September 28th, 1964 I was hired by a major international corporation. How did Charlie know? God knows and that was good enough for me to just continue to trust and obey Him. I answered an ad in a Milwaukee newspaper for a city licensed maintenance and construction electrician. I got the license and was hired. In order to attract me to this job I was offered the same hourly rate I received at the company I was leaving behind; which was above the pay structure of my new employer. With God all things are possible.

In Psalm 27, David quotes the Lord saying that "He orders the path of His blessed one and delights in his ways." I know that God, the Creator of the whole universe, who knows every star, also knows the secrets of my heart and my thoughts; why not give Him everything and receive from Him what He knows is best for me. I can't even begin to count the stars on a clear night without getting dizzy or falling asleep. What an awesome God I serve; giving my heart to Him was the best move I have ever made. When I have these outbursts of joy, I wish I could convince everyone around me to believe in Jesus Christ and that there is absolutely no better way of life.

During the first few weeks of employment I sensed some antagonism from my co-workers. I was told that my fellow workers got wind of my pay rate. If they had planned to push me out, I knew that they would fail; and soon the working environment turned into one of camaraderie.

Before accepting this position, I had considered attending Marquette University to further my education in the electrical engineering field. I was accepted, but changed my mind after considering my strenuous time schedule. In my heart I knew that I possessed what it would take to pursue a professional career; however, not at the expense of my highest priorities. Early in my marriage I had decided that my family took first priority after my God, a decision I have never regretted. The year 1963 had other eventful surprises in store. The most exciting was that Martha was expecting a baby. Again, like we did with our two boys, we prayed over the baby, believing that God would be pleased to richly bless His new creation.

On November 7th, 1963 our daughter Lilly was born at St. Joseph's Hospital in Milwaukee, Wisconsin. I praised God for rewarding us with a girl, in addition to our precious boys. In the same year, we decided to buy a house. A construction company that was offering to build homes with only a five percent down payment seemed the right way to become homeowners. When we sold our home in Argentina, the buyer had asked to pay a remaining balance at a later time. I shared with him that my parents would most likely follow us in 1963, and I agreed with his request. When we signed the contract with the builder, I was counting on the cash that was due to me from Argentina.

After my parents arrived, my mother handed me a note from the buyer stating that he refused to pay me the balance unless certain new stipulations were met. My first reaction was an angry one; but mother quickly added that the Lord has incredible ways to compensate our losses when we are willing to forgive people for hurting us and continue to trust

Him with all our heart. I believed mother, who had experienced God's love and kindness all of her life. I never again heard anything from this former colleague.

It was absolutely awesome how God responded to our prayers. I even received a check from the Wisconsin Tax Department, notifying me that I had overpaid them on my taxes. It was difficult convincing my friends that I was telling them nothing but the truth. God's wonderful blessings just poured upon us; our Father loves to surprise His children!

In November of 1963, while shopping at a local drug store for several items for our new born baby, I was shocked to hear an announcement that President John F. Kennedy had been shot while riding in a motorcade in Dallas, Texas.

During the years 1963 and 1964 we helped several family members immigrate to America. My brother George and his family, my brother Luis and family, my parents and Martha's parents, all found their new home in Milwaukee. Additionally, a number of our church friends from Argentina showed up in Milwaukee. After living in our first rented home for two years, we moved into our own brand new home.

Shortly after arriving in Milwaukee, Pastor John asked me to join the board of deacons. This did not go over too well with some of the senior members. I did not feel that I was pushing myself into any position and after accepting the offer, I knew I was going to win over those who felt that I was too young and inexperienced.

Martha and I agreed that Milwaukee was a great place to raise a family. We lived only a few miles from Lake Michigan and from many wonderful parks. There was a wealth of many things to enjoy in Wisconsin. With regard to restaurants; there was a good selection with a great variety of ethnic menus. Martha established wonderful friendships among the ladies' group and the choir members. Our children found their place in Sunday school. We wanted to be what Jesus prepared us to be wherever we are; light in this dark world and salt on our morally decaying earth.

We truly experienced the love of Christ from those who sacrificially offered their time and means to make our transition a delight. We have countless memories that cannot be forgotten. In fact, every loving deed is recorded in heaven. Our son Carl was placed in first grade and as is the case with most children, it did not take long for him to learn English, thus adding another language to German and Spanish. We considered ourselves a happy family. Enjoying our frequent trips around the State of Wisconsin with its beautiful lakes and great campgrounds in our 1959 Chevy Parkwood station wagon became a way of life. We loved to sing and praise the Lord; singing and hearty laughter became an integral part of our family. We greatly enjoyed the outdoors and before long we were out shopping for a camper. It was such a great way to enjoy God's creation.

One day in 1968, while responding to a trouble call at my job, I was paged to report back to my shop. I was told that my Papa passed out while shopping at our favorite deli and was now being transported to the Milwaukee County Hospital. Not knowing the difference between passing out and passing on, I thought he had died. Instead of condolences, I was told to take the rest of the day off and take care of my dad. Papa recuperated quickly from a stroke and I was able to pick him up for sightseeing trips around greater Milwaukee. Papa was truly happy, and countless times he expressed his gratitude for being back in the United States, after more than sixty years.

In 1969, we decided to become American citizens. It was the law at this time that immigrants could not become US citizens until they had lived in the US for five years. After attending citizenship classes we were sworn in; a very important step in our Americanization process. My picture showed up in our company's periodical, while my boss was handing me an American flag. After years of keeping my mouth shut and my eyes and ears wide open about my professional background, I gradually began to share some of my past corporate experiences. I was asked to hire electricians and organize our own electrical department. My management instinct began to resurface, and I enjoyed every minute of it.

In 1971, I was offered a position with the business expansion group which had embarked on a major construction project that would cover the entire country. In 1975, we sold our home in the city of Milwaukee and moved into a lovely stone house located in the Milwaukee suburb of Brookfield.

Chapter Sixteen

Papa Departs for his Heavenly Home

I noticed that my Papa's health began to deteriorate. After an in-depth medical exam, it was decided that he undergo surgery. The prognosis was not good, and the doctor predicted only several months of life. Working so close to the Milwaukee County Hospital, allowed me to visit Papa during my lunch time. Those were the most precious moments in our relationship in terms of learning more about my dad. I was glad that I had urged him a couple of years prior, to record his life's story. He gave his three sons and my mother a hand-written copy of his autobiography.

Papa did not complain about anything while in the hospital. At times he would ask me for some ice cream and he loved it when I came to visit him with one of his favorite delights in my hand. Sometimes, when I took Papa for a ride, he would meet with some of his good friends from our church, who loved to treat him with some delightful snacks. One time he shared with me, with a smile, that one of them had treated him with a glass of special wine. I am grateful that my parents modeled the importance of handling this often touchy matter with love and tolerance. A glass of wine for special occasions was welcomed in our home and we appreciated not being judged by fellow Christians.

Papa's condition deteriorated to the point of requiring life supporting equipment. One day, on one of my daily visits, I saw Papa sitting in his bed, with his head down and eyes closed. As I moved close to his bed he motioned his hand, indicating for me to sit down on his bed. After a few minutes, he lifted up his head and looked at me with a beautifully radiant countenance, and shared what I know was a wonderful vision.

"Harold, I noticed when you came in, but I did not want to lose track of the vision. I saw this great, serene body of water. At the horizon, I saw a bright light reflected across the surface of the water. And then, slowly rising from the horizon, I saw this head appear and I immediately knew it was Jesus, my Lord. He rose up higher and I saw His arms outstretched and then His echoing voice sounded so clearly; 'Ludwig, come home.'" By his radiant face and beautiful smile I knew my Papa was overwhelmed, joyfully looking forward to meet his Lord. He requested that all life-supporting equipment be removed. At that moment the doctor walked through the room and I told him my father's wish. He looked perplexed and walked away.

When I returned after work, I was glad that his wish had been carried out. Interestingly, not long before, my dad had shared with me that he wished to live a few more years; but now he was totally prepared for his new, eternal home! Within the next five days his physical condition deteriorated rapidly. I leaned over to get close to his face so I would not miss any words. Papa whispered; "Harold my son, I am going home to be with the Lord; I will see you in heaven; please look after Mama." The next day, while my mother and Martha stood at his bedside, Papa left this world. Praise God for his glorious departure. Not long before, Papa told me that George, my younger brother, will come into the fold; meaning that he would accept Jesus Christ as his Lord and Savior. Praise God, he did.

Chapter Seventeen

On the Move Again

My new job required a moderate amount of travel to various construction sites as well as our corporate headquarters in Manhattan, New York. Leaving my family behind was always a difficult experience. My boys were teenagers and Lilly was eight years old. I was blessed with a loving and godly family; something I certainly did not take for granted. Upon my return from business trips I was received with loving surprises. Sometimes Martha had the tape recorder running to capture the welcoming scenes. To hear how my children helped Martha in my absence was very rewarding. Our God is indeed a loving and caring Father, always providing our needs and also our desires. He loves to bless His children in ways that we do not even dare to ask.

"Oh, God our Father, You are so kind and generous; open our understanding and greatly increase our faith so that we dare to move beyond our self imposed limitations. I pray Father that people around us will sense Your love through us and be encouraged to seek You, the almighty God and Jesus Christ the only way to You."

Christians are often hesitant to ask God for what they desire. But God states in His Word that if we delight ourselves in Him, He will grant us the desires of our heart. (See Psalm 37:4) The deeper our will is anchored in our Father's will, the more rewarding our lives will become. In fact, it becomes our delight to walk daily in intimacy with our Shepherd, the Lord Jesus Christ. However, this relationship requires our obedience and willingness to fully open our hearts to Him.

During the month of November 1976, I was notified that our vice-president wanted to present his plans to the business expansion group; of which I was a member. A great deal of our business planning had to be coordinated with the engineering and architectural group, located at our corporate headquarters in New York City. Consequently, our boss decided to move our group to Manhattan. As one who grew up in a major metropolis, I did not mind working in a large city again, and felt honored by the offer.

Chapter Eighteen

Stricken with Grief

In December of 1976, while still living in Milwaukee, without any prior warning signs, Martha, my dear wife, was advised by a well known surgeon that she needed to undergo a radical mastectomy. The surgery was performed in January, on the day of Jimmy Carter's inauguration as president of the United States. Martha was showered with prayers from all directions. I was perplexed and, falling on my face, I desperately sought answers from my heavenly Father.

This was the first time that the joy of the Lord, which always filled my heart since I was miraculously healed in 1959, turned into deep sorrow. I was shocked by the doctor's diagnosis. After crying my heart out before God, I jumped to my feet, and with His joy restored, I returned to Martha's bedside at St. Joseph's Hospital, in Milwaukee, Wisconsin. According to the surgeon's report, the surgery was successful.

What was I to do about the offer to move to New York? I could hardly concentrate. Unending questions flooded my mind. I laid everything before the Lord in prayer. "Father, I need your help; You promised that You would never leave nor forsake me, no matter what the situation. I will continue to trust You with all my heart and love You with all my strength." I brought my concerns to our next deacon meeting and asked for direction. The majority of my brethren suggested that I decline the company's offer. We had established a caring relationship and as the head of the board, they asked me to stay in Milwaukee.

Furthermore, my aging mother would certainly need my help. I informed my boss about my predicament and my regrets of having to turn down their generous offer. The offer included relocation by July 1977, after selecting a place of residence from one of three states; Connecticut, New Jersey or New York.

I continued to ask God for wisdom and guidance. When I presented my situation to my mother, her response surprised me. "Harold, my son, if your job is transferred to Manhattan, New York, you need to consider moving along." Thank God, Martha's condition improved and the surgeon released her for our move. However, Martha had to submit to a rigorous period of rehabilitation. When I informed my bosses that I had reconsidered the company's offer, they were pleased. No doubt, God was still in charge. "Give me your heart, My son, and the way will open before you," I perceived God speaking to my heart.

God is a rewarder of those who diligently seek Him; and I was totally committed to doing just that. But my understanding of the truth of the Bible was limited to what I was willing to accept as applicable to me personally, in every situation. If I was to be a "vessel for honor, sanctified and fit for my Lord, prepared for every good work," as I frequently asked Him; (2 Timothy 2:21) then I needed to open every area of my innermost being to the Holy Spirit. This process does not come to us automatically; it is activated through childlike faith and obedience.

The department in charge of employees' transfers suggested that we consider Middlesex and Monmouth counties for our new location and to stay away from Mercer County where real estate prices were considerably higher.

With Martha and our children looking forward to an exciting new adventure, we drove around Central New Jersey, while praying up a storm. We strongly believed that there was a house on the market, just for us. Martha put her foot down and emphatically declared; "You will not commute to New York by bus, but only by train." She remembered my commuting by train to downtown Buenos Aires, which was more reliable than the bus. I had to smile while wondering where we would find our house. We unanimously decided to investigate Mercer County.

When we came to Princeton Junction, NJ, we walked up to the train station and at that moment an Amtrak train was rolling in. I studied the train schedule and was impressed that it took only forty-five to fifty minutes from Princeton to Manhattan, NY. Compared to my commuting experience in Buenos Aires, this seemed like flying.

We stopped at the closest real estate office, and the agent told us that a two story Colonial house had just been listed; in fact, it was not even advertised. We went to look at it and, in one accord, we exclaimed; "this is our place." Our son Gus came running out of the house, all excited after he saw an in-ground swimming pool in the back yard. The owner was a United Airline pilot, who had been transferred to the state of Washington. We made an offer that was accepted.

Singing and praising God we returned to Milwaukee. To my delight, my company sold our home in Brookfield, Wisconsin for more than what was agreed upon for our new home on the east coast. As we prepared for our move, we reflected on the many wonderful experiences we enjoyed during our fifteen year stay in picturesque Wisconsin, surrounded by friends and relatives. I was particularly grateful that my brother George and his family lived in Milwaukee and were willing to look after Mama. Through the years, we made frequent trips back to the Midwest where we had left behind many delightful memories.

My salary was generously adjusted to the increased cost of living around the New York metropolitan area. In the past, I never asked for a raise; I just believed that by leaving money matters to God I would always be surprised. He said it in His word; I believed it and that settled it for me!

Excited to move into a new adventure, we embarked in establishing new friendships. Prior to moving east, I investigated the possibility of transferring our church membership to a sister church in a location nearest to our new home in New Jersey. The closest one was a half hour drive from West Windsor, our home township. All five of us found our place in that church and, for four years, it became our spiritual home. Our boys taught Sunday school, Lilly played the piano, Martha became active in the ladies missionary group and I accepted the positions of a deacon and adult Sunday school teacher.

After four years of attending the Baptist church three to four times a week and watching Martha's physical condition weakening, we decided to visit an Evangelical Church within one mile from our home. This became our next spiritual home. I was asked to join the board of elders and Martha and our children, again, found their place in this church in various activities. I soon adjusted to my commute to Manhattan. I decided to attend Bible school to further my knowledge of the Holy Scriptures and the comfortable Amtrak train rides afforded me the opportunity to do my school assignments.

The train station was only ten minutes from home and the township provided a very convenient parking lot for local residents. My office was located on the 37th floor of 6th Avenue and 52nd Street, near the Rockefeller Center. Having the choice to, either walk twenty two blocks from Penn Station, or take the subway; I mostly chose to walk.

The strategic location of our office building, with underground connections to many businesses, provided convenient access to many points of interest. In a relatively short time, my colleagues and I became familiar with Midtown and Lower Manhattan. Sometimes, while comfortably relaxing on an Amtrak seat, I was reminded of the four mile, ten minute commute to work in Milwaukee and how, at times, I would get annoyed by one single traffic light.

In April of 1979, Martha began to feel pain in her lower back and we decided to see her doctor who recommended that X-Rays be taken. With the test results in his hand, the doctor laid his arm on our shoulders and said; "I am very sorry to report that the disease has advanced into Martha's spinal cord." While I broke down in tears, my precious wife comforted me and lovingly said; "Honey, everything is in our Lord's hand." Her inner strength absolutely amazed me. When I watched her walk with great difficulty, while holding on to my arm, I stammered words of gratitude to God for her courage.

Our lives began to slow down. Many things that were on top of our "honey-do list" began to lose their urgency and new priorities were established. I believed what I experienced in my walk with Jesus Christ over the years, would now be put to the test. My faith and trust in Him were beginning to take a major upswing; and so did my love for God and people. It may sound unreal, but my heart began to connect with my Father's heart; there was no other way to explain this deep joy, accompanied with the inner assurance that He loved me beyond my comprehension. This gave me an extra measure of strength.

Martha's condition was treated with Chemotherapy. After the negative side effects had subsided, her condition improved to the point that she was able to function fairly well. However, we were faced with questions, many of which could not be answered. I wanted the Holy Spirit to fine tune my spirit and my soul to the point of being able to clearly discern my Shepherd's voice. As did the apostle Paul, I decided that nothing shall move me away from pursuing my calling and to finish my course with joy, and the ministry that I have received from my Lord Jesus Christ, without regard to what may come into my life. Jesus promised that His sheep will hear His voice and follow Him. (John 10:4) Jesus calls His own sheep by name and leads them. He goes before them; and the sheep follow Him, for they know His voice. They will by no means follow the voice of strangers (John 10:4,5).

Surrounded by all kinds of inner and outer voices, I needed to be saturated with the Word of God, knowing from the words spoken by Jesus Christ that only God's truth will set me free. And whom the Son makes free will be free indeed (John 8:32,36).

I want to encourage you to pursue intimacy with our heavenly Father through faith in His Son Jesus Christ, and you will be rewarded with such peace and joy that this world with all its goods cannot offer.

I value wise counsel from Christians who are committed to walk with the Lord Jesus Christ while enjoying intimacy with God. Through the many years since my conversion to the Lord, I have learned to avoid arguments that lead to extremes. Not that I close my ears to what many sincere Christians are struggling with; but I love to share what I have learned without expecting people to accept something they are not ready for. Aware of my own shortcomings, I prefer to listen rather than allowing myself to be lured into a trap of the enemy. The process of learning to listen while keeping my mouth shut was and still is an arduous path.

One day, while still attending the Baptist church in New Jersey, I was asked by one of the pastors whether I expounded Calvin's or Armenian's theology. Never having been confronted with this question before, I answered that

I was a disciple of Jesus Christ and that His Gospel is the basis of my beliefs. Of course, I had learned about the lives and beliefs of these men of God. The question I was asked was related to losing our salvation and the gift of eternal life. In my mind I thought we can best settle this argument while in heaven. I hope to shed some light into this often hotly debated issue by sharing some personal experiences.

I remembered that the dear pastor of my first and only church in Argentina expounded an Armenian theology. I truly loved Uncle Conrad, but I know that he was not very happy when challenged in his theology. I spent many hours in his home asking endless questions; he treated me like a son. Over the years I came to the conclusion that I do not like the tension of the extremes, specifically in theological matters. I wanted to walk with Jesus, at His side; not ahead, nor behind Him, so I could listen even to His whispers. During times when our church had no pastor, Brother Alfred would teach and preach in addition to directing our choir. He was a very gifted man. I liked his soft mannered style and his loving disposition. To this day I often wonder why some preachers have to shout through their entire sermon, when they have such great sound systems.

Brother Alfred was a widower and there was a period when he missed a number of services. Rumors spread that he was dating a lady who owned a gift shop in town, but was not a Baptist. All kinds of rumors provided plenty fodder for the gossip mill, to the point that many in the congregation believed that he fell from grace and was on his way to hell. For years I refused the thought that Brother Alfred was lost. Several years later, I was informed of his death. To me this remained an unresolved matter for years. Deep in my heart I felt that someday the Lord would resolve this conflict in my mind.

On my first return trip to Argentina, after living in the USA for twenty two years, I met a good old pastor friend. I asked him what he knew about Brother Alfred's relationship with Jesus Christ, and he shared his experience: "I sat at his bedside during his last hours of life, and I can assure you that he was reconciled to his Lord and had a peaceful departure from this earth." I was very happy that God satisfied my heart's desire.

I was now assured that if someone becomes a Christian by publicly confessing Jesus Christ as Lord and Savior, he has eternal life. If he decides to live his life without Christ, he will be relentlessly pursued by the heavy hand of his Master and will finally be reconciled to him. I have seen it on more than one occasion while sitting at the bedside of dying Christians. Praise God, our loving heavenly Father, for His faithfulness and His infinite love and grace.

After the doctors assured us that Martha's condition went into remission, and following a desire that I had entertained for years, I decided to continue to pursue my studies at the Bible School in Manhattan. Classes were held on evenings in a nearby church, so I was able to walk from my office. Of course, it meant that I would be out till late evening hours, twice a week. Over the following three years I was able to complete sixteen courses. By then it was the year 1982. After a medical examination, we were told that the disease had progressed into Martha's lungs. In July, we decided to travel to Florida, as we did every year. It was not without difficulties, as Martha's overall condition rapidly deteriorated.

As of September 1982, Martha was totally confined to her bed. Consequently, I had to request hospice service in addition to visiting nurse service, provided by Princeton hospital. In order for me to leave home at 6 AM to commute to my office, ladies of our church generously provided covering for the two hours before and after the nurse's schedule. I was overwhelmed by all the various ways we were blessed by our dear friends. Even delicious meals were brought to our door. Our Lord promised that every loving deed offered in His name will be rewarded,

Our pastor and the members of this loving fellowship truly walked their talk and so much more. My children were spread out around the country. Carl in Chicago, Gus in Cincinnati on job assignments, and Lilly was attending Bible College in Edmonton, Alberta, Canada. At one point, my mother came from Milwaukee to help me. At seventy-five she was no longer a spring chicken, but she did a great job. Her delicious cooking skills had not diminished one bit.

In spite of having so much on my plate, trying to keep things going, I had an incredible amount of energy. Sleeping in intervals with a total of no more than five hours daily and commuting to my office in New York was more than people could understand. My mother often said: "Boy, you look so slim." It was awesome how generous my bosses were in giving me the freedom to arrange my time schedule according to my personal needs. I had people come to my office, asking me how I was able to keep my composure in this difficult predicament. These were precious opportunities to share my confidence and total trust in God. Some took my testimony to heart and accepted Jesus Christ as their Lord and Savior.

As Christmas arrived, I was grateful to have my children and their loved ones back home. Before their arrival I placed a record player under Martha's bed, in order to record this last important event in Martha's life. We had the most precious Christmas ever, just by being around Martha's bedside. Her joyful attitude and solid inner strength encouraged us all. It amazed me how the nurses wanted to spend time, sometimes hours, just sitting next to her bed to hear her testimony for Christ.

Our pastor, as often as he came to visit her, would walk into the room saying: "Martha, my dear friend, I came to be comforted." Martha usually responded with a smile. My precious wife was not a complainer. She often said that it was her heart's desire to love and please the Lord. She was fully aware that she was leaving this world to be with Jesus Christ and had no fear of death. After Christmas, Lilly had to fly back to Bible College in Northwest Canada for her exams, and my sons returned to their out of state jobs. These were heart breaking experiences, to leave their precious Mom, knowing that they would not see her again on this earth.

As February 1983 approached, the doctor predicted that her vital signs would fail in about two weeks. Carl's wife was expecting her second child to be delivered in a few days. It was Martha's last wish to hear about our new grandchild's birth.

On February 2nd Martha told me that her vision was becoming blurred while she was reading a devotional with the author's initials H.G.B. She handed me the sheet and said: "I want you to know that this poem expresses my thoughts, as I look forward to meeting my Lord Jesus Christ soon." The title of this article is "When I am Gone:"

We are....willing rather to be absent from this body, and to be present with the Lord. (2 Corinthians 5:8) The pale specter of Death with his cruel sickle of sorrow is no respecter of persons. He reaps the aged-"the bearded grain"-as well as the tender flowers of youth. If you have recently suffered the heartache of bereavement, be assured that your saved loved one is now alive and enjoying the bliss of heaven's realities. Barbara C. Ryberg has written a beautiful and consoling poem in which she envisions a saint in glory speaking words of comfort to grieving relatives here on earth.

When I am gone, remember that I am with Jesus;
Then do not mourn because I've passed away.
Life holds so much grief and disappointments.
And will you cry because I did not stay?
'Tis only for a spell we must be parted;

Not many years on earth to us are given.
And when my Savior tells me you are coming,
I'll go with Him and welcome you to Heaven.
Grieve not because the eyes that looked upon you.
Shall never see you face to face again;
Rejoice, because they look upon the Savior,
Who gave His life to ransom sinful men.
Weep not because I walk no longer with you.
Remember, I am walking streets of gold.
Weep for yourselves that you for a while must tarry.
Before the blessed Lord you may behold

You can take comfort in the fact that your Christian loved one is experiencing the unending delights found in the presence of Jesus. Therefore, do not selfishly wish he were back on earth. He is so much better off; absent from the body and present with the Lord.

Martha wanted to write with her own hand what she believed in her heart; and while I supported her body she wrote; "To my Honey, my children and grandchildren: I came across this nice poem and I want you to know that it expresses my belief when I will be in Glory with my Lord."

Jonathan, our grandson, was born in February of 1983 and a few days later, Martha went into a coma. During the following ten days we had two snowstorms; eighteen and fifteen inches. Looking out of the front window I saw practically nothing but snow. Returning to Martha's bedside became harder every day as I could no longer converse with her. Of course, I knew that she could hear me. No one else was around, except Prince, our American Eskimo dog. He did not want to leave Martha's bedside; he knew that something was wrong.

Spending hours meditating and watching Martha's breathing gave me plenty opportunity to reflect upon the nearly forty years since I first met her in Sunday school.

Sensing the pain of separation, I was unable to imagine what life would be without my beloved and faithful friend. What did my heavenly Father have in store for me? It was really difficult to plan without Martha. However, I always found comfort in God's Word: "I know the thoughts I think about you, says the Lord; thoughts of peace and not of evil, to give you a future and a hope. Then you will call upon Me, and pray to Me, and I will listen to you. And you will seek Me and find Me, if you search for Me with all your heart" (Jeremiah 29:11-13). The Lord's abiding presence in all areas of my life was the most gratifying experience.

During the time when Martha was still able to communicate with me, she asked me how I would be able to pay for all the many incurring expenses; but quickly added that she was aware that I would completely trust our heavenly Father. She knew that, when I approached a seemingly impassable obstacle, that I would find a way through it. Shortly after that conversation, I left for a business trip. When I returned on Wednesday, my colleagues informed me that a company memo was circulated, offering natural death insurance for spouses of full time employees, without prior medical examination. The response had to be returned by Friday. While filling out the form I had to turn on my "windshield wipers" to clear my eyesight.

I was overwhelmed by my Fathers goodness. When I informed Martha about it, she smiled and said; "I knew the Lord is faithful." The words of Scripture came to mind that says; "The king's heart is in the hands of the Lord, like rivers of water; He moves it wherever He decides" (Proverbs 21:1). I thought; "Yes, Amen." He can even move a whole company, including an insurance company, in order to provide for His loved ones. Our heavenly Father will not let His faithful servants go empty handed. My faith took another big leap.

On February 15, 1983 I was visited by a good friend, one of our church leaders. While sitting in the kitchen, involved in a wonderful conversation, I kept an eye on Martha, who was in the adjacent family room. At one point I interrupted our conversation, as I noticed that she had stopped breathing. Martha had indeed left to meet her Lord in Heaven to enjoy everlasting life, at 7:10 PM at age 50.

My dear friend was deeply impacted by this sad moment and wanted to help me in whatever way possible. I was convinced that the Lord had sent him at the right time. All necessary arrangements for Martha's burial at Princeton, NJ cemetery were handled flawlessly. With so many friends and relatives sharing our grief, it was truly a blessed experience for my children and me. "Thank You my God and heavenly Father for my precious children." They all returned to their respective places. I was grateful that Lilly would soon live with me.

One of my first priorities, after the funeral, was to catch up on my journal. Without it I would not have been able to remember what I considered important for the future. Suddenly, there was an intense knock on the front door. Who was there—but my next door neighbor and another friend from church; with pail and broom in one hand, she ordered me up to my bedroom to catch up with much needed sleep. When I woke up twelve hours later, the house was clean. For one who only slept five to six hours daily, this felt like being on vacation.

Chapter Nineteen

"The Year 1983 in Retrospect"

I wrote this article on my first Christmas without Martha. The great preacher Dwight L. Moody said: "There are three kinds of faith,

1. Struggling Faith; is like a man floundering and fearful in deep water.
2. Clinging Faith; is like a man clinging to the side of a boat.
3. Resting Faith; Finds a man, safe inside the boat, strong enough and secure to reach out and help others. This is the faith that I am praying for."

"Lord, I thank You for the twenty-eight years of a happy and fulfilling marriage to Martha, after years of friendship. I also thank You for making the difficult years bearable and for not giving up on me. I know they brought me closer to You. Keep me, Father, on the path of righteousness all the days of my life, so that people will be touched by my testimony and receive Jesus Christ into their hearts. I know that after a night of sorrow, a day of joy will follow."

I heard about Christians who, after severe trials, experienced depressing inner conflicts; such as anger, lack of enthusiasm, bitterness and guilt. Well, I had a taste of most of them. Sometimes it seemed as though the enemy would unleash forces of darkness trying to destroy me or disrupt my quiet time with the Lord. At times I wondered—what happened to the joy that was mine for so many years. All kinds of evil thoughts pervaded my mind, but I knew that my Redeemer lives, and that one day, Oh glorious day, I will see Him in glory. (Job 19:25)

I kept praying what became part of my daily request for many years to come: "Restore to me the joy of Your salvation and uphold me with Your generous Spirit" (Psalm 51:12).

Then slowly but deeply, joy began to fill my heart again; and I knew that Jesus Christ was fighting the battle against the forces of darkness for me. "Father, You know my heart; I am willing to submit it to You for Your cleansing and complete restoration." I sensed an inner voice telling me that I will come through this time of sorrow and adversity as pure as gold. (Job 23:10)

"Martha, I miss you; your smile, your hearty laughter, your loving and tender care for me and for our precious children. I know how much you loved our Lord and Savior Jesus Christ; friends and neighbors heard your testimony and your invitation to believe in Him for their salvation. I miss your hand that I used to hold when praying together."

"Our children are a reflection of your life; the fruit of your efforts is evident in them. Thank you so much Martha dear. Christ is glorified; and that is what we always desired. You have obtained the reward of your faith in the glorious presence of God; the struggle against the enemy, the 'prince of this world', has ended for you."

Dr. Faris D. Whitesell said: "Physical sufferers, rightly oriented with God, learn things that others miss. They come to a more correct evaluation of what is really worthwhile in life; their spirits are chastened, their motives are purified, their sympathies are deepened and their characters are sweetened."

"It is evident, that the knowledge we obtain from God comes through hard dealings, not merely from hearing or reading of God's Word or from experiences of others. We begin to know what He requires of us, what He wishes to remove from us, and what it is that He desires to accomplish in us;" says Watchman Nee.

Reflecting upon what Jesus Christ did for me on the cross, brought great comfort in times of inner pain. His triumphant resurrection from the grave, followed by His ascension and glorious reception by the Hosts of Heaven, and now seated at the right hand of God, provides the daily comfort to move on in my life. I have determined that, with God's help and in the words of the apostle Paul; "I will fight the good fight, I will finish the race, and I will keep the faith. Finally, there is laid up for me the crown of righteousness, which the Lord, the righteous judge, will give to me on that Day, and not to me only but also to all who have loved His appearing" (2 Timothy 4:7,8).

Chapter Twenty

After a Night of Sorrow, a Day of Joy Will Follow

On December 2nd, I attended a Messiah concert, sponsored by a nearby Bible College. I was invited by my next door neighbor who had unsuccessfully attempted to connect me with some lady friend of hers. Since this was not the first invitation, I decided to oblige. To my surprise, she had also invited some friends; a widow and a gentleman, who somehow ended up sitting together.

As I watched them get into a lively conversation I remembered that had I seen this widow before in our church and I caught myself getting a little jealous. After returning to our seats after the intermission, I was oblivious to the fact that my neighbors played a little trick on me. Somehow, they maneuvered me into the seat next to this cute looking widow. She introduced herself as Jean. I still wonder to this day, how my neighbors were able to pull this one off behind my back. After the concert, my neighbors invited us to a light dinner. Again, they succeeded in bumping me into the seat next to their widow friend.

During our table conversation, I learned that Jean's 50th birthday had been the day before. I mustered the audacity to ask her to see her driver's license to verify her age. We departed and no follow-up ensued. I purposely stayed away from any commitments prior to the first anniversary of Martha's departure to heaven. Furthermore, I had decided to be available for my daughter Lilly who was living with me. Other reasons came to my attention that kept my thoughts away from getting remarried any time soon or perhaps not at all; so I thought. Do I believe that our Father often smiles at His children when they miscalculate situations? I believe He does; and that helps me to relax.

Even if or when remarriage became a consideration, I had no idea at all whom I would consider the God-given woman. My next door neighbor and other well meaning friends wanted to assist me in my selection, but "I knew my credentials" and I was in no way going to yoke myself unequally, no matter who or what came onto my path; period. Furthermore, I was an elder in my church and had no intention of jeopardizing my reputation as a "good Christian." In addition to the above reasons, I had already purchased a flight ticket to Buenos Aires, Argentina, for a three week stay, primarily to visit Martha's surviving parents and other relatives and friends.

However, as was the case more often than I like to admit, God intervened with some specific directions. They were given to me clearly and objectively so my mind could process them accordingly. In order to have scriptural confirmation, I was directed to the Apostle Paul's letter to the Philippians Chapter three verses 7-9. The emphasis was on his determination to put off all things that in any way may hinder his relationship with Jesus Christ. "But what things were gain to me, these I have counted loss for Christ. But indeed I also count all things loss for the excellency of the knowledge of Christ Jesus my Lord for whom I have suffered the loss of all things, and count them as rubbish that I may gain Christ and be found in Him, not having my own righteousness, which is from the law, but that which is through faith in Christ, the righteousness which is from God by faith."

In retrospect, I believe that the Lord brought me to a point in my relationship with Him where I was willing to totally trust in His divine providence for every situation — no matter what the outcome. Frankly, this came as no surprise, because I had asked the Lord for some time to help me come to the point of total surrender to Him. It was at this point that God surprised me with the unexpected.

Around mid February 1984, I was on a business trip to Milwaukee, Wisconsin, with plans to lead a conference on energy conservation. During the flight, and while reviewing my notes for the conference, I perceived, what I recognized as the voice of my Shepherd: "Pursue Jean." I admit that at times we can be doubtful about the source of an inner message; so I asked the Lord for clarification. In order to better follow the Lord's direction and to protect myself from the devil's deception, I decided to keep written records. Of course, if this was from the Lord, I will not hesitate to pursue this invitation! Being in Milwaukee also gave me the pleasant opportunity to visit my mother, my brother and family, as well as friends.

Many preconceived notions, prejudices, and unnecessary Christian traditions had to be sacrificed in preparation for a new relationship. It amazed me how old habits began to fade. Through my bi-cultural background I inherited a number of pleasantries that refused to succumb to the process of my Americanization, because they actually helped me in my interaction with people; so I thought. God must have smiled again at the list of requests that I laid before Him.

Jean and I attended the same Non-Denominational Church in West Windsor, NJ, near my home. She was teaching Sunday school and I served as an ordained elder. Very discreetly, I approached her at the book table and asked if I could be of any help in her search for a book. She was looking for information about the church's Constitution and By-Laws. We had just updated them so I was able to answer her questions. Then Jeanie said: "I don't know if this is the right Church for me." "Yes, it is," I quickly replied, not knowing her from "Eve." We had a brief chat near the book table, and I quickly returned to my "greeting the people" assignment, while that inner voice; "pursue Jean" echoed in my mind. Later, (after three encounters) I wrote Jeanie (as I like to call her) a brief note containing three questions.

By now I knew she worked for a well known publishing company as the treasurer's Administrative Assistant. The first question was the most important for me. Her reply came promptly; "During my morning quiet time with the Lord, the Holy Spirit directed me to Psalm 40 verse 8; 'I delight to do Your will O my God, and Your Law is within my heart.' This is the answer to your first question," she wrote. Questions two and three were practically answered by the first.

"Lord, if it is her desire to delight herself in You and Your word is within her heart, then she is Your choice for me. Thank You for Your clear directions."

I also learned that Jeanie had been a widow for fourteen years. Her husband Thomas died at age forty-one; Jeanie was thirty-seven. It was a very traumatic experience to live through and raise two precious daughters, ages 12 and 14.

Before leaving for Argentina for a three week visit, I exchanged a number of interesting telephone conversations with Jeanie followed by a couple of delightful dinners. We seemed to be in tune with each other in many ways. I was able to snatch a photograph from her before I rushed to the airport. Was I already bitten by a love bug? If so, I needed to handle this situation discreetly. Jeanie's heartfelt desire for more of Jesus Christ was in harmony with my heart.

Chapter Twenty-One

Jeanie Shares Her Story

My dear husband of twenty-four years (although, in all honesty, it only seems like five) has asked me to share my experience of how the Lord orchestrated our marriage.

I became a widow in my thirties, losing my first husband to cancer at age forty-one. He was a wonderful husband and father; however, I was left with the responsibility of raising our two daughters, Charissa and Debbie, ages fourteen and twelve.

Sad, to say, this loss was not my first experience with the early death of a loved one. During the 17 years of my first marriage to Tom, seven of his nine siblings died before old age. Rumors circulated that a "death curse" was made against this Irish clan, resulting in many premature deaths. I am strongly persuaded to share what I experienced relative to this declaration.

Harold and I were saturated with so much information in the 1990's and more than one of the ministries covered Generational Curses. It was during that period, while we were living in our summer home, that I was awakened out of troubled sleep at about 1:00 AM. I remember sitting upright and waking Harold telling him "I heard a voice instructing me to read Deuteronomy 28, there's a death curse on Tom's family." Harold was now fully awake and he knew what Deuteronomy 28 was all about...blessings and curses. He read the whole chapter and before we went to sleep, we decided to call our dear Counselor friend in Florida. Mainly...what do we do with this revelation?

Early the next morning I called Anne in Florida, and related what had transpired; her immediate response was "Jeanie, I need to talk to Harold and you shouldn't be on the phone." Needless to say, I became pensive and fearful of...what did she have to say to Harold that I couldn't hear? All the while, she instructed him with various Scripture verses and how he was to pray over me. She had no doubt the death curse passed onto me because, through marriage, I was bonded to Tom.

Unfortunately, we waited two days because a dear couple was visiting until Thursday morning. So, Thursday morning we committed ourselves to intense prayer. Harold was instructed to close any open windows or doors as there may be some manifestations.

I sat in a chair and he stood behind me with his Bible and various verses he was to pray over me. He began with prayers for protection and then he proceeded. As he was speaking words of Scripture over me, this ungodly howling and shrieking began to emanate from my mouth. (Harold is now sweating profusely.) Along with the strange sounds out of my mouth, I began to experience a sensation of countless pins and needles starting from the top of my head, down to my waistline and slowly moving down each arm and finally out of my finger tips. The sounds and the prickly sensation then stopped and I was engulfed in total peace. Some tremendous power of darkness left my body. Harold, now totally relieved, including myself, could not stop praising the Lord for my freedom.

As follow-up, Harold and I told my two daughters of the situation and he asked permission to pray over them. They consented and he prayed and broke any curses coming down the generational line off them. We were so thankful they did not experience any manifestations.

I'd like to incorporate a small portion of my life with Tom. I would like to honor his memory in that he was a dedicated caring husband and a loving father. His nurturing helped to build a strong foundation for Charissa and Debbie. He believed in a united family, especially concerning our faith. He was raised a Roman Catholic and I was brought up in the Russian Eastern Orthodox Church. Tom willingly converted to my faith since his attendance in his church was erratic. He did not want a split in our family due to religious beliefs.

I'd like to share two specific areas which I believe will touch someone "searching for more."

Christmas day was always special for us. Sharing gifts with our children, wonderful fellowship and dinner with our families and, finally, sitting by the Christmas tree later that evening reflecting on the events of the day. We'd always come up with the comment, "how come we feel some kind of vacuum deep inside us?" As you'll read in my story, that vacuum was filled in 1976. This fulfillment in my life was the result of a quest that started early in my childhood. Like, who am I, what's my purpose in life and what is this search and seeking all about?

I know Tom had a heart that was also seeking to be filled. During the two years after he was diagnosed with cancer, he was able to maintain his job until the last two months before he died. The last week of his life, I believe, was one in which every night at 11:00 PM, he had a visitation. He would excitedly exclaim that Jesus had entered the room, and he felt at total peace; while my heart beat was escalating at a rapid pace. I could not see the apparition, but I did not deny it because of what I saw reflected on Tom's face. I believe, regardless of the fact we were not familiar with the need to be born-again as Jesus teaches us, this faithful man went home to be with Jesus.

I was unprepared, challenged and did my utmost to care for these girls as a single parent. I thank God they never went through a period of teenage rebellion. However, the new role of single parent brought out a part of me I call the "Sergeant"—that endeavored to cover the missing male authority in the girls' lives. To this day, on rare occasions, when Harold notices the return of the "Sergeant," he accepts it with humor. In hindsight, I realize I tried to compensate for the missing father image in my daughters' lives.

I was extremely busy being mother and father to these girls and they surely were keeping track of me. I'm very grateful that the Lord blessed me with siblings and a widowed mother who were there for me when I needed help. I will never forget how my sister Margie cared for my daughters, after school, while I was busy at my job.

Early in my life the Lord blessed me with a loving and faithful friend, Dottie; who is still a wonderful and trustworthy friend to this day. She was there through "thick and thin;" and was a beautiful example of the love of Jesus. Harold and I had an extraordinary experience with her while she was visiting us at our cottage near a beautiful lake. As we stood on a hill overlooking the water, close by was an awesome flowering bush. Out of the blue, flew a beautiful butterfly who began to circle around Dottie three times. It then alighted on the bush. Dottie loves birds and nature and she began to speak words of love to the butterfly. She then leaned over and kissed it on its' wing. Slowly thereafter it began its ascent over our heads. I regretted that we failed to have our camera with us. However, some events in life are supernatural, intended only for our eyes. I wanted to put this experience in my contribution to the book, as Dottie knows

Jesus, and it's amazing what the love of the Lord can do; bringing about the "kissing of a butterfly."

It's amusing how roles reverse when you're a single parent and your children begin to question you as to: where you're going; with whom and what time you'll be home. It wasn't until years later I found out my younger daughter, Debbie, could not go to sleep until I was home from my outing. Even though her older sister tried to persuade her to go to bed, she waited by the living room window until she heard my car safely in the driveway. I regretted what I put her through and even asked for her forgiveness. She's a precious daughter and has forgiven me for many of my shortcomings and I have a great relationship to this day with Debbie and her family.

There was also an episode with Charissa that took place while she was attending college. I made arrangements to meet a widowed girlfriend at a Single Set dance in Washington Crossing, PA. The dance ended at 11:30 PM and I headed home. I disliked the part about driving late at night by myself, so I accelerated the gas pedal and was going about 10 miles over the speed limit. In a matter of minutes, blinking red lights were behind me and I immediately pulled over. As the officer questioned me about my "speeding," I honestly told him I was in a rush to get home. I had shut the engine off, but left my lights on. After he completed checking my registration he decided that he would give me a "warning" instead of a ticket. I was more than thankful that he extended some mercy to me.

I proceeded to start the car without any success. It was evident the battery was dead. The officer was apologetic in that he was not allowed to "jump start" my car. Did I have anyone who could come out to assist me? Did I? Well, I had a daughter at home, fast asleep—but I knew she had a set of cables to jump start my car. There was a phone booth right near my car and the officer waited until I called Charissa to come and help me out. She did—although not too happy to roll out of her warm bed at midnight to come to my rescue. The officer stayed the whole time and I was so grateful we were not left alone at that time of night. We laugh about it now; however, Char was a lifesaver for me that night and she's still a wonderful daughter, along with her husband and son.

During the fourteen years of widowhood, I attended many Single Set Groups such as Parents without Partners, a week at a Christian Retreat for singles and periods of dating which never resulted in anything positive.

In the early 1980's I finally gave up my search for a husband. I followed the advice of a friend who encouraged me to pray and claim Isaiah 54, verses 4-8 for my life: "Do not fear, for you will not be ashamed; nor be disgraced, for you will not be put to shame; for you will forget the shame of your youth, and will not remember the reproach of your widowhood anymore. For the Maker is your husband, the Lord of hosts is His name; and your Redeemer is the Holy One of Israel; He is called the God of the whole earth. For the Lord has called you like a woman forsaken and grieved in spirit, like a youthful wife when you were refused, says your God. For a mere moment I have forsaken you, but with great mercies I will gather you."

In essence, I relinquished my life to the Lord and asked Him to help me accept my single life. As a result of this commitment, I began to accept my position in life and had no desire to remarry. I was now at peace and looked forward to the plans God had for my life.

Briefly, I'll reflect back to a period of time before I made that commitment to the Lord. In the 1970's, a dear friend Marie encouraged me to place an application at a major publishing company where she held a prominent position. At that time I was employed by three surgeons and I loved my job. However, the erratic schedule caused some concern for me. I needed to have a 9 to 5 job because of my daughters' after-school activities. So, with my friend's reference, I applied, was interviewed and accepted for employment.

It was during that time, specifically July 1976 that I experienced a personal encounter with the Living God at a Praise and Worship Conference in Vineland, NJ. My long search to fill an unknown vacuum in my heart was filled by the Lord Jesus Christ. Words cannot adequately express the joy, peace and love showered upon me. This included a deep desire to read and study the Bible.

Shortly thereafter, two Christian women who worked for this firm were introduced to me. Barbara heard me sharing with a co-worker my marvelous conversion experience and she anonymously sent me a Living Bible through the inter-office mail. The second one, Carol, became my spiritual mentor. Both women were important in my early walk with the Lord. The first friend, Barbara, is still in my life; whereas my mentor went home to be with the Lord. Carol was an important link in my life because she was the next door neighbor to Harold Alfredo Geil, the author of this book.

Carol approached me one day in the summer of 1983 and asked me to pray for her neighbor, Harold, whose wife passed away in February 1983. Her face reflected genuine concern. She told me that Harold purchased a sporty, white Camaro Berlinetta and was wearing a brown suede cap on his head (not his usual attire). Was he now in mid-life crisis mode? Carol was particularly concerned he would be the target for an adventurous young woman.

I met Harold and his wife, Martha, when I attended the same non-denominational church. He was an elder in the church; a man well respected by many. I certainly did not want him to fall into the wrong hands. So...my prayers went something like this; "Lord Jesus, please keep Harold safe from any scheming women (especially the real young ones), for the Holy Spirit's wisdom and discernment and for the Lord's protection in all areas of his life."

It was during this time of prayer that Carol began to invite me to various functions where she also invited Harold. I was aware of the purpose of her invitations and declined one after the other. I was happy and at peace with my life. I thought to myself, "dear friend, don't do me any favors, my desires of the past for remarriage are gone. I'll respect you, but I won't be a part of your schemes."

It was December, right after I celebrated a "landmark" birthday that Carol invited me to a Messiah Concert at a local Bible College. Some other friends were also invited. It was a blessed performance. For the first half I sat next to one of the other invited gentlemen. However, after the intermission, Harold was suddenly maneuvered, by Carol's husband, into the seat next to me. How clever, I thought, but he's not going to impress me. Wrong!

I saw Harold in church thereafter. One Sunday, after the service, I expressed my concern about the church's views on certain doctrines. I also stated I was not sure if I belonged in that church. Wrong! He suggested we meet for a cup of coffee to discuss my concerns. Shortly thereafter we went to a nearby restaurant to enjoy our planned cup of coffee. Instead, we indulged in a four hour dinner with non-stop sharing.

After that night, my personal journal recorded: "What's happening to me? My still waters were deep and peaceful; one encounter with this man and the waters are stirred up!" I didn't like the reactivation of emotions—especially toward men. I prayed to accept my single life and I did. What was happening here?

Within a week I received a second invitation to dine at a quaint restaurant that was originally a railroad car. Again, we practically closed the place as we talked for hours on many subjects—especially what the Lord had done and was still doing in our lives.

It was after the third encounter with Harold that I received an interesting letter from him. In essence, the letter posed three questions. I answered them as honestly as I could. The first question was a spiritual one. I responded; "while having my devotions this morning I was led to the book of Psalms, and the answer to your question is found in Psalm 40:8 'I delight to do Your will, O my God, and Your law is within my heart.'"

This man had a serious, committed walk with the Lord and did not want to continue with any relationship with a woman, unless it was planned by the Lord. That resolve prompted him to put out a "fleece" to the Lord, (as Gideon did in the Old Testament of the Bible) resulting in the letter with the three questions.

When I think back to the importance of that letter, I definitely see the hand of God leading me through the Holy Spirit. My responses gave him the green light to further pursue this relationship.

I've always had a deep desire in my heart to reach out to those in pain; either physical or emotional. When I reflect back to the years before I met Harold and see how many books in our library deal with healing of the wounded heart, I'm amazed how the Lord was preparing me for the ministry that evolved in the early 1990's. I was so surprised when Harold shared with me that he had asked the Lord to get him out of the corporate world into full time ministry to the brokenhearted. This indeed was a confirmation that our marriage was planned by our Maker.

Now back to Carol's request for intercessory prayer for her neighbor. I smile when I reflect upon the answer to my prayers in that I became the subject for God's answer to the petitions for Harold Alfredo Geil.

I truly know how much God loves me. He brought Harold Alfredo into my life, the perfect match for me! I'm so blessed to have an extended family. Thank you from the bottom of my heart, Lil, Carl and Gus and their precious spouses and children for accepting and loving me all these years.

Chapter Twenty-Two

My First Visit Back to Argentina

As the aircraft approached the terminal at the Ezeiza airport in Buenos Aires, I recognized many smiling faces. This was an exciting experience. At one end of the continent I was bitten by a love bug, and on the other, overwhelmed by a wave of many years of emotionally charged memories. The bulk of my luggage consisted of used and new clothing, destined for the needy. Martha's parents lived in a nice apartment in my home town, a suburb of the capital city of Buenos Aires. This became my base of operation for three weeks.

I was very eager to find out what had transpired in Argentina as a result of the spiritual revivals of the 1950's and thereafter. I needed to speak with people in regard to their experience about the Pentecostal and Charismatic revivals in my home town, the city of Buenos Aires, and other suburbs. I wondered if a softening of the Fundamental Evangelical resistance to the revivals with supernatural manifestations had occurred, which drastically had changed the spiritual landscape of Argentina, and even spilling over to neighboring countries.

In spite of well documented reports of millions coming to Christ, the responses were a mixture of skepticism and excitement, depending with whom I spoke. I was not happy at all by what I experienced, even in the company of my best Christian friends.

Many of the Christians, who criticized what they really did not understand, suffer from spiritual stagnation. In one specific home of a friend that I knew from Sunday school I saw something that moved me to tears. I walked from Martha's parents apartment to what I remembered was my friend's address. I rang the bell and waited and waited some more. As I looked around at the neighborhood I had a feeling of heaviness, a sense of gloom; nothing uplifting.

This is Henry's home, my friend whom I had recommended for the Military Equestrian Team, back in 1952. Suddenly out the front door, way in the back of the house appeared this doubled-over woman. She could hardly lift her head high enough to look at me. I could not understand a word she spoke. I shouted out my name and she just uttered some totally unintelligible words, but I knew she had recognized me; it was Henry's mother. A moment later, Henry put his arm around me and, after a brief conversation I noticed that something was wrong with my friend. We agreed to meet the next day for a more in-depth conversation.

After we sat down for lunch, I knew that a blanket of deep depression was keeping him in inner captivity. I saw something in him that I was going to experience on a much broader scale in our future ministry to God's brokenhearted people. As I walked away, I broke out in tears, completely aware that Satan had practically destroyed this family of five. How can this situation be reversed? Not by human effort; only by genuine love that emanates from our Father's heart, combined with the healing of man's heart. I spent many hours with Henry, but now it was time to continue with my visits.

I went to my dear cousin's home and spent several meaningful days. She was convinced that I came back to Argentina to search for a wife. Bertita, my cousin, let me know that she had already chosen the right partner for me. After she started to describe this candidate, I interrupted her to thank her for her effort; and at that point I pulled out the photograph that Jeanie had given me before I left the USA. After my cousin looked at the picture for a while, she said; "She is really pretty;" and gave me her approval. That meant a great deal to me, because this lovely cousin is like a sister to me.

Whenever I asked questions about the revivals in the greater Buenos Aires area, in the company of either relatives or friends, I encountered doubtful responses. I refused to get involved in arguments, because I realized that it would only result in deeper divisions; neither would trying to convince them through lengthy philosophical dissertations bring about the desired results. My frustration was mostly fueled by their lack of at least considering what I was convinced had been the work of the Holy Spirit. But who was I to try to convince people when it took me years of learning in my walk with Jesus that it was all about the heart of man connecting with our Father's heart.

My own heart had to be purified for the flow of God's love. I wanted immediate action, like some of Christ's disciples wanted Jesus to bring down fire from heaven to take care of the doubters. I finally decided that I would come to my own conclusions, regardless of the opinions of others. Most people look at the outward appearance anyway, whereas God looks at the heart. There was more for me to learn about the heart of men and how the devil stirs up conflict, specifically between those who have been saved and redeemed by the Blood of the Lamb. I continued to appeal to my heavenly Father for wisdom; while it saddened me, at times even upsetting me, that so many otherwise mature Christians chose the "teachings of men" over the truth of God's Word. I know that it has a lot to do with the fear of men.

One day, an old friend picked me up for dinner. In the past, he was one of the contenders for Martha's heart and was angry at me for beating him in his pursuit. For many years he avoided me and if I came too close to him for comfort, he would let me know by his looks that he was done with me, period. All attempts on my part to restore our friendship, had failed. Now that I was sitting in the car next to him, forty-five years later, I took the opportunity to extend an olive branch; it worked, and our friendship was restored.

There is another chapter related to this story. His sister had long attempted to cultivate a romance with me, but Martha became my first choice. I was so relieved that this long, drawn out matter, was wonderfully resolved on this side of heaven. When we arrived at this very familiar restaurant, I was surprised to see a group of people sitting at a long table. These were my seventh grade classmates from the German school I had attended. Most of them I had not seen since 1944. We had a great time, and they were surprised when I called out all the names on our 7th grade roster. Some of them were absent. Asking about their whereabouts, I was told they had disappeared during the military regime that overthrew President Peron.

In order to investigate other matters of importance to me, I went to visit Siemens, my last employer before I left Argentina. After the guard announced my arrival to the Personnel Department, I was escorted to a conference room where I was cordially welcomed by a number of managers and old friends, some very dear to me. A lively conversation ensued and after a few minutes, a woman entered the room with a huge smile on her face. It was Agda, my dear and faithful secretary. This was certainly an emotional encounter. We recalled some precious moments and briefly touched on some of the highlights of the past. I was delighted to learn that her faith in Christ was still strong. I knew that I would see her in Paradise which Jesus Christ promised to all those who have given their lives to Him, but I was truly delighted to see her one more time on earth. During the period I was the department manager we had such wonderful conversations, often of a spiritual nature that affected many people in the company. Our need to be light and salt in a dark and spiritually hungry world overwhelmed me.

For a brief moment, the thought crossed my mind that had I stayed in Argentina or moved to Germany, the opportunities for promotions in this company would have been excellent. Did I have any regrets? Not for a moment. I was absolutely convinced that it was the Almighty God who opened the way for me in every respect.

The plant manager invited me to a tour of the plant. As we approached what used to be my department, I was absolutely elated when I saw my dear blind friend Alex, sitting at the same work place that I had prepared for him. The entourage stayed behind while I slowly walked up from behind my friend, laid my arm around his shoulder and said; "Ola, Alejandro, mi amigo, como esta?", (Hello, my friend Alex, how are you?) Very happily surprised, he responded; "Senior Geil; usted volvio?" (Mr. Geil, you came back?). I was absolutely amazed how he instantly recognized my voice, after twenty two years! He immediately told me that he was married, had children and lived within walking distance from the plant. I was grateful for his strong faith in Jesus Christ. I believe that all these wonderful experiences will be fully celebrated in Heaven. When I rejoined my friends I thanked them for this treat.

Another highlight of this trip that greatly blessed me was the opportunity to be the guest speaker at my old Baptist Church for several meetings.

Through a constant flow of letters, Jeanie and I were able to develop a wonderful relationship, even while separated by thousands of miles. I soon received an inner confirmation that Jeanie and I were meant for each other. Martha's parents, who readily approved of our relationship, were delighted to handle the very active mail traffic. Sometimes, two or three letters would be delivered at the same time and my in-laws wouldn't see me for a good while.

With the increasing excitement of God's latest miraculous provision for my future, it became harder for me to endure a full three week stay, in spite of a full schedule. But the day of my return finally arrived and my cousins took me to the Ezeiza airport. I was moved by the crowd that had gathered for my return to the United States.

Jeanie was waiting for me at the Princeton Junction train station, but found herself on the wrong side of the tracks. Desperately looking for a way to cross over, we met in the middle of the tunnel, out of the public's eye.

Obviously, I was unable to keep this latest excitement from my friends at work. I invited Jeanie to a party hosted by our vice-president and, by observing their faces; I was delighted with my choice. "Harold's Americanization process is really advancing rapidly," was one of their comments.

Jeanie, who was raised in the Russian Orthodox Church, had an awesome encounter with Jesus Christ in 1976, which instilled in her a hunger for a deeper relationship with God that has not diminished to this day. Some nominal Christian relatives invited her to a Charismatic Christian conference, held in Vineland New Jersey. During the worship time she was overwhelmed by the presence of the Holy Spirit and filled with great joy. She told me that this was by far her most awesome encounter with the living God. She was changed forever.

She didn't realize what was really happening at the time; but she knew that this was supernatural and after that experience her life took a totally different direction. Her immediate desire was to purchase a Bible. Mysteriously, a Bible landed on her desk at work; and from that moment on she became an avid reader of the Word of God. When Jeanie shared this experience with me, I was exuberant that we had found each other.

Although I had a heart relationship with my heavenly Father for many years, Jeanie enriched my life in many ways. Her Eastern Orthodox Christian background stimulated me to learn more about this tradition and I was pleased with what I discovered. Since my teenage years I believed there are true and faithful believers in Jesus Christ in every Christian denomination. Also her mother's Russian background, with a rich cultural and political history, truly fascinated me. I watched several movies related to Russia and was touched by their art, music and their ornate churches.

Her mother was born in Galicia, an area in Europe that was part of the Austrian-Hungarian Empire. My maternal grandparents lived in that part of Europe before they returned to Germany. The greatest percentage of inhabitants in the Kingdom of Galicia was Ukrainian. The other ethnic groups were Russians and Germans, in addition to other groups. Living conditions were very hard which forced many people to move to other countries. Jeanie's Mom left with her family through Hamburg, Germany, for the United States in 1921, at age twelve.

When Jeanie shared her exciting story about our relationship with her daughters Charissa and Debbie (age 28 and 26), they were surprised and cautioned their mother to take her time. By her excitement they were concerned that she was rushing into this relationship too fast, and reminded her how she had cautioned them to exercise good judgment. They realized the futility of their attempts to slow her down and obliged. The moment I met Jeanie's daughters and their families I took them into my heart. Later they told their mother: "Mom, you did not tell us that he had an accent." During my stay in Argentina, Jeanie gave a public testimony of her faith in Jesus Christ, and received believer's baptism, as an act of her obedience to the Lord, on May 5th of 1984.

We began to talk about getting married; but I was hesitant to set a date because my daughter Lilly was still living at home. Jeanie and I quickly agreed to welcome her to stay with us for as long as she wished. Interestingly, soon thereafter, she started a friendship with Ridgely, a wonderful Christian, who later became her husband. This meant that father and daughter were dating at the same time.

Our wedding date was set for September the 15th, 1984. Family members and friends helped to make this event a wonderful celebration of love. My son Carl did an excellent job as master of ceremony keeping the guests in "stitches." I was elated when I saw a side of him that I was not fully aware of. Jeanie's reply with Psalm 40:8 to my initial questions became our marriage theme Scripture verse. "We delight to do Your will, O God, Your word is within our hearts."

Jeanie had her eyes on the island of Bermuda for our honeymoon. We followed through and made reservations at the Sonesta, a beautiful beachfront hotel. We had a fantastic time on this gorgeous island.

Every passing day seemed to confirm that this was a divine arrangement. Not only the melting together of our hearts, but watching our children and their loved ones uniting into one harmonious family, left no doubt that the Lord was involved.

Upon our return we resumed our respective jobs. Jeanie with the publishing company in the Princeton New Jersey area, and mine in Manhattan, New York City, which separated us by a distance of seventy five miles. Two years later I suggested that Jeanie consider early retirement, if she so desired. After fourteen years of employment with a prestigious publishing company; the latter seven years working for the treasurer, it took her only seconds to accept my offer. This only increased my desire to retire from the corporate world and serve the Lord Jesus Christ, preferably helping hurting people.

Jeanie's father was born in Hamburg, Germany to a family of seven children with a long history of living in that city. He left his family for the US in 1920, for reasons that could never be established. After his passing, her Mom gave me a stack of letters and documents from her husband, and I was encouraged by family members to obtain records of possible survivors. I contacted the police headquarters in Hamburg and two weeks later I was notified that my letter had been forwarded to the Census Bureau for further investigation. This was good news.

To Jeanie's family's great surprise we learned that a good number of relatives had survived the war. Three siblings of Jeanie's father were still living in Hamburg. This awakened in us a desire to visit Germany. Jeanie and I brought our request to the Lord in prayer and left it with Him. I have had many experiences of God's faithfulness as I waited upon Him. His responses to my heart's desires were overwhelming. Our Father loves to surprise His children; and the timing is always perfect.

Since my childhood, my parents often surprised me by walking up to me, while holding their hands behind their back. I had to guess in which hand they had a surprise for me. Sometimes I had to guess several times before getting my reward from one of their hands. God, our loving Father wants to surprise us more then we can imagine. However, when His hands move toward us, we will find something wonderful in both hands.

As our mutual desire for a deeper relationship with our heavenly Father increased, new doors opened before us. We wanted everything God planned for our lives, and determined to be obedient to Jesus Christ. However, unconditional surrender to the Lord of Lords, our Shepherd, has a price tag. Were we willing to pay the price? Jesus said: "He who overcomes shall inherit all things, and I will be His God and he shall be My son" (Revelation 21:7).

Trials and tribulations, filled with controversies, are a way of life for those who want to fight the good fight, finish the race and keep the faith. Our strength comes from the Lord as we bear the fruit of the Spirit; Love, Joy, Peace, Patience, Kindness, Goodness, Faithfulness, Gentleness, and Self-Control (Galatians 5:22). Our awareness of the devil's subtle devices to derail us from the path of righteousness helped us in our understanding of God's ways. Equipped with a strong armor and an awesome spiritual weapons arsenal at our disposal to overcome any obstacle coming into our path, Jeanie and I asked God for wisdom, knowledge and courage for the journey ahead of us. We had no more than a tiny inkling of what was waiting for us out there.

In 1985 we decided to renovate our house in the Princeton area, with a plan to sell it the following year. It was remarkable how God lined things up for us. Jeanie was excited to have a husband who was not afraid to make decisions, even under incredible circumstances. I was convinced that, if the God of the universe is with me, whatever comes from the opposite direction must meet His requirements, period. I also knew from the Bible and personal experience that, it is in the midst of hardships that we are equipped for even greater assignments. I learned that if I want to become a more effective soldier of the Cross, I must be willing to endure what can only be learned in the darkest hours of our lives; namely, through the path of humility. "It is not till sinful self is slain, that Christ can fully reign" (Ref: Harold Geil 2000).

In 1986 we moved to Bucks County, Pennsylvania. This move extended my commute by half hour each way, for a total of four hours a day, including the elevator ride to the 37th floor. One day, while on my lunch break, I felt persuaded to write a "letter to the Lord," stating my heart's desire. I believed that I was delighting myself in the Lord and, consequently, He would give me the desires of my heart. This is what the Holy Spirit moved King David to write in Psalm 37 verse 4. Moreover, Jesus said "If you abide in Me, and My words remain in you, you will ask what you desire, and it shall be done for you" (John 15:7). I believed the Word of God, and that settled it for me! After outlining my plans in specific details, I prayed over the letter and filed it for later reference. The main topic of my request to the Lord was that I would be out of the corporate world and in my Father's business at age 58.

In 1987, Jeanie and I planned a trip to Europe, with specific stops in Germany and Switzerland, leaving by the end of May. Around that period, rumors began circulating around the office that the company planned to move the corporate office to Texas. Two days before our departure to Europe, the chairman of the board invited all corporate employees to a musical at Radio City Music Hall, across the street from our office. Following the program, the chairman announced that by May 1st of the following year, we would move to Texas.

A memo was released later, stating that any employee, at least fifty-seven years old, with a minimum of twenty years of seniority by May 1st, 1988, would be qualified for early retirement with full benefits. I was overwhelmed, to say the least, that I would be 57 years old by April 16th, 1988, two weeks before the deadline. Not only did God beat my request for early retirement at age 58 by one year, but He also provided monetary compensation beyond my expectations.

Our three week, four thousand kilometer trip across Germany and Switzerland was fantastic. Our most important stop was Hamburg, where we met three siblings of Jeanie's father and other family members. It was a very emotional experience for Jeanie, as one of her uncle's reminded her of her father who had died in 1960.

We had the opportunity to visit many sites and enjoy unforgettable interactions with people across two beautiful countries. As I pondered on my past experiences traveling through Europe in 1952, shortly after the ravages of World War II, I was astonished to see the fruit of restoration.

Upon our return from Europe, we systematically made plans for a dream that became reality— to become what Floridians call "snowbirds." This meant spending six months in Florida and the other six months in Pennsylvania; in other words, escaping from the extremes. This required that we needed two homes.

Our summer home was established in 1987 by the purchase of a rustic, two story cabin, located in a densely wooded area, near a lake outside of Quakertown, Pennsylvania.

As we allowed our remodeling imagination to go wild, we ended up with a pretty quaint summer home; a haven of rest for many weary pilgrims. Next, we sold our townhouse and purchased a large condominium on a small island in South Pasadena, across the Boca Ciega Bay from St. Petersburg Beach, Florida. This was a beautiful place with two wrap around balconies overlooking the water; a lovely beach on one side and a swimming pool and tennis courts on the other.

We were aware that many people would have their "heads spinning" trying to keep track of our journey; but to Jeanie and me it was a thrilling experience. In order to receive appropriate spiritual nurture, we attended two churches; one up North and another in Florida, with different Evangelical affiliations. We believed the Lord was leading us in several directions in order to acquire experience relative to healing for His brokenhearted people.

Soon after we were directed to a leader's conference held in Ft. Worth, Texas, under the leadership of a well known evangelist. While traveling to the conference, we discussed whether we should become members of a large Evangelical

Church we were attending since we moved to Florida. Neither Jeanie nor I were able to come to a conclusion.

During our stay in the Dallas area, we visited a pastor friend who invited us to his church. The service was very informal and began with congregational prayer. Then, people began to share personal testimonies. But, what followed greatly surprised both of us. A middle aged couple stood up and he gave a message in a strange language. Then another person gave the interpretation and said: "There is someone here who is undecided regarding church affiliation; the word from the Lord is that you take up membership in that church." I was beginning to get "hot under my collar" and looked at Jeanie, while she was looking at me.

I knew then and there, that this was something supernatural, which had awakened my curiosity since my youth; however this subject required God's timing for its fruition. Jeanie and I decided to move in God's ways no matter what the consequences. Even during our drive back from Dallas to Florida, we were recounting our experiences like two kids coming home from an exciting adventure. This conference of approximately 4,000 church leaders, marked the beginning of a long period of training for what became our prayer ministry to the brokenhearted.

I thought that—if this is what the sixties are going to be like, then I believe that Jeanie and I are heading for a long life; because we were convinced there was fruitful Kingdom activity awaiting us. I was awed when I perceived a message in my heart; "I am your Protector, your Defender and your Provider." With this assurance, why worry about our future?

Upon our return to Florida, we decided to become members of the church we were attending. Shortly thereafter, I was asked to lead an adult Sunday school class. I gratefully accepted the invitation and knowing that I was going to invest my heart in this wonderful assignment, Jeanie and I were surprised by the rapid increase in attendance.

Jeanie's interest in getting to know the country I came from, prompted us to plan a trip to Argentina, at the end of 1989, followed by a second one in 1991. This gave both of us ample exposure to the ongoing spiritual revivals in Argentina, and a good opportunity to sort out opinions of men from what we believed to be a mighty move of God's Holy Spirit. The newspapers of Buenos Aires published a variety of news reports and editorials that prompted us to seek out some of the leaders.

One particular ministry claimed over one hundred thousand followers with all kinds of supernatural healings, signs and wonders. They were meeting in an old theater building with services from six in the morning to midnight. I called the office and left a message that I was here from the United States and wanted to meet the leading pastor. When we returned to the hotel there was a message from the church office inviting us to come to meet the pastor at 2:00 PM.

What we found completely overwhelmed us. I knew the city well, but this was above and beyond what I had ever seen. We made our way through hundreds of people, many sitting or sleeping on sidewalks, waiting to get into one of the services. We finally managed to get through the door and were escorted to the office of the evangelist. A young, dynamic pastor greeted us with a typical Argentinean bear hug. His wife joined us minutes later. He shared how he came to know Jesus Christ and how miraculously he obtained favor with the Argentinean president who helped promote his ministry. After our meeting, and in the company of his wife, they imparted God's blessings upon our lives and our future ministry. For years I had their photograph on my prayer wall, together with dozens of pictures of people that we pray for daily.

During our stay in the city of Buenos Aires, I was eager to meet people with opinions on both sides of the spectrum. While the majority of the public welcomed this visitation of God, there was no shortage of those who either just raised their eyebrows or harshly criticized what they considered a hoax. As I mentioned earlier, my exposure to spiritual revivals dates back to the mid-fifties. I believe God has enriched my life through so many experiences, as painful as some may have been, in order to establish a good foundation for our ministry. I was careful to stay clear from theological extremes. "Walk with Me and I will show you the way" seemed to surface in my mind. The world needs to see what is genuine; the counterfeit does not accomplish much of anything, and before long the true colors will surface.

Again, just like during the revivals in the 1950's, I saw wonderful signs and miracles that made me grateful for God's love and compassion for His hurting people. But too many times I saw little change in the lives of Christians who had received miraculous healings. Some had even lost what they received and now seemed angry at the world, and sometimes even at God. Jeanie and I became convinced that, unless the heart is healed from all kinds of deep hurts, the enemy will try to finish his destructive work.

It is for this and other reasons, there is much tension and downright animosity within the Body of Christ. Unfortunately, the enemy is determined to create infightings and divisions within churches which have moved many Christians into extremes, with all kinds of sad consequences. This situation has strengthened our resolve to move ahead with our ministry and leave the outcome in our Father's hands.

We traveled extensively through the country from the breathtaking Iguazu waterfalls near the jungle of Paraguay and Brazil in the North, to the southernmost tip of Argentina; Ushuaia, Tierra del Fuego. We returned to the United States, full of excitement and ready to share with our friends at church, what the Lord had done in our hearts. Some were eager to hear our testimony; however, there were others who seemed to shun us. Jeanie and I could not understand what was happening; we had so many exciting things to share that we were convinced would bring glory to God.

The next Sunday the church invited a guest speaker, a well known Evangelist, who was introduced as a graduate from a fundamental Evangelical Seminary. To my great surprise, he spoke about the spiritual revivals in Argentina and shared that he was born there to American missionaries. After the meeting I walked up to him and addressed him in our Buenos Aires Spanish language. He gave me a big hug and said: "What are you doing in this church?" He took me aside and prayed a moving prayer over me in Spanish. Jeanie and I became increasingly aware that far too many Christians have no doubt that great signs and wonders were manifested during our Lord's earthly ministry, but refuse to believe that they are for today!

As a result of so many new experiences in the Kingdom of God, we agreed that the importance of being equipped with the gifts of discernment and wisdom were essential for our ministry. Faced with the sad reality of unbelief in the supernatural manifestation of the Holy Spirit in many churches, and aware of the devil's deceptive schemes, we were determined to move forward in what we believed to be God's direction. Jeanie and I were convinced that we had to be further equipped for what our Father had in store for us.

We wondered what our next move would be. One of my mother's wise sayings popped into my mind: "The donkey outgrew his stable." As a rapidly growing teenager, my mother knew it was high time to sew new clothes, when arms and legs outgrew my shirts and pants. As always, we brought our dilemma to the Lord, who already knew where He wanted to relocate us. Jeanie opened the church section of the Yellow Pages and saw this large framed ad and the following Sunday we visited an Episcopal Church involved in the Renewal Movement.

Their warm welcome absolutely surprised us. After two to three visits, we knew that this was our next station. Our hearts connected in a way we had not previously experienced. What we learned in this church further stimulated our desire to start a ministry to bring God's healing to His people.

Chapter Twenty-Three

The Birth of Fullness of Christ Ministries

Long before our ministry became reality, God had planted the seeds into my heart. The desire to help hurting Christians become whole and fruitful disciples of Jesus Christ was implanted within me since my late teens. I learned early in life that God delights to intervene supernaturally encouraging us to move on to higher grounds, while enjoying intimacy with Him. My unquenchable desire to share Christ and His Gospel was nurtured by the flow of God's love and joy into my whole being. At the same time, I was aware that my testimony had to be a reflection of my walk with the Lord, in order to bring glory to God. The walking out of the old into the new, became a very real process, which the Scriptures refer to as; "This is the will of God, your sanctification" (1 Thessalonians 4:3).

With Jeanie joining her life to mine, I was happy that she was ready and in full agreement with this joint venture. In fact, she brought the gifts and talents that the Lord had blessed her with, as she accepted Christ as her Lord and Savior. With my Baptist background of having enough water to be fully immersed in baptism for the cleansing by the water of the

Word of God; combined with Jeanie's baptism with the Holy Spirit and fire; (Matthew 3:11b) we were now equipped with the right combination to "steam" along for our Lord.

Joining the traditional church in Florida, who had experienced a spiritual renewal, was the right step for our training, for what later became Fullness of Christ Ministries, Inc. The husband and wife who founded this church were our dear friends for years to come. As a well trained professional counselor, she took us "under her wings" and provided us with hands-on-training. Within a short period of time, she began sending people to us for prayer ministry. Recognizing our need for more intense preparation, we first attended three courses in Biblical counseling at Elijah House, Inc. followed by training received from various well known healing ministries.

It was during our time at this traditional church, from 1992 through 1995, that the Lord surprised us with what was to become the most amazing miracle in our ministry by leading Mary (not her real name) into our lives. She came from an extremely abused background. Mary became our first spiritual daughter and, to this day, we are amazed how the Lord brought about this relationship. Jeanie and I were not "childless" or lonely. God blessed us with a combined family of twenty four, not counting our siblings. But through the grace and love of our Lord Jesus, hurting people were drawn to our hearts. We learned through so many experiences, that it was the absence of true and nurturing love that wounded the heart of the child. Consequently, only God's love can truly restore the heart of the adult. The number of spiritual daughters and sons grew from year to year.

Mary's childlike faith has inspired us through the years since she came into our lives. Through all the unbelievable horrors that she suffered, her faith in Jesus Christ never faltered. With hardly any formal education she is indeed one of God's "walking miracles." A licensed professional counselor diagnosed her with severe Dissociative Identity Disorder and Satanic Ritual Abuse. Mary's counselors asked that we pray for her healing. I believe that it was through the infinite love of God and His healing power that Mary found her freedom. Jesus said: "Whom the Son sets free is free indeed." Mary has been equipped with gifts and talents that enable her to bless others. We consider ourselves blessed by having Mary in our lives. Through many tears and sleepless nights, combined with endless telephone calls at any time of the day and night, I consider her now a "Watchman on the Wall," as well as one of our spiritual "vigilantes."

Our church leaders welcomed the flock to a weekly pot luck supper in their home. As was the practice, hot and cold meals were provided by the group. This precious couple had such a warm, loving heart for the less fortunate that one couldn't help but feel at home. One specific Friday, Jeanie and I decided to prepare a batch of German potato pancakes. What we didn't know is that after Mary tasted one of these pancakes, she liked them so much that she almost overindulged herself. Not only did Mary love these pancakes, but she called Jeanie and me the "Pancakes" for years to come.

When a Christian commits his or her life to Jesus Christ, with a sincere desire to follow Him obediently, he will undoubtedly confront Satan, the enemy of Christ and his church. This is what happened to Jeanie and me, not only through Mary's situation but through others as well. We were determined not to be overcome by the enemy, but submit to God, and resist the devil, knowing that he will flee from us. (James 4:7) God will equip every obedient follower of Jesus Christ with discernment to identify the evil schemes of Satan and the power to overcome him. The battle is the Lord's. Our duty is to be so intimately united with Him that the power of the Holy Spirit can move us in His direction.

One of Satan's most lethal characteristics is deception. The apostle Paul warns us not to be ignorant, "lest Satan should take advantage of us; for we are not ignorant of his devices" (2 Corinthians 2:11). The Lord has used Mary on various occasions to protect us from deception. She would be prompted by the Holy Spirit to call and let us know that during her midnight prayer time she perceived the Shepherd's voice with a message for us.

The following experience has helped Jeanie and me to wait patiently on the Lord when confronted by Christians who staunchly oppose supernatural manifestations of the Holy Spirit. This takes more than natural human effort; it takes godly wisdom combined with perseverance and a heart full of God's love.

One day while in Florida, we were pleasantly surprised by a visiting evangelist friend from Argentina. I knew him since I was a teenager. He was the secretary general of the South American wing of an international Christian radio and television ministry, and was accountable to his mission board located in Germany. One day he attended a Charismatic church service that deeply affected his life. His wife was happy with her husband's joyful disposition and his renewed commitment to his ministry. But this change did not come without heart break. Someone in his town saw my friend attending these charismatic meetings and reported him to the mission board. The response came immediately. The members of the board voted unanimously to fire him from his position without any delay.

This radically changed the course of his life. Thank God that the Lord is our protector, defender, and provider; He will never ever leave nor forsake those who sincerely trust Him. The Lord blessed my friend beyond his highest expectations, in every sense. Over twenty years later, he received an invitation to visit Germany. During this trip he was invited to an old friend's home where he met the members of the mission board that had fired him. With the exception of the chairman who had since died, every one asked for his forgiveness.

Jeanie and I were excited to hear the story of another faithful servant who decided to trust God without keeping any resentment against those who had treated him as a stranger. While we were enjoying his company, my friend looked at Jeanie and said; "Jeanie you look like you want to ask me a question." "Well", Jeanie said; "I wonder if there is something still missing in my walk with Jesus Christ?"— To which my friend responded; "I know what it is." At that moment he stood up and with a smile said; "You need your prayer language." Jeanie was excited while I was getting restless. Wait a minute, I thought; this is going too far and too fast. But I didn't have a chance to voice my opinion. It was already beginning to happen.

My friend instructed me to interpret the words that he was going to pray over Jeanie in Spanish. What ensued the next several long minutes can only be understood by those who lived through this process. While I was interpreting my friend's prayer, Jeanie began to sputter unrecognizable words that sounded like some strange foreign language. Puzzled by what was really happening, I began to perspire while wondering who would exclude us from their company. I am convinced now that the Lord was smiling while I was getting irritated. God had many more surprises in store for me.

The ability to hear the voice of our Shepherd and distinguish it from other voices is paramount for a successful ministry in the Kingdom of God. I needed to hear from God in order to make wise decisions about our future. The number of people seeking help increased in Florida, as well as in Pennsylvania, and as we moved into our mid-sixties we wanted to be where and how we could be most fruitful. Additionally, the "snowbird commute" began to take its toll on us and our car. Consequently, we went to our Lord for counsel.

The Lord knows that I am not the kind of guy who can spend hours upon hours lying before Him. I am action oriented, and I am glad that He knows my weaknesses. I am absolutely convinced my Father hears me, and deeply loves me. He has a totally different concept of time that is beyond my comprehension. I praise God that He does not miss one single request; and when it seemed otherwise, I found out later that He just gave me enough time to get rid of another "beam from my own eye" (Matthew 7:3).

Jeanie and I did not give up in our pursuit for more of Jesus Christ. When He left this earth He told His disciples, and us, that all power is given to Him in heaven and on earth. These words had a profound effect on my entire life; I took Him by his words. Reading the Holy Scriptures without believing its content was inconceivable. I know beyond any doubt that Jesus wants us, His followers, to be equipped with power from above.

My craving for more of Him is something that God had placed in me; it does not have its source in me but in God's heart. It is the expression of my gratitude for what Jesus did for me through His suffering, before and on the Cross. His glorious resurrection, His grace and infinite love for me, propel me into every day from the moment I wake up. However, before you assume that I am some holy man walking around with a huge cross on my chest, I must declare that I know my shortcomings, and I need His grace and mercy for everyday living.

Jeanie practiced her newly acquired prayer language in her daily quiet time with God. When she emerged from what I call her "inner sanctum," I could see a change in her face; there was a radiance that exuded from her countenance. I knew this precious woman very well; and whatever the Lord did on that day through His messenger from Argentina, powerfully affected her life. Now—I felt a little bit like an outsider.

Early in the morning on December 7th, 1994 during my quiet time with the Lord, He spoke with these words to my heart: "Start a church fellowship in Bucks County, Pennsylvania; there will be about twelve people with you." Someone may wonder in what language the Lord speaks to me when I am equally proficient in three languages. My answer may sound funny, but I think it's a mixture of all three, combined with a heavenly language.

At this time, we were still commuting between two States and I wondered how the many details necessary to bring this call into reality, would come about. However, nothing is impossible for God, including the sale of our homes, the move and so much more; so, I asked the Lord for a confirmation of His message.

About two weeks later, while on a very early walk in the woods surrounding our summer home, these clear words came to me; "Go to your friend Bill's church this Sunday." We visited there only one time, so I called my friend for directions. As Jeanie and I walked into the lobby, a gentleman approached us and asked if I was Pastor Jim. I was informed their pastor was in the hospital and the church leader asked the Conference for a substitute, who was unknown to the church. Pastor Jim gave a wonderfully anointed message that touched my heart. After he finished he said; "I am going to do something different this morning." He pointed his finger in our direction and while he stepped down from the platform, said; "From the moment this couple walked into the church, the Lord gave me a message for them."

I was overcome with a strange feeling while all eyes were upon us. Even right up to the moment when he stopped next to us, I was hoping that he was referring to the couple behind us. He laid His hands on my shoulder and said; "Thank You Lord for this brother; thank You for his love and heart commitment to You." Then he said; "This message is in response to your request; get ready, for this will be your calling and the purpose of your life." I was stunned; this man didn't know me from Adam, I thought. There was no doubt in my heart that Jesus had answered my request for a confirmation. A time of praise and worship followed and someone handed us an audio tape of the service.

In early January 1995, we returned to our home in Florida, just in time to escape a major snowstorm. A few days later, during her devotion with the Lord, Jeanie was journaling what the Lord laid upon her heart. The gifts that Jesus has blessed Jeanie with, combined with her wonderful disposition, are a valuable asset to our ministry. When Jeanie read the content to me I could not hold back tears of joy.

I quote from Jeanie's journal: "My dear child. I hear all your requests-the verbal ones and the unspoken. Be still and listen for My quiet still voice. I will direct your path and show you the way you should go. I want you to listen carefully because very soon I will show you the person who will sell your property. I am pleased that you trust Me to show you step by step the way you shall go. I Am a God of order and not of confusion. Be alert to the sign I shall give you; and the two of you will be in total agreement regarding these signs. Be watchful, because the adversary roars like a lion and he would like to devour you; but I will not allow it. My right hand is and will always guide you and protect you. Stand back and see what your Lord will do."

Shortly thereafter, one morning while we were getting dressed, someone knocked on the locked door and shouted; "Anybody home?" The door opened and a young woman walked in, totally surprised when she saw us. "I thought your place was vacant as indicated by the tag on your keys that you had left with the real estate office. I was just hired by the Realtor that you listed your home with and I am here to look at your property." By what she told us we knew that this was orchestrated by the Lord. The second couple that came to see our place made an offer.

Our condo had been on the market for two years, without any success, while similar condos around ours were selling for more money. God's timing is perfect, while ours is limited to our five senses. By mid-May we put our furniture in storage and moved into our summer home in Pennsylvania.

After God's call to start a church fellowship in Bucks County, PA, we asked Him for a house in Doylestown. God's timing and His awesome choice of what He knows is best for His children, is absolutely overwhelming.

With our hearts set on God and our feet firmly on the ground, we keep following His directions. Our Father makes us aware when we stray in our frail humanity and we quickly submit to His fine-tuning. It is our desire to share our joy in the Lord with people who are still poking in the dark, not knowing which direction to take. Though often invisible to the human eyes; God will reward those who diligently seek Him. "But without faith it is impossible to please God, for he who comes to God must believe that He is and that He is a rewarder of those who diligently seek Him" (Hebrews 11:6).

In July 1995 we purchased our present home, a lovely cape cod in Doylestown, Bucks County, Pennsylvania. Again, Jeanie and I were elated to see our Father's hand bringing this all about. It would be absurd to describe the entire unfolding of our relocation process as anything other than divinely providential. Our first worship service was held in our recreation room in November of 1995, with eleven people attending. Our daughter Lilly was our worship leader.

After our fellowship grew to over twenty, we decided to rent a meeting hall in town. We truly enjoyed ministering our Father's love to our little flock. As the attendance increased to over forty, with many asking for personal prayer counseling, it became evident that a change was imminent. Jeanie and I saw the great need for personal ministry and our hearts longed to see God's people healed. As a result of a fully scheduled ministry week, we decided to discontinue our Sunday services at the end of 1998.

We saw the fruit of our prayer ministry grow, not only in the number of people seeking healing, but in their relationship with Jesus Christ and their interaction with people. The healing of the heart brings indescribable freedom for God's children, enabling them to become light and salt to the world around them. The outflow of our Father's love will become so obvious, that people will know that we are Christ's disciples. The only one who does not like this heart transformation is Satan. His plan, after losing someone to Jesus Christ, is to keep him in a state of spiritual apathy.

As wonderful as spiritual revivals are, with all the accompanying signs and miracles; unless hearts are set free by our willingness to surrender all to Jesus Christ in obedience, God's anointing will lift and what remains will be as sounding brass or a clanging cymbal. (1 Corinthians 13:1). However, this does not discourage me to continue to pray daily for God to pour out His Spirit upon all flesh to renew the Church of Jesus Christ and prepare her for the return of our King of Glory. I believe that the fruit of our intimacy with our heavenly Father will be manifested in a wholesome balance between the natural and the supernatural. Our passion for God must find its outlet not only through our praise and worship of Him, but also in our sincere concern for those Jesus Christ died for.

In September 1997, our prayer ministry was officially incorporated with the following Mission Statement.

Our Desire: To introduce people to the only God, through a personal relationship with His Son, the Lord Jesus Christ (Romans 10:9).

Our Purpose: To glorify God and the Lord Jesus Christ in the power of the Holy Spirit (1 Peter 4:11).

Our Commitment: To share the teaching and healing ministry of Jesus Christ with the needy and brokenhearted (Luke 4:18).

Our Experience; "And they went out and preached everywhere, the Lord working with them, and confirming the Word through the accompanying signs" (Mark 16:20).

Chapter Twenty-Four

Overwhelmed by the Holy Spirit

Throughout the many years since I dedicated my life to Jesus Christ, I have always believed what the Scriptures teach about the Holy Spirit as the third Person of the Godhead, the Trinity. I understand that it is the Holy Spirit, who regenerated me, indwells and anoints me, empowers and sanctifies me, and bears witness to my spirit that I am a child of the most High God. (Romans 8:16) He helps me and gives me joy; He discerns the Scriptures for me, gives me wisdom and gifts, and helps me to bear fruit to the glory of God. In summary, the Holy Spirit forms Christ in me, so I can live my life through Jesus Christ and become more like Him. I consider my relationship with Jesus Christ and God, my Father, with the help of the Holy Spirit, to be alive and exciting. This reality helps me to overcome whatever the enemy tries to put into my path trying to separate me from my heavenly Father.

However, my heart's craving for more of God and His kingdom was not satisfied by mere teachings of men. I loved the Holy Scriptures and through my daily reading I received strength and comfort. Attending Church on Sundays and Bible study groups during the week, supplemented by choir practices, and other church related activities provided what I needed to sustain my spiritual life. I thank God for wonderful teachers and godly mentors that helped me in my walk with Jesus Christ.

But in spite of this rich background, I longed for something more than what I saw in my Christian surroundings. This inner thirst for more of God was not something painful or distressing; not at all. I found great pleasure in the Bible and if I failed to understand what I was reading, I would ask the Lord for wisdom and revelation. Sometimes the answers came, and other times I walked away puzzled by what I read. In this pursuit for a greater understanding of the Bible, I found myself ahead of some of my Christian friends.

The apostle Paul was and still is to me, one of the most fascinating characters in the Bible. So much went on in one person's life, that I have not exhausted my interest in this ironclad man with a heart of gold, even to this day. His fervor for the God of Abraham was insatiable. As a prestigious Pharisee he was determined to spare no effort in eliminating any teachings that were not in strict alignment with what he thought was right; he just knew it all, or so he thought. It was while on his way to Damascus to bring to trial those who were following Jesus Christ that his life fell apart. He came under a blinding light and as he fell off his horse, he heard a voice from heaven.

The account is recorded in the book of Acts chapter nine; "And as he journeyed he came near Damascus, and suddenly a light shone around him from heaven. Then he fell to the ground and heard a voice saying to him, 'Saul, Saul, why are you persecuting Me?' And he said, 'Who are You, Lord.' And the Lord said, 'I am Jesus, whom you are persecuting. It is hard for you to kick against the goads.' So, he trembling, and astonished, said, 'Lord, what do You want me to do?' And the Lord said to him, 'Arise and go to the city and you will be told what you must do'. And the men who journeyed with him stood speechless, hearing a voice but seeing no one. Then Saul arose from the ground, and when his eyes were opened he saw no one. But they led him by the hand and brought him into Damascus. And he was there three days without sight and neither ate nor drank."

God restored Saul's eyesight and changed his name to Paul. His erstwhile opposition to Jesus Christ transformed him into the most powerful and successful missionary to the Gentiles. His encounter with the Lord, in my understanding, is an illustration of our rejection of the supernatural power gifts of the Holy Spirit and the manifestation of signs and wonders in our time. It deeply concerns me that Christian leaders continue to insist that the power gifts and all kinds of signs and wonders have ceased.

By insisting on this incredible lie of Satan, they keep many otherwise faithful believers from pressing into all things God has for them. This is a matter of great concern as they fail to understand that a Christian's continued opposition to our blessed Holy Spirit will have grave consequences. The apostle uses the words; "For this reason many are weak and sick among you, and many sleep (have died)" (1 Corinthians 11:30). Although the reference here is in connection with Holy Communion, there are enough references in the Bible in regard to serious consequences for stubbornly resisting the ministry of the Holy Spirit who came to do the works of Jesus.

Paul's compatriots, the Pharisees who confronted Jesus Christ, give us an insight into their hearts and their role as leaders of the people of Israel. The more I read about the conduct of the Pharisees and their interaction with Jesus, the more I see them reproduced in the church of Jesus Christ today. Nothing in God's economy happens by accident; everything fits in His overall plan for His creation. So do the Pharisees.

The lives of the Pharisees were thrown into disarray by the appearance of Jesus Christ in their midst. According to their interpretation of the Holy Scriptures, Jesus' claim to be the Son of God was absurd. In fact they attributed the miracles of Jesus to Beelzebub, a name for the devil (Matthew Chapter 12).

Jesus responded by warning them that they were blaspheming the Holy Spirit; "Therefore I say to you, every sin and blasphemy will be forgiven men, but the blasphemy against the Holy Spirit will not be forgiven men." These words of Jesus have brought controversy and confusion not only to people in His time, but all through the church age to this day.

Is there a parallel between the Pharisees of Jesus' time and some church leaders in our time? Have the supernatural manifestations of signs and wonders caused similar reactions among contemporary church leaders? Given the gravity of standing in the way of the Holy Spirit's ministry, I cannot help but be deeply concerned about those who dare to harden their hearts. I have been confronted with this subject countless times and heard many interpretations from well meaning Christians. I do not claim to have a theological answer to every question regarding this subject. However, I will continue to share what I have learned through the years of my relationship with Jesus Christ and the Holy Spirit, as well as from interacting with Christians through our Prayer Ministry. The Bible teaches us that the Holy Spirit can be:

Grieved; Ephesians 4:30
Quenched; 1 Thessalonians 5:19
Resisted; Acts 7:51
Rebelled against; Isaiah 63:19

We do not grieve a policeman when speeding; he just gives us a ticket. Nor do we grieve a judge when we misbehave; he simply hands us a sentence. We can only grieve someone who truly loves us. We can certainly grieve our parents.

The Holy Spirit was sent by our heavenly Father to do the works of Jesus after His resurrection and ascension to heaven. "But the Helper, the Holy Spirit, whom the Father will send in My name, He will teach you all things, and bring to your remembrance ALL things that I said to you" (John 14:26). Jesus also said that he who believes in Him will do the works that He did, and even greater works than these will he do, because I go to My Father" (John 14:12).

Certainly our finite minds are unable to understand the Holy Trinity, specifically when it comes to the Holy Spirit. Though described as a Person our brain "threatens to explode" when attempting to comprehend the Holy Spirit. I always end up totally awed when meditating about the Holy Spirit and His role in the universe. What I can grasp is that He does the works of the Father and the Son without taking any credit for Himself. This alone, without any other understanding, moves me to fall prostrate before my Father, praying that He will protect me from ever grieving or quenching the Holy Spirit again. From His tenderness represented by a dove, to his power to move mountains, the Holy Spirit was on the scene before the creation of this world, as mentioned in Genesis 1:2.

Having lived in Argentina for thirty-one years, I was exposed to spiritual revivals that brought great excitement to many people, while others were disturbed and still others became outright nasty. After I moved to America I was told by some church leaders that the supernatural power gifts as listed in First Corinthians chapter twelve had ceased after the Bible was completed. This was new to me, as I had never heard this from my forefathers, who had their Christian roots in the Protestant Reformation. In fact, since I was brought up in Martin Luther's Bible, I read in his personal comments, that though emphasizing the authority of the newly translated Scriptures into German as the foundation of the Christian faith, he was positive when it came to the supernatural power gifts.

I learned that not much is accomplished by arguments. So, I took a deep breath and moved on. I never heard anything like this from my parents or from any of the many German and Spanish Christian books I read earlier in my life. There was much more I was to learn and experience about the Kingdom of God and what often well meaning Christian leaders have taught in their churches.

I thank and praise God that He has chosen to reveal the deep things of His Kingdom to those who sincerely seek wisdom and desire intimacy with Him. The apostle Paul writes: "Where is the wise? Where is the scribe? Where is the disputer of this age? Has not God made foolish the wisdom of this world? God has chosen the foolish things of the world to put to shame the wise, and God has chosen the weak things of the world to put to shame the things which are mighty; and the base things of the world and the things which are despised God has chosen, and the things which are not to bring to nothing the things that are, that no flesh should glory in His presence. But of Him you are in Christ Jesus, who became for us wisdom from God-and righteousness and sanctification and redemption-that, as it is written, He who glories let him glory in the Lord" (1 Corinthians 1:20, 27-31).

Encouraged by absorbing God's Word daily, I was learning that through the sanctification process of the Holy Spirit, the Lord was forging my character to become more like Him. No matter what distraction came into my life, I needed to keep my heart anchored in God. I had to accept the fact that even those who opposed or criticized me were there for a purpose. In the school of hard knocks, I learned that the path to humility will lead to brokenness, which leads to greater spiritual strength and authority, and ultimately to a free flow of God's love through my heart.

This was not an easy path for me to choose, when my sinful nature often sought to overtake other Christians. I knew what my mother would have said about my overactive zeal to move to the top: "Remember my son, God will not allow trees to grow into heaven. When they grow too tall, He will clip off the top; and if you fly too high, He will clip off your wings and you will plummet to the ground." I am grateful that when things seem to get too tight, I can laugh at myself by dipping into my forefather's wisdom and sound humor.

God wants us to be overcomers, for he who overcomes shall inherit all things; but certainly not at the expense of others. As I pondered about the Pharisees' inconsistency between their outward appearance and the state of their hearts, I began to see some similarities in my own life. This led me to believe that the Holy Spirit's sanctification of a believer in Christ can be seen as a three phase process: Pharisaic, Brokenness, and Outflow of God's love and power.

The Pharisaic phase often surfaces after our conversion to Jesus Christ. We believe that we have been saved by grace through faith and that it is a gift of God and not the result of our own effort (Ephesians 2:8,9). We also believe that we have been created in Christ Jesus for good works that have been preordained by God and are now encouraged to walk in them. I have no doubt that many sincere believers have done and are still doing what they believe God equipped them for. However, there are times when our walk is not in line with our talk. We tend to hide behind masks, pretending to be more spiritual than our fellow Christians.

I know that during the first twenty years after my conversion, I have often displayed pharisaic characteristics. In my zeal to please God and convey truth to my fellow Christians, I realized that my lack of biblical understanding of the truth, led me to grieve, quench, and sometimes resist the Holy Spirit. The Pharisees claimed that their rejection of Christ's deity was based on biblical truth, when in reality they got their information from teachings of men. Similarly, either through ignorance or downright stubbornness, many Christians have rejected the works of Jesus as manifested through the Holy Spirit.

Even to this day I get frustrated at otherwise mature Christians, who choose to close their hearts to what so obviously is the outpouring of God's spiritual power. I thank God that He has not left me in my ignorance, but in His grace kept moving me on to higher grounds. Firmly believing that Jesus is who He claimed to be, I continued to ask Him to reveal His truth to me.

At the beginning of 1993, while still living in Florida, Jeanie purchased a Christian book. Some of the author's teachings were not in line with what I believed. Over the years, she purchased hundreds of good books that helped us in our ministry to the brokenhearted. But this one, I was not willing to read, so I asked her to return it. I was still struggling with my impressions about the revivals in Argentina and elsewhere. I believed that God, our Father, actively intervenes in the affairs of men through the Holy Spirit, but I objected to the methods and the responses of Christians who left their church to run after something that excited them.

One of the statements in the book that most irritated me was that; "if you don't speak in tongues, you are not born-again." I truly loved God and had committed my life to Jesus Christ, only to hear that "nonsense" from those who so obviously were still "drinking milk" (Hebrews 5:12,13). Of course, my reaction to their immaturity was anything but loving. Over and over again I heard the voice of my Shepherd; "By this all people will know that you are My disciples, by the love you have for one another." The beauty of having this heart connection with our heavenly Father is that He will not leave us orphaned; but will comfort and help us move into a deeper understanding of His word.

A year later, we returned to the book store and while Jeanie walked through one aisle, I went straight to the book I had rejected, and read about the author's background. I purchased it, returned home and read it in two sittings. I reflected on how I had judged the author simply by his outward appearance and based on other Christians' opinions. Through God's grace I repented from what I thought was my sound Christian judgment.

Chapter Twenty-Five

An Awesome Vision.

On January 11th of 1994, I woke up at 2:00 AM and could not fall back to sleep. I thought that the Lord woke me up to pray, so I asked Him to let me experience the presence of the Holy Spirit. Then, at 3:00 AM, half awake and praying, I saw and experienced what I believed was a vision from the Lord. It was unusual. I wanted to speak but my jaw felt numb; I was unable to move my body. What I saw next was undoubtedly a vision; something difficult to express in mere human words, unfolded in front of me. I was not asleep neither was I awake; it was something like an in-between state. My eyes turned to the clock; it was 3:15 AM. Suddenly it became dark all around. I looked for the light switch, but my attempt to turn on the light was to no avail. Soon the darkness turned into something so beautiful and majestic that I find no words to describe it. I saw a large white fountain, and out of the center emerged a crystal clear stream of water, engulfed in a bright shining light and as it grew larger and taller, it looked like a gigantic lily.

Then the entire area was filled with beautifully sparkling lights that streamed out of this flower like an erupting volcano. What followed absolutely delighted me. I was lifted out of my bed and carried out of the bedroom and slowly moving down this stately stairway of what looked like cherry wood. This was so awesome, I felt like I was sitting on a flying carpet. At the bottom of the stairway I was placed on the floor while I heard this gentle, but firm voice saying; "do not grieve, quench nor resist the Holy Spirit." I got up and slowly walked into my prayer room.

As I approached my room I sensed that someone was behind me; I fell on my face in adoration and thanksgiving and immediately I knew that my heavenly Father was allowing me to experience the presence of the Lord Jesus through the Holy Spirit. I perceived the voice of my Shepherd again; "Write a prayer of repentance for grieving, quenching and resisting the Holy Spirit, and for rebelling against Him; and share this with every church leader I will send your way." I left my prayer room to go for a walk around our beautiful Island, while the words written at the end of this chapter came to my mind.

The vision I experienced was about supernatural life and the power of the Holy Spirit. Jeanie and I started to act upon our newly invigorated faith; and wonderful things began to happen. Spiritual gifts were manifested; when we laid hands on the sick, they recovered; when we opened our mouths in obedience, prophetic words brought encouragement to those we ministered to and when confronted by evil spirits we cast them out in the name of Jesus Christ of Nazareth, and they left.

Through the gifts of knowledge, wisdom and discernment of spirits, the Holy Spirit enabled us to determine open doors that the enemy had used to harass those who were brokenhearted. Their hearts were healed, opening the way for the love of God to flow into their lives.

As the Lord continued to work in my heart, my perspective of the ministry of the Holy Spirit widened tremendously. I began to acquire a better understanding of human reactions during spiritual revivals. Before, I would rush to judge things that were offensive to my orderly perception of spiritual matters, whereas now I am more cautious in my evaluation, lest I be found to resist the Holy Spirit. Skepticism is not a noble virtue for a Christian; it stands in opposition to real joy and the truth of the Holy Scriptures, and robs us of the child-like faith that Jesus wants us to possess in order to enjoy intimacy with Him and His Father.

One way to be freed from this ugly trait is to praise and worship the Lord. It helps us to ignore the devil's lies and focus on what God has for us in a certain situation. Of course, we are to be alert and exercise sound judgment in evaluating doctrines lest we are deceived by the enemy. As the fruit of the Holy Spirit; love, joy and peace began to mature in my heart; I surged above the ugliness of unbelief, doubt and skepticism.

Without a cleansed and sanctified temple, the glory of God cannot be properly manifested in a Christian's life. At best we may enjoy some momentary bliss that will be gone before long. Holiness is the work of the Holy Spirit; it is formed in us through death and resurrection, through repentance and forgiveness. The old is replaced with the new; not by trying to make the old better. Jesus said; "Verily, verily, I say to you, unless a grain of wheat falls into the ground and dies, it remains alone; but if it dies, it produces much grain" (John 12:24). We must surrender all our being to our Lord Jesus Christ; soul, spirit and body, so that the Holy Spirit can transform us into His image, thus enabling us to think, speak and act more like Him.

"I beseech you, therefore, brethren, by the mercies of God, that you present your bodies (your whole self) a living sacrifice, holy, acceptable to God, which is your reasonable service. And do not be conformed to this world, but be transformed by the renewing of your mind, (heart) that you may prove what is that good and acceptable and perfect will of God" (Romans 12:1,2).

What is it that upsets some Christians when someone in their midst shares his delight about spiritual revivals with supernatural manifestations? I am convinced that our Father's main purpose for the mighty move of His Spirit is to target our hearts. There are so many Scripture accounts about the hardness of the hearts of men. From a gentle breeze to refresh those who walk in obedience, to a mighty hurricane that breaks the prison cell of those in captivity; the Holy Spirit is in perfect unity with the Father and follows His directions.

Those who see the changing hearts will shout for joy, but the critics will only see chaos and miss the best. What they see with their physical eyes or hear with their physical ears, does not line up with their theology, often acquired by doctrines of men. Thank God that He is faithful in dispensing His grace through the ever increasing number of revivals across the globe. However, there are sufficient warnings in the Holy Scriptures for those Christians who stubbornly choose to climb up the dangerous ladder of grieving, quenching, resisting and rebelling against the Holy Spirit.

Prayer of Repentance for:

Grieving the Holy Spirit: "Do not grieve the Holy Spirit of God by whom you were sealed for the day of redemption" (Ephesians 4:30).

Quenching the Holy Spirit: "Do not quench the Holy Spirit" (1 Thessalonians 5:19).

Resisting the Holy Spirit: "You stiff-necked and uncircumcised in heart and ears. You always resist the Holy Spirit; as your fathers did so do you" (Acts 7:51).

Rebelling against the Holy Spirit: "In His love and in His pity He redeemed them; and He bore them and carried them all the days of old. But they rebelled and provoked His Holy Spirit" (Isaiah 63:9,10).

"Dear heavenly Father; I come before You and acknowledge that I have sinned against You, by resisting the Holy Spirit's work of sanctification in my life. I repent from the sins of unbelief and stubbornness, and ask for Your forgiveness. I believe your Word that says; 'Rebellion is as the sin of witchcraft, and stubbornness is as iniquity and idolatry' (1 Samuel 15:23a).

I surrender myself, spirit, soul, and body as a living sacrifice to the sanctifying work of the Holy Spirit. Teach me Father, to think with the mind of Christ, and help me to speak and act as is pleasing to You. Help me not to judge Christians with whom I may still disagree and teach me Your truth in a fresh way. I believe that the Holy Spirit is reviving the Body of Christ in ways that are often beyond my limited understanding. I receive Your forgiveness with thanksgiving and I praise and love You with all my heart. In Jesus' name;" Amen.

Chapter Twenty-Six

Speaking with New Tongues?
No thanks

On March 11th 1995, during my quiet time with God, He impressed upon my heart the need to write what I had learned about the speaking in Tongues and later incorporate it into my book. This was certainly not an easy task and, before I was able to start, I was tormented by inner conflicts. I was aware that my sinful mindset was in conflict with my spirit or my heart. My rational mind was not satisfied with what it could not understand. From the words of the apostle Paul I know that; "The Spirit Himself bears witness with our spirit that we are children of God, and if children, then heirs; heirs of God and joint heirs with Christ, if indeed we suffer with Him that we may also be glorified together" (Romans 8:16,17). I quickly reasoned myself out of anything that would stir up controversy.

In Ephesians 1:13,14, Paul writes; "in Christ you also trusted, after you heard the word of truth, the Gospel of your salvation; in whom also, having believed you were sealed with the Holy Spirit of promise, who is the guarantee of your inheritance until the redemption of the purchased possession, to the praise of His glory."

Romans chapter eight became one of the most important Scripture lessons for my understanding of not only my need to submit to the teaching of the Holy Spirit, but to obediently follow His instructions for my walk with God. This was a tedious and lengthy process, but worth pursuing.

Listening to the voice of my Shepherd and following Him obediently was my heart's desire. Consequently, I wanted to be careful not to hastily reject something that would enrich my relationship with Him and my fruitfulness in the Kingdom of God. I also spent much time in Paul's first epistle to the Corinthians chapters one and two; and God blessed me with a deeper understanding of the struggle that was raging between my natural, carnal mind and the mind of Christ that needed to take control of my whole thought process. Having gone through this important transformation process has helped me to be aware that the real battle for the supremacy of the Holy Spirit in the Christian's life is in the mind.

It began to dawn on me that the conflict between my natural mind and the mind of Christ, currently active in my heart, could only be resolved by obediently submitting to the renewing work of the Holy Spirit, through the power of the Word of God. There were no short cuts; neither was there any way around the fact that my natural mind is only able to receive and comprehend information coming from my five senses; whereas my spirit receives revelation from God.

Does this conclusion mean that reason and logic are to be discarded? Absolutely not; they just become subservient to the Holy Spirit. More light was shed on this subject as I spent time reading, studying and obediently submitting to the Word of God, the Bible. The enemy intensified his attack on my natural mind; "You have enough controversial information in your book; you do not need more. Furthermore, you are already fluent in three languages; why overload your mental computer?" The adversary did not spare any tricks to restrain me from writing about my experiences in this book. Thank God, the conflict subsided after I commanded Satan and his cohorts to leave me. Joy returned and I was able to proceed with my writing.

Interestingly, while busy writing, I was reminded of Martin Luther who threw his inkstand at Satan who repeatedly tried to disrupt his translation of the Bible into the German language. The ink stain on the wall of the Wartburg Castle has been preserved to this day.

I never believed that the power gifts of the Holy Spirit, as listed in 1 Corinthians 12:4-10 had ceased; in fact, I'm excited when I see them active in the Church of Jesus Christ and in our lives. However, the gift of speaking in new tongues had intrigued me for many years, but I did not know how to relate this gift to contemporary Christianity. Rather than getting involved in a theological study, I will simply share some personal experiences.

As I shared earlier, I was raised by godly parents who never mentioned that certain gifts of the Holy Spirit were not available for the church today. In fact, they believed the entire Word of God. In my home church in Buenos Aires, the subject never really surfaced until a Pentecostal church was established by American missionaries only a few blocks from our Baptist church. Now things began to change to the point that our church became polarized, when a number of our people attended this newly established church, bringing back all kinds of "new doctrines." Needless to say, our congregation had its own brand of revival; except it was a major revival of the natural mind that was offended by what was happening. Frankly, I was caught in the middle of it all.

As a member of the church board I had to work myself through this confusion. To make matters even worse, another "trouble spot" surfaced a few miles away, when Pentecostal missionaries from America started what turned into a great spiritual revival, with major rallies conducted in a giant soccer stadium. Trucks and bus loads of people stormed to these meetings, which were now covered by the press. Needless to say, the attendance in our church diminished which caused no minor consternation. We had our hands full.

Frankly, in a way, I began to like this new agitation in our church, because I thought this may shake us out of our spiritual stagnation. However, the responses of some of those super excited Christians provided fodder for those who were opposing the whole movement. "You are not a born-again Christian unless you speak in tongues;" was one of the most offensive statements I heard. Some of these Christians were in positions of leadership, which did not help me in my search for answers. Of course, I contributed my share of criticism to this major affair that was beginning to awaken hundreds of thousands of people who were storming to the stadium to watch "los americanos" (the Americans).

Furthermore, it was rumored that most of the crowd were considered to be less educated people, which strengthened my resolve to stay away from it. This, of course, is utter nonsense; as if education has anything to do with the ability to receive the things of the Spirit of God. As a result of what I saw and heard about the gift of tongues, I was getting a bitter taste in my mouth. However, the ensuing conflict in my heart was not appeased; because I was not ready to "dump out the baby with the bathwater."

After moving to the United States, the confusion about the power gifts, specifically the gift of tongues only increased. Why in the world can the Church not settle this issue once and for all and get on with the job of bringing people to Jesus Christ? Either we believe that the Lord is pouring out His Spirit upon all flesh or we don't and leave those who do alone. Obviously, while the Bride of Christ is still in this world, it is no more likely for this issue to be resolved, than Satan to be bound before his God-assigned time. From my own observations I am convinced that the adversary is more involved where the anointing of the Holy Spirit's power increases. Complacent Christianity offers the enemy a time of rest. As I mentioned earlier, when revivals come, the power encounter with the Holy Spirit brings confusion to those who resist the work of the Holy Spirit, because of what they observe in peoples' reactions.

One day while in the company of a dear pastor of a Charismatic Church, he told me I was one of the very few Charismatic Christians that he knew who did not speak in tongues. I was not aware that I was a Charismatic Christian; however, I was not a bit offended. Ever since the movement began I wanted to be part of the move of the Holy Spirit— but, if possible, without the controversy.

I was not ready for what my friend had in mind for me. I saw in his eyes that he was getting ready for the big move. I said; "my dear friend, I don't need a new language, I already have three. I love the Lord, and I am happy the way things are in my life." With my teeth tightly closed and my lips hardly moving, I whispered; "leave me alone."

However, I couldn't explain why I felt so uncomfortable whenever my friend came too close to me. Usually, when convinced that something was not for me, I would simply ignore the matter and move on to something else. During my friend's next trip to America, things again got very uncomfortable; it was the time when Jeanie got her gift while I had to translate the entire process. I shared this and other related experiences in the chapter "The Birth of Fullness of Christ Ministries."

Over a period of nearly two years, I was directly exposed to my own precious wife's prayer language, and I began to enjoy it because I liked what I saw in Jeanie. It was not only the gift in itself, but her sweetness and the way she went about it that touched me. She was truly becoming a vessel for honor, sanctified and fit for her Master, the Lord Jesus Christ, preparing her unto every good work (2 Timothy

2:21). It became very obvious to me that the Holy Spirit was transforming her heart, enabling the outflow of God's love to people around her. It was so unpretentious and unthreatening; so different from what I had experienced since the spiritual revivals in Argentina in the mid 1950's.

Needless to say; this intensified, first my curiosity and later my interest in the gift of tongues. But I still wondered how I could benefit from what I still thought was the most controversial gift of the Holy Spirit. Continuing to search the Scriptures I read and re-read Paul's first letter to the Corinthians chapters 12, 13, and 14 and could not find anything that I could see as an excuse to abstain from this gift. I was surprised when I discovered that Jeanie had the freedom to control the flow of her gift; something which concerned me. Could this manifestation pop up anytime, anywhere and unannounced, making me look like a fool? Then I read that Paul stated that it was the least of all the gifts. Well, if so, why bother and I walked away from it. But I couldn't; the more I tried the more it haunted me.

I went back to the Bible, to the apostle's words; "I will pray with the spirit, and I will pray with the understanding. I will sing with the spirit, and I will also sing with the understanding. For if I pray in a tongue, my spirit prays, but my understanding is unfruitful" (1 Corinthians 14, 15). This meant that the natural mind is not actively involved in that prayer. Wow, this is getting too risky.

But can the mind think other things while the Christian is praying in the spirit? Who forms the words and sounds in his mouth? What happens during that kind of praying? Are we opening ourselves to strange spirits? I wanted to know answers to my questions. Who can I ask the many questions that invaded my mind when so many of my contemporaries wanted no part of it?

Some of the most pious ones warned me that I could easily get involved in transcendental meditation and other

Eastern religious practices that would land me right in Satan's territory. If I would ask Pentecostal and Charismatic friends about the gift of speaking in other tongues, they wanted to baptize me in the Holy Spirit and convince me that there is ample proof in the Bible for this practice; and that would destroy my reputation as a sound believer in Christ. I was convinced that the Holy Spirit was all in and around me. What was left for me to do? Ignore the matter and walk away from it? I tried that many times before and it did not work; certainly not after I was "stung" in my heart by what I soon learned was the Holy Spirit Himself. Then I reasoned for a while and came up with the brilliant thought that; if the gift of tongues is the least of all the gifts, why not start from the least and then move up to all the other power gifts? My spiritual eyes began to open, my heart received light and the entrance of God's Word granted me understanding.

The restlessness that had plagued me for decades was beginning to subside. Praise God for His mercy and unending love for me. It was my heart that my Father was after; He wanted all of it, without any reservations. After seeing many people coming to Christ, either one at a time through my personal testimony or through church services, rallies, or major moves of the Holy Spirit during revivals, I finally received an answer to a nagging question; why is there so little lasting fruit in the lives of believers in our Lord Jesus Christ? Why do so many begin with a bang and soon there-after fizzle out? I began to see it in my spirit and confirmed by the Holy Spirit that it is all about our hearts and our will-ingness to allow Him to remove all hindrances, all blockages that prevent the free flow of God's love, through the Holy Spirit.

It is only through our Father's powerful and thoroughly transforming love that the Church of Jesus Christ can deeply affect the world. His end-time outpouring of the Holy Spirit upon all flesh is in progress. I believe that we will see complacent Christians and entire churches move under the fire of the Holy Spirit, powerfully affecting our decaying society.

During the season of struggling with the gift of tongues, and trying to find my way through this controversial and divisive subject, I was reminded of something Corry Ten Boom shared during one of her visits to our church in Milwaukee. She stepped up to the pulpit with a flashlight in her hand and while greeting the congregation, she tried to turn on the flashlight without success. Her simplicity and good humor had everybody's attention riveted to her attempt to turn on this thing that was not responding to her directions.

Then she proceeded to unscrew the lens and to her "surprise" a piece of cardboard that was caught between the light bulb and the battery fell onto the pulpit. That very simple demonstration became her teaching theme and it is still alive in my mind and heart over thirty years later. Far too many Christians are unaware of what blocks their hearts from the free flow of the Holy Spirit and the Father's love. Unfortunately, teachings of men still take precedence over the voice of our Shepherd who seeks to direct us through the Word of God and His Holy Spirit. The consequences of this absence of clear directions in the Christian's life are very obvious. Thank God, that through an increase in a genuine desire to be firmly anchored in Christ, many Christians are finding their way to our Father's heart!

In April 1993, after seeing the gift of tongues active in my own home for quite some time, I shared with Jeanie that I was ready to have our fellowship pray over me to receive this gift. This was the usual time we planned our return from Florida to our summer home in Pennsylvania. Our customary potluck dinner hosted by our dear friends and mentors John and Anne, the leaders of our church, was the appropriate place to express my prayer request. After dinner, Anne asked; "does anyone have a special prayer request?" During the silence that ensued, I decided to "chicken out."

At that very instant, Jeanie, who was oblivious to my change of mind, raised her hand and shouted; "My hubby Harold has a prayer request." There was absolutely no way of escape; I was in for the ride. I took a deep breath and whispered; "here I am Lord, help me." I was asked to sit on the "hot seat" and suddenly the group went into action as Anne gave instructions; "let everybody gather around Harold and while we will make a joyful noise to the Lord, he can practice his prayer language."

As I submitted to the Holy Spirit's leading by activating my vocal cords with the words Abba, Abba, strange sounds began to issue from my mouth; it felt like a sputtering engine before warm-up. Obviously, the joyful noise of my dear friends drowned out my mind's ability to figure out what was happening; this was the purpose of the noise; my natural mind was not to interfere with the Holy Spirit's work in my spirit.

I was experiencing what I had learned, that it is in the spirit that we receive revelation from the Holy Spirit, while our carnal mind may be confused. After briefly reflecting upon my strange predicament, I came to the conclusion that it was time for my inquisitive carnal mind to submit to the Lord. I had complete peace knowing that I was under the anointing of the Holy Spirit. After practicing for a while I began to enjoy it. The joyful noise around me changed into thanksgiving and praise to God. After we came home Jeanie asked me with a smile; "Are you going to practice your prayer language before bedtime?" After overcoming all hurdles, it became part of my devotional time with the Lord.

If anything broke in me that evening, it was pride. Our move into the other supernatural gifts of the Holy Spirit came with a lot less pain. This experience marked the beginning of a completely new understanding of the ministry of the Holy Spirit in the Kingdom of God on earth. My faith took a great leap and my relationship with the Lord Jesus

Christ became very endearing. I know deep within me, that He is my best Friend and as such I can trust Him with all my heart. The Word of God became more plausible as the Holy Spirit revealed deeper truths to me. Fifteen years later, I am still convinced that it was my heavenly Father who opened the eyes of my understanding to what He has provided for the church of His beloved Son.

So, have I become a crusader for or against the Holy Spirit's power gifts? or do I spend hours speaking in tongues? Do I believe that Christians who are endowed with specific power gifts are more mature than others? My answer is no to all the above. What I do believe is that if we humble ourselves under the mighty hand of God and properly exercise the gifts that God has chosen to grant us, He will reward us through becoming better servants to our brethren in Christ and to the world around us. Christians who overemphasize certain gifts of the Spirit tend to neglect the need for the healing of their hearts. It is the Fruit of the Spirit (Galatians 5:22,23) that equips us for this world and the world to come; the signs and wonders that follow us, will confirm the power of the Word of God, while here on earth.

Are you still struggling with the reality of the power gifts of the Holy Spirit and its value in the body of Christ? If so, let me encourage you with the following words of Scripture: "So then, after the Lord had spoken to them, He was received up into heaven, and sat down at the right hand of God. And they went out and preached everywhere, the Lord working with them and confirming the word through the accompanying signs" (Mark 16:19,20).

Some Christians may argue that verses 9-20 are lacking in a few of the oldest versions of the Gospel of Mark. However, most of the oldest versions contain them. I am grateful that the Gospels and the book of Acts, as well as many accounts throughout church history, testify of the Holy Spirit's powerful manifestation through signs and wonders. When

I checked Martin Luther's old German Bible comments in reference to these verses, he states: "Since the Bible is available to all people, signs and wonders are not as necessary as in early Christianity. However, when they manifest, we need to be open to them." Jeanie and I have decided to exercise whatever gift the Holy Spirit bestows upon us, and stay away from arguments.

For every friend we lost after our transition into deeper mysteries of the Gospel, the Lord added several new ones; and after a while some of the old ones rejoined our ranks. Satan is well aware of the intrinsic power of the supernatural gifts and will do everything he can to confuse Christians who are open to the move of the Holy Spirit. Stop worrying what people may think and ask God to fill you with His divine love to overflowing and you will see His truth affecting people's hearts.

Beware, the real battle is in the carnal mind. It insidiously tries to keep you from addressing the blocking issues of your own unhealed heart. "Every argument and every high thing that exalts itself against the knowledge of God…as well as every thought must be brought into captivity to the obedience of Christ" (2 Corinthians 10:3-6). Godless thoughts, entertained in our minds, become imaginations and sin is conceived; and if not quickly confessed, the enemy will establish strongholds through which he will be able to harass us.

Of course, Jesus wants us to "be wise as serpents and without malice as doves." We need to be aware that our adversary, the devil, is able to counterfeit what God creates, including signs and wonders. Here is where godly wisdom is required in order to discern that which is genuine from what is false. Be aware that through either pride or ignorance, the devil can blind us to his wicked devices and sooner than we realize it, we may swallow his bait. After Satan lost his position in heaven, he is still under God's jurisdiction and cannot move beyond His parameters. The enemy may be allowed to sift us as wheat for a specific learning season in our sanctification process; but after we repent from our wrongs, our Lord will turn what Satan meant for evil into something good. (Read about the Apostle Peter's experience with Jesus, Luke 22:31-34).

Until the Lord gives me new directions, I will use what I believe is a prayer language in my personal devotions. At times, Jeanie and I find ourselves in specific intercessory prayer sessions when we sense the need to express something in an unknown language. The Holy Spirit prompts us and we follow His directions. However, we do it very discreetly so as not to irritate those around us who are "strangers" to supernatural manifestations.

I have also experienced in several Christian gatherings, how a message was given in a language other than English, through which someone present from another country would receive directions from the Lord in his native language. It pleases me when these situations are properly handled by the leaders.

I am well aware this subject can become a controversial and even divisive issue that is often treated with contempt and consequently kept out of churches. However, this grieves the Holy Spirit and will eventually lead to spiritual apathy, which was Satan's purpose in the first place.

Since the enemy of God and the Church of Jesus Christ is still roaming around this earth, we must be aware of his wicked devices and protect ourselves with the weapon arsenal that the Bible outlines for us. The enemy has broad knowledge of the dealings of mankind and is specifically interested in those who believe in Jesus Christ. Deception is his most powerful means to attack Christianity. Painful pitfalls can be prevented through a more intimate relationship with our Lord, in conjunction with greater knowledge of His Word, the Bible. This needs to be emphasized repeatedly.

Jeanie and I have frequently experienced that the precious Blood of Jesus Christ, the Lamb of God, is an aberration to Satan and his minions. Combined with His holy and powerful name and the Word of God, we have awesome protection against attacks of the enemy. However, we must be aware that Satan is a legalist and, as such, has a right to harass us when failing to address sinful issues. Jesus is our "Sin bearer;" the only One who can cancel the power of sin (Revelation 12:10).

There is indeed mighty power in the name and the Blood of the Lamb!

Many Christian leaders and entire ministries have fallen under the cloud of deception. I have witnessed this tragedy in Argentina and in the USA, and it saddens me to see Christians getting hurt by trusting those who are themselves blinded by the tricks of the devil. All of us are vulnerable to the forces of darkness; it is therefore essential to open ourselves to one another and have our hearts healed.

The second part of this book is basically a collection of articles, originally written in the 1990's for the purpose of giving the reader an illustration of God's sanctification work in my life. I believe that this material can be used to teach Christians to become vessels for honor for the outflow of our Father's love. While emphasizing that my relationship with the Lord Jesus Christ is an exciting journey, I am aware that my old, sinful nature has not lost its potential to fall into temptation and must therefore be surrendered to Jesus Christ daily!

Part II

The Outflow of our Father's Love

A sequel of Bible teaching articles, originally written in the 1990's

Introduction

Military armies celebrate victories after the enemy has been defeated. The war is over; a peace treaty is signed, prisoners of war exchanged, and eventually normal relations between countries are restored.

However, there is a war, fought in the unseen world that has been raging relentlessly since the creation of mankind, and will not cease until Satan, the instigator of evil and arch-enemy of God is bound and cast into the bottomless pit. In the New Testament of the Bible, the apostle John gives us a description of this event in the book of Revelation; chapter twenty, verses 1-3.

"Then I saw an angel coming down from heaven, having the key to the bottomless pit and a great chain in his hand. He laid hold of the dragon, that serpent of old, who is the Devil and Satan, and bound him for a thousand years; and he cast him into the bottomless pit, and shut him up, and set a seal on him, so that he should deceive the nations no more till the thousand years were finished. But after these things he must be released for a little while."

All through the Old Testament period, we see a relentless tug of war between good and evil, because man had fallen under the jurisdiction of Satan, as the result of his disobedience to God, his Creator. Every attempt by God to restore fellowship with the crown of His creation was countered by man's disobedience to Him, thereby giving Satan the legal right to harass, oppress, and torment mankind with the sole purpose to destroy what God had created.

Yet God, in His infinite love, did not give up on His redemptive plan for mankind. Through the obedience of a man called Abraham, who turned his back on pagan worship, God was able to gather a people for Himself whom He called Israel. Although a great number of them continued to rebel against the Lord, there were those who decided to follow Him. This only increased the resolve of the devil to keep men under his dominion.

This tug of war continued through the centuries, while God communicated with his people Israel through prophets, judges and kings, until the greatest event in the history of this universe took place. God sent His only begotten Son Jesus Christ into the world, to gather for Himself an army of believers, whom the apostle Peter calls "…you are a chosen generation, a royal priesthood, a holy nation, His own special people, that you may proclaim the praises of Him who called you out of darkness into His marvelous light; who once were not a people but are now the people of God, who had not obtained mercy but now have obtained mercy" (1 Peter 2: 9,10).

No matter how intensely the name of Jesus is ignored or abhorred in our days, the day will come when He will return to this earth as He promised as King of kings and Lord of lords and everyone will see Him no matter where they are. The apostle Paul, in his letter to the Philippians 2: 9-11 writes:

"Therefore God also has highly exalted Him and given Him the name which is above every name, that at the name of Jesus every knee should bow, of those in heaven, and of those on earth, and of those under the earth, and that every tongue should confess that Jesus Christ is Lord, to the glory of God the Father."

When Christ returns to set foot in the land of Israel, He will rule over a kingdom of peace for a thousand years. As the Prince of Peace, He will be seated on the throne of David in the holy city, the New Jerusalem and establish it with judgment and justice.

"For unto us a child is born, unto us a Son is given; and the government will be upon His shoulder. And His name will be called Wonderful, Counselor, Mighty God, Everlasting Father, Prince of Peace. Of the increase of His government and peace there will be no end, upon the throne of David and over His Kingdom, to order it and establish it with judgment and justice.

From that time forward, even forever. The zeal of the Lord of hosts will perform it" (Isaiah 9:6, 7).

We live in a time of unprecedented turmoil. Practically every day we could be disturbed and fearful by what we hear and read in the news. However, we who believe in Jesus Christ can be reassured that He will return soon to take us out of this world to be with our heavenly Father for all eternity. This awesome truth should fill us with unspeakable joy and hope, able to face every day.

I grew up in a home and attended a church where believers in Christ encouraged each other with words of Scripture. Their hope of eternal life in Christ provided the foundation for joyful living. Of course, things were not perfect, but in retrospect I dare to say that it was the familiarity with the Bible and the willingness to live godly lives that gave Christians the ability to overcome difficulties. I remember the many ways people went out of their way to help each other, visiting the sick, celebrating "love feasts" with the ladies cooking most delightful meals; in other words, Christians enjoyed each other's company. They were aware that we, as followers of Christ, are pilgrims on this earth, waiting for a much better future. The apostle Paul, in

1 Thessalonians 4:13-18 writes about our need to be well informed about our future:

"But I do not want you to be ignorant, brethren, concerning those who have fallen asleep, (died) lest you sorrow as others who have no hope. For if we believe that Jesus died and rose again, even so God will bring with Him those who sleep in Jesus. For this we say to you by the word of the Lord, that we who are alive and remain until the coming of the Lord will by no means precede those who are asleep. For the Lord Himself will descend from heaven with a shout, with the voice of an archangel, and with the trumpet of God. And the dead in Christ will rise first. Then we who are alive and remain shall be caught up together with them in the clouds to meet the Lord in the air. And thus we shall always be with the Lord. Therefore comfort one another with these words."

All who believe in Jesus Christ will at that moment, receive a new body, which Paul calls; "the redemption of our body;" Romans 8:23b, and in 1 Corinthians 15:51-53 he writes; "Behold, I tell you a mystery: We shall not all sleep, but we shall all be changed- in a moment, in the twinkling of an eye, at the last trumpet. For the trumpet will sound, and the dead will be raised incorruptible, and we shall be changed. For this corruptible must put on incorruption, and this mortal must put on immortality."

From that moment on, and for all eternity we will have glorified bodies just as Jesus received after His resurrection. This is absolutely awesome, to say the least. Just as God created every planet and star in the sky by the power of His spoken word, so countless believers in Jesus Christ will receive new, glorified bodies and join their souls and spirits in the presence of God. In regard to the end-time turbulent events Jesus said; "Now when these things begin to happen, look up and lift up your heads, because your redemption draws near" (Luke 21:28).

However, while still on this earth and looking forward to Christ's return, we must be faithful to our Lord's injunction to love one another as Christ loves us, so that we can be salt on the earth and light in a dark world. Our world needs to see the unconditional love of our Lord Jesus Christ reflected in us.

I pray every day for God to bless America, and I believe in a mighty outpouring of the Holy Spirit to revive His church, empowering her to bring in a great harvest of souls. When this happens, we may even see a socio-political invigoration of our society.

During a period of over sixty years I had the privilege of serving as Sunday school teacher, youth leader, elder, deacon, and adult Bible teacher, in several Evangelical churches in Argentina and the United States. In 1995, my wife Jeanie and I established Fullness of Christ Church and I served as the lay pastor until 1998, at which time we decided to dedicate our time to minister God's healing power to the brokenhearted. Amazingly, God always took us far beyond of what we were able to imagine. We have learned, and are still learning, to walk with Jesus Christ; not running ahead of Him, nor staying behind, but walking side by side with the Lord, attentively listening to His voice. Of course, it took years, if not decades; but the reward of obedience is exciting.

The wealth of experiences gathered during a lifetime cannot be contained in one single book. I will attempt to highlight in the second part of this book, what I consider essential marks of a Christian who seeks to enjoy intimacy with the Triune God; Father, Son Jesus Christ, and the Holy Spirit.

Part two is essentially a collection of articles written at different times and are not in chronological order. Consequently, you may notice some scriptural repetitions. If you wonder why I have quoted so much Scripture, it is because I have learned and experienced that not just the letter but the Spirit of the Word of God has the power to transform lives.

Chapter One

How You Can Know that God Loves You

Have you ever wondered what will happen at the very end of your life, and where you will be after you die? Has it ever occurred to you, that much of what you read in the Bible applies to you personally? Do you know that God, the Creator of the universe, wants to become your loving Father? Can you envision yourself in the presence of God and the Lord Jesus Christ, overwhelmed with joy and gratitude, ready to receive your Lord's reward?

If you consider yourself a Christian, but you do not enjoy a personal relationship with the only true God, and are not sure whether you are on your way to heaven, you need to make a decision.

I would love to show you how to enjoy a relationship with God, our Father, so you will have the inner assurance that when you leave this world, you will be with Him forever.

The sacred Word of God, the Bible, teaches us how to find the way to Jehovah, the only true God. When God created man in His likeness, with the ability to choose between good and evil, Satan, the archenemy of God, was determined to lure him under his evil control. God called the first man Adam, and later gave him a wife whom He called Eve. To this day, every person born into this world has been given the opportunity to choose between good and evil, or heaven and hell. Adam and Eve exercised their free will by listening to the lies of the enemy, who deceived them into eating fruit from the only tree that God had forbidden them to eat; namely the tree of the knowledge of good and evil. As a result, they reaped the consequences of their disobedience, bringing upon themselves and all mankind, first spiritual and later physical death, as God had warned them.

Everything God wants us to know about Him, has been recorded in the Holy Scriptures, the Bible and through the work of the Holy Spirit we will be led into a deeper knowledge of Jesus Christ, who is the Eternal Tree of Life. The devil has not changed since the day he succeeded in deceiving the first couple in the Garden of Eden; namely, to believe his lies and thus forfeiting God's promises. Praise God that through faith in Jesus Christ the way to the eternal God is open to all who accept His invitation; "I Am the resurrection and the life, he who believes in Me, though he may die, he shall live. And whoever lives and believes in Me shall never die" (John 11:25-27).

Nobody in this world or in the unseen world, except Jesus Christ, can bring us back home to our Creator. Jesus said of Himself: "I am the way, the truth, and the life. No one comes to the Father except through Me" (John 14:6). God sent the Lord Jesus Christ, His only begotten Son into this world; and after suffering the most agonizing pain ever inflicted to a human being, He died on the Cross and shed His Blood for the sins of the whole world. On the third day, after His crucifixion, He rose from death and after forty days, in the presence of many eyewitnesses, Jesus Christ ascended into heaven to return to His Father.

If you are ready to accept Jesus Christ as your Savior and Lord I invite you to pray the following prayer with a sincere heart:

"Dear God, You are holy and I am a sinner. I confess my sins and repent for my disobedience to You. I believe that Jesus Christ shed His blood on the cross for all my sins and that He rose from the dead to grant me eternal life. I believe that Jesus ascended to the glory of His Father from where He will return to establish an eternal Kingdom, ruled by Him and his Bride, the Church. I accept your forgiveness with thanksgiving. Thank You for hearing my prayer; in Jesus' name, Amen."

The apostle Paul declares "that if you confess with your mouth the Lord Jesus and believe in your heart that God has raised Him from the dead, you will be saved" (Romans 10:9). Share with someone what you did; begin to read the Bible and attend a church where the Gospel of Jesus Christ is preached.

In the following article I want to show you how your relationship with Jesus Christ can reach deeper dimensions, adding great joy to your life.

Chapter Two

Seeking a Deeper Life in Jesus Christ

If you desire to enjoy a rich and powerful relationship with the risen Lord Jesus Christ, that you may have observed in other Christians; let me help you by sharing how God transformed my life:

Seek Him fervently in prayer...

Tell God in your own words that you desire to know Jesus Christ, His beloved Son, more intimately. The works of Christ are performed here on earth by the Holy Spirit; He is our Helper, our Comforter, our Protector, our Provider, the Discerner of the Word of God, and much more. Remember, when Jesus promised His disciples that when He leaves them He would send them another Comforter.

Jesus said: "I will pray the Father, and He will give you another Helper, that He may abide with you forever, even the Spirit of truth, whom the world cannot receive, because it neither sees Him nor knows Him; but you know Him, for He dwells with you and will be in you" (John 14:16,17).

As a believer in Christ, your spirit was made alive to commune with your Father; Christ, the hope of glory lives in you (Colossians 1:27). I knew this in 1943 when I invited Jesus into my heart; but it was not until 1959, after I surrendered myself, body, soul, and spirit to the Lord, that my life took an exciting new direction. I asked the Lord to flood my entire being with the Holy Spirit and have full reign in my life.

Ask Jesus to flood your whole being with the Holy Spirit and He will do it. Pray; "Come Holy Spirit, permeate my whole being with Your presence; renew my mind by teaching me to function with the mind of Christ (1 Corinthians 2:16). I take my carnal mind to the Cross where it belongs. Father, I thank You that You will help me to live to Your glory. In Jesus' name;" Amen.

Read God's Word regularly and devotionally, submitting to His teaching...

When you enter the pages of His holy Word, leave behind all opinions of men. In a short prayer, ask the Lord to cleanse your mind of anything that will keep you from understanding the unadulterated Truth of His Word. (Read 2 Corinthians 10:3-5). Remember, God has declared it, and the believing heart will accept it as written. Sometimes we read the Scriptures and wonder whether certain things are really available to us today. If you truly seek to understand deeper truths of God's Word; be patient, and delight yourself in the Lord. In due time He will give you the desires of your heart (See Psalm 37:4).

Ask the Lord to illumine your spirit...

...so that you can come to the proper understanding of His Word. "Oh, send out Your light and Your truth! Let them lead me; let them bring me to Your holy hill and to Your tabernacle" (Psalm 43:3). One of the most difficult things for us is to wait patiently for the Lord. We are so action oriented and geared to expect immediate results that waiting for something can be an agonizing experience. However, in our walk with the Lord we must learn to wait for Him in order to prevent hurtful pitfalls. "Wait on the Lord; be of good courage, and He shall strengthen your heart; wait, I say, on the Lord" (Psalm 27:14).

I have often looked at this verse with impatience. I kept waiting and waiting, trying to muster up courage while still waiting. It was not until it dawned on me that the Lord wanted to strengthen my heart and heal it, so that waiting on Him would become a lot easier.

Whatever God grants you, will be measured by what you are willing and prepared to receive. Nothing is wasted in God's economy. Your outstretched arms and your open hands and heart will be filled to overflowing. Jesus said: "I have come that they may have life, and that they may have it more abundantly" (John 10:10b). The Holy Spirit, our Instructor and Helper, will open your understanding for God's Word and will impart wisdom to you, not available to those without Christ, because; "The fear of the Lord is the beginning of wisdom, and the knowledge of the Holy One is understanding" (Proverbs 9:10).

The reading of other books, no matter how good they may be, should never replace devotional Bible reading. If this is happening to you, you may be suffering spiritual malnutrition. You may have been at a party preferring to indulge in snacks because you anticipated a poor meal; but let me assure you, in God's royal feast there is no lack of absolutely delicious food.

Bible commentaries and dictionaries may be good sources for archaeological or historical information. However, the opinions of the authors, in regard to doctrinal matters, should only be considered if they prompt you to submit to the Holy Spirit's discernment of the Bible.

God's refreshing response to your yearning for more of Him, will bring great joy to your heart. Your sincere quest for intimacy with God will intensify day by day.

Pray with King David:

"O God, You are my God; early will I seek You; my soul thirsts for You; my flesh longs for you in a dry and thirsty land where there is no water. So I have looked for You in the sanctuary, to see Your power and Your glory. Because Your lovingkindness is better than life, my lips shall praise You. Thus I will bless You while I live; I will lift up my hands in Your name. My soul shall be satisfied as with marrow and fatness, and my mouth shall praise You with joyful lips" (Psalm 63:1-5). When the heart is healed, our mouth and lips will bring forth blessings, and people will know that we mean what we say, because our countenance reflects our inner connection with the Lord.

God's Word will become sweeter than honey; "How sweet are Your words to my taste, sweeter than honey to my mouth" (Psalm 119:103). This will increase your desire to serve the Lord. You need to press in and persevere. It is essential that you spend time in the Word of God every day; even reading a few verses or a chapter will edify you. I wrote Bible verses on small cards and carried them with me to work to feed myself with the Word every opportunity I had. Through the years I collected over three hundred verses. I have tasted the sweetness of God's Word and experienced its supernatural power that has sustained me for many years.

I cannot contain the joy of the Lord; I have to share it with those who are hungry for God and the deeper truths of His Kingdom. This is not only a heartfelt desire; it is a mandate for me. "For everyone to whom much is given, from him much will be required" (Luke 12:48). Of course, we must be wise stewards of the time allotted to us by God.

Let me assure you; there is a delight in serving those in real need. Many times I heard the Lord speaking to my heart; "Take care of my people and I will take care of you and what is yours."

As an illustration, I will share an experience from our prayer ministry. Phil, (not his real name) was a man in his early thirties, who was diagnosed by medical professionals with Paranoid Schizophrenia. Jeanie and I brought him to our home, mainly to shower love on him. We bought him a Bible and had him read Scripture verses from my packet that I collected over the years, while in the corporate world. I also wrote a prayer for the healing of the brain, because we believed that the Lord would honor our prayers. When we first met Phil, we could not keep eye contact with him. His head and eyes would shift from one side to another; while his speech was incoherent, at times. In the beginning, we spent a lot of time laying our hands on him in prayer, believing that the Lord would do what Jeanie and I were not able to do in our own strength.

Aware of the fact that we are not professional counselors, we trusted God with all our hearts in every situation. Gradually, we had our friend read several Scripture verses and highlight them in different colors. He was very cooperative; but we had to exercise patience with his inability to follow our instructions. Our reservoir of patience had to be replenished daily.

After several months of guiding Phil along the Lord's healing path, we began to see slight improvements in his behavior. At times, we would take our friend out for lunch; which he absolutely loved. We saw in his countenance that he trusted us and he began to receive the unconditional love that we extended to him. Over the years we have seen wonderful progress in his condition; by then Phil had highlighted over three hundred Bible verses. He is now reading from them in his time with the Lord. "The entrance of Your Word gives light; it gives understanding to the simple" (Psalm 119:130).

The path of obedience to Jesus and His word may become treacherous at times; but our loving and caring Shepherd will always surround us. His Word promises that God will never leave us nor forsake us (Hebrews 13:5). Overcoming hardships will always be rewarded by an inheritance; "He who overcomes shall inherit..." In the book of Revelation we read at least eight times that those who overcome shall inherit a promise. Let me encourage you to: "Arise, shine; for your light has come! And the glory of the Lord is risen upon you. For behold the darkness shall cover the earth, and deep darkness the people; but the Lord will arise over you, and His glory will be seen upon you" (Isaiah 60:1,2).

You may still think these promises are not for you; be assured, you are as important to God as every other child of His. He loves you so much that He sent Jesus to die for you personally. He shed His Blood to wash you clean from all your sins and then He rose from death to grant you eternal life to be enjoyed while here on earth and then for all eternity. Jesus said so:

"This is eternal life, that they (you and I) may know You, the only true God, and Jesus Christ whom You have sent" (John 17:3). Christians who accept Jesus Christ as their Savior and then live their own lives thinking that all these beautiful promises the Bible speaks about are meant for heaven, are deluding themselves. They must be reminded that all Christians must appear before the Judgment Seat of Christ, to give account of all their works, good or bad. The present life is our preparation time for our heavenly assignments. (Read 2 Corinthians 5:10 and Hebrews 4:13)

We were dead in sins, separated from God; but through faith in Jesus Christ we are alive and will not die, but live forever. God's plan for your life is to transform you into the likeness of Christ to enable you to glorify Him. In fellowship with Jesus Christ, you are entitled to use His name to take authority over the adversary. You will be able to live above your circumstances and not be squashed by them. It is lamentable that so many Christians live defeated lives; they are missing out, literally robbed of the indescribable joy that Jesus promised those who are obedient to Him. "These things I have spoken to you, that my joy may remain in you, and that your joy may be full" (John 15:11).

The absence of the Lord's abiding joy can often be attributed to the Christians' failure to read the Word of God devotionally and pray consistently. We need to understand that there are no shortcuts to a victorious life. The character of Christ must be "implanted" in us, replacing our sinful nature that belongs on the Cross. It is a lifelong process. If we harbor resentment and unforgiveness, we cannot live joyfully; our lives must reflect what we believe. I will share a lot more in this area of unforgiveness in later chapters. The devil wants to keep your hands tied to your back; his purpose is to defeat you. He knows that he lost you to Jesus when you accepted Him as your Lord, but he will relentlessly attempt to keep you spiritually impoverished, thus making you ineffective in God's Kingdom.

The Holy Spirit will convict you of sins, bad habits, or compulsions to commit sins that will hinder and disrupt your fellowship with the Lord. You may observe other Christians practice certain things that seem harmless; but remember, God's standard for righteous living is often very different from what we understand. We tend to be either too stringent which may cause us to judge or condemn ourselves or others, or we are too lenient which may open the door to Satan to harass us. He is a legalist, make no mistake; he knows when he is given the right to torment us through our unconfessed sins, or our failure to forgive others. (Matthew 18:34,35)

I was often shocked when the Holy Spirit brought something to my attention after I asked Jesus to reveal thoughts and intents of my heart that were out of alignment with God's truth. (Read Hebrews 4:12,13) Only the Lord truly knows our hearts; "The heart is deceitful above all things, and desperately wicked; who can know it? I, the Lord search the heart; I test the mind, even to give every man according to his ways, according to the fruit of his doings" (Jeremiah 17:9,10). Whenever you sense that something is not right in your heart, I suggest you pray Psalm 139:23, 24. You cannot wear out the Lord with your requests; He is always there for you, ready to show you His way for your specific situation, because what seems right to you may not be what the Lord has purposed for you, which is always much better than what you can figure out in your limited understanding.

If the Holy Spirit convicts you of a sin, lay it before Jesus; mention the sin by what it is in your own words and ask Him to forgive you and then turn away from it. Receive His forgiveness with thanksgiving. Tell the Lord: "I receive Your forgiveness with thanksgiving." The path to forgiveness is always open; "If we confess our sins, He is faithful and just to forgive us our sins, and to cleanse us from all unrighteousness" (1 John 1:9). The Blood of Jesus, the Lamb of God, washes away all our sins.

Jesus loves you more than you will ever understand, and when He asks you to give up something for his sake, He will most certainly fill that "vacuum" with something that will make you a lot more effective for His Kingdom; and you will love it. God never intends to make you miserable; I am sure you knew that; He wants you to be complete in Him. "God the Father of our Lord Jesus Christ has blessed us with every spiritual blessing in the heavenly places in Christ" (Ephesians 1:3).

Thank God, that He has ignited in your heart a desire to obediently follow Jesus. If you continue to thirst for more of Him, He will respond accordingly; remember: "ask and you shall receive;" which tells you; if you do not ask you will not receive. "But, what if what I ask is not meant for me?" you may wonder. Does it bring you closer to the Lord? Does it make you more effective in God's Kingdom? Does it give you peace? And then, most importantly, is it backed up by the Word of God? If so, go for it, and thank God for the answer, even though you may not "see" immediate results. "Now this is the confidence that we have in Him, (Jesus) that if we ask anything according to His will, (everything I mentioned above is according to His will) He hears us. And if we know that He hears us, whatever we ask, we know that we have the petitions we have asked of Him" (1 John 5:14,15).

"What man is there among you who, if his son asks for bread, will give him a stone? Or if he asks for a fish, will he give him a serpent? If you then, being evil, know how to give good gifts to your children, how much more will your Father who is in heaven give good things to those who ask Him" (Matthew 7:9-11). Continue to press in; Jesus will be delighted in you, and you will impart blessings to those He brings into your life. There is no limit to His blessings upon you, and at the end of your earthly journey you will be received by Jesus in His heavenly Kingdom as a faithful steward.

The work of the Holy Spirit to transform you into the likeness of Christ is called sanctification. This process will continue for the rest of your life until you reach perfection in the presence of Jesus Christ. (See Philippians 1:6) The transformation process will be more effective and less painful when we willingly submit to our Lord. It is sad to observe Christians who are living their own life after they opened their hearts to Jesus. It is almost as if they are saying to God: "thanks a lot for your salvation; I will see You in heaven;"..and the time in-between is lived according to their own understanding.

"Do not be deceived, God is not mocked; for whatever a man sows, that he will also reap;" the apostle Paul writes to the Christians in Galatia. And then he clarifies it: "For he who sows to his flesh will of the flesh reap corruption, but he who sows to the Spirit will of the Spirit reap everlasting life" (Galatians 6:7,8).

I believe there is a great deal of ignorance among Christians in regard to this important fact; perhaps due to lack of clear teaching.

I am convinced, that the primary reason for the alarming apathy among Christians, and the resulting spiritual impoverishment, is due to their indifference toward the Holy Spirit, the third Person of the Trinity. Grieving, quenching, resisting, and rebelling against the Holy Spirit are alarming signs of an apostate church and of impending judgment, if not repented from and confessed as sin. It is also a call to us who truly love the Lord, to intensify our cry to God for a mighty Holy Spirit revival in our lives, in our churches, and in our land.

When we stubbornly close our minds and hearts to the persuading voice of our Shepherd, we must be reminded by His Word, that we will fall under His pruning knife (Read John 15:1-11). The Holy Spirit seeks to penetrate every secret chamber in our heart to bring greater freedom to our lives.

This has frequently been my own experience; true freedom from the enslavement of sin gives you victory over your carnal nature, over the world, and over Satan. The world, the flesh, and Satan, with his wicked cohorts, will exercise great pressure upon you. But remember, "For whatever is born of God overcomes the world. And this is the victory that has overcome the world—our faith" (1 John 5:4).

Jesus tells us: "These things I have spoken to you, that in Me you may have peace. In the world you will have tribulation, but be of good cheer, I have overcome the world" (John 16:33). (The sinful system of this world is under Satan's dominion). The devil cannot overcome you as you cling to Jesus. Friends, and even other Christians, may caution you about "fanaticism;" they may oppose what you believe and try to keep you at their spiritual level.

Be Watchful...

God tests us to build us up; but the devil tempts us to destroy us. Be alert, the enemy will try to convince you that everything is "fine" with you; there is no need to press in. He will come to you with "good advice" through people you had not expected. But your commitment is first and foremost to Jesus Christ, your faithful and true Friend.

If you desire to be and to have everything God has in store for you, you cannot compromise. After you tasted the infinite goodness of your Father, you don't want to return to superficial Christianity. Your friends do not understand this, unless they too are seeking the deeper things of the Lord. The apostle Paul tells us: "For we do not wrestle against flesh and blood, (people) but against principalities, against powers, against the rulers of the darkness of this age, (the world system) against spiritual hosts of wickedness in the heavenly places" (Satan's abode) (Ephesians 6:12).

Satan, the enemy of Christ and His Church, who is also called the prince of this world, can disguise himself as an "angel of light;" read 2 Corinthians 11:14. He will fool many into accepting false teachings. He can cause great harm to inadvertent Christians; but he cannot triumph over you if you stand firmly against him in the power of Jesus Christ and His Gospel.

Though still allowed by God to create problems in this world, Satan has received his ultimate sentence at Calvary's Cross; and through Jesus' triumphant resurrection we can appropriate His power to resist the enemy. It is possible, as you grow in your relationship with the Lord, that you may find yourself restricted in your present church. We do not all grow at the same pace. God deals with us as individuals and He has a plan for every child of His. I can share from my own experience that if the Lord touched your life in a very special way, He is most likely responding to your yearning for more of Him.

Whatever you share in your fellowship must be seasoned with the love of Christ. Some people, particularly in the leadership, may come up against you and challenge your understanding of the Word. Be aware; many of us have received distorted teaching and need to "unlearn doctrines of man" in order to receive what the Holy Spirit teaches us through prayerful and diligent searching of the Scriptures. No one in the Body of Christ has a clear understanding of the full council of God; we will be students until the end of our earthly pilgrimage.

However, we can differ in our opinions and still maintain a loving fellowship with one another. There may come a time, when the Lord will lead you out of your church into one that better represents your new understanding of the Truth, and rejoice with you for what the Lord has revealed to you. But you need not decide hastily; the Holy Spirit knows where he wants you. "Wait on the Lord; be of good courage, and He shall strengthen your heart; wait, I say, on the Lord" (Psalm 27:14).

Your continued growth in the Lord does not come without tensions from within yourself. Along with your desire to be more like Jesus, you will find another force pulling in the opposite direction. The apostle Paul was very aware that this was happening to him. The Scriptures calls this the lust or the desire of the flesh, the old, sinful nature of man. Paul said: "For what I am doing, I do not understand. For what I will to do, that I do not practice; but what I hate, that I do.

For I know that in me (that is, in my flesh) nothing good dwells; for to will is present with me, but how to perform what is good I do not find" (Romans 7:15,18).

What Paul describes is what happens inside a Christian who is pressing-in to know Jesus in a deeper dimension. It helps us to understand our frustration when we fail in "our efforts" to please the Lord. In fact, we may condemn ourselves and might even be ready to give up. In reality, God is waiting for us to give up so He can begin His work in us.

Let's continue with what Paul is saying in chapter seven, to find the answer to our frustration. In verse nineteen he says: "For the good that I will to do, I do not do; but the evil I will not to do, that I practice." Does this sound familiar to you? It certainly does to me. I remember my frustration while struggling with these issues. Sometimes it is not the flesh but the enemy who tries to keep us from doing what is right. I have this problem even while writing this manuscript. However, I know when it comes from the evil one; because I want to write and I desire it with my whole being and he tries to frustrate my efforts. I take authority over him in the name of Jesus and command him to leave me. I also need to put on the full armor of God every day. (See Ephesians 6:13-17)

Now, let's read the conclusion the apostle draws from his frustration. In verse twenty he writes: "If I do what I do not want to do, it is not I but the sin that dwells in me." In the following verses Paul clearly establishes the fact that there are two forces or two laws inside us struggling against each other. The old sinful nature, our soul, is fighting against the new nature, our spirit, which came alive through faith in Jesus Christ, and is now indwelt by the Holy Spirit. The apostle is teaching us through his own experience that we don't really have a "free will." What we do have are two laws working in us pulling in one or the other direction; and obviously the stronger one will usually win. Consequently, we are either for God or against Him; there is no "neutral" ground. "He who is not with Me is against Me, and he who does not gather with Me scatters abroad" (Matthew 12:30). The aim of the Holy Spirit is to bring us to the realization that we will enjoy the victory over our flesh, over the world, and over the enemy when we allow Jesus to reign supreme in our whole being, spirit, soul, and body.

I do not know what circumstances are presently surrounding your life. You may be stuck in a swamp right up to your chin. If so, I can identify with you; I have been there. But I quickly realized that the only one who really wanted me there was the devil; and I was not about to give him a chance to harass me. I quickly cried out to Jesus, and in His name I told the adversary to flee from me; and, glory to God, he left.

You and I have the best credentials in the whole world. Jesus told us to go into all the world, share His Gospel and use the power of His name to advance His Kingdom. Thank God we do not have to "buckle under" when the enemy attacks us. Our Shepherd will never abandon us. However, it would not be scriptural if I told you that the path of a committed Christian is a rosy one; it is not. What I will tell you is that Jesus is properly equipping you so you can make it through your difficulties; not in your strength, but in His. When in the midst of a trial, our minds are so preoccupied with all its implications that we are unable to "see" what goes on in the spiritual realm. But no matter how difficult the situation, your faithful Shepherd is absolutely aware of everything that concerns you. He knows your name; the faintest cry, the most desperate gesture, every word of complaint or accusation, the most exasperated call for help and the silence that often seems to follow; absolutely everything is known to Jesus. He is all-knowing, all-present, all-powerful, never-changing, and therefore you may know that "He will never leave you nor forsake you" (Hebrews 13:5b).

Listen to what Job said in the midst of utter calamity: "Look, I go forward, but He is not there, and backward, but I cannot perceive Him; when He works on the left hand, I cannot behold Him; when He turns to the right hand, I cannot see Him. But He knows the way that I take; when He has tested me, I shall come forth as gold. My foot has held fast to His steps; I have kept His way and not turned aside. I have not departed from the commandment of His lips; I have treasured the words of His mouth more than my necessary food" (Job 23:8-12). You cannot handle your circumstances alone; call upon the Lord and tell Him:

"Dear Father God, I am tired of living in fear and defeat; I desire a deeper communion with You, and I long to have Your peace and joy. Please forgive me for looking to myself or others and not to You. Reveal to me anything in my heart that is hindering true fellowship with You, and I will confess it. (from Psalm 139:23,24) I commit my whole life into Your hands. Renew my mind and help me to receive Your Word in my heart; transform me by the power of Your Holy Spirit. Thank You Father; in Jesus' name" Amen. You can rest assured that God will hear you and in His perfect timing you will begin to see order in what you perceived as disaster.

At the end of Romans chapter seven, Paul is grateful to God for bringing light to his understanding of what was going on inside a believer; and in chapter eight he makes a dramatic declaration that greatly encouraged countless Christians through the centuries:

"There is therefore now no condemnation to those who are in Christ Jesus, who do not walk according to the flesh, but according to the Spirit....For those who live according to the flesh set their minds on things of the flesh, but those who live according to the Spirit, the things of the Spirit. For to be carnally minded is death, but to be spiritually minded is life and peace. Because the carnal mind is enmity against God; for it is not subject to the law of God, nor indeed can be, so then, those who are in the flesh cannot please God. But you are not in the flesh but in the Spirit, if indeed the Spirit of God dwells in you. Now if anyone does not have the Spirit of Christ, he is not His" (Romans 8:1; 8:5-9).

I pray that you are beginning to see how important it is to mature in Christ, so that you can cease from your own selfish works and allow the Holy Spirit to prompt you to think, speak, and do what is pleasing to the Lord. I believe you will be in a better position to understand Romans 8:28: "And we know that all things work together for good, to those who love God, to those who are called according to His purpose." Jesus will equip you for service. It is not easy to "change gears" and begin to act in the Spirit. Years of following the dictates of a certain mind pattern have created such a routine that we often put up a fight when changes come our way. All too often, while in the midst of a hardship, we may think it is the end of the world; things just couldn't get any worse. But after we come out of the dark tunnel, we see the light and realize that God had us surrounded by his mighty angels. It is through difficulties that our faith is forged.

After we have tasted the loving-kindness of our Lord, we need fellow Christians along our path of life to share our ups and downs and encourage one another to overcome and celebrate victories. The apostle Paul declares "I have fought the good fight, I have finished the race, I have kept the faith. Finally, there is laid up for me the crown of righteousness, which the Lord, the righteous Judge, will give to me on that Day, and not to me only but also to all who have loved His appearing" (2 Timothy 4:7,8). The Lord wants to bless each one of His children with everything He has planned for them, but we need to ask Him just as children ask their loving parents and be willing to receive it with a grateful heart.

From my own, as well as many other Christian's experience, I believe that the subject of the renewing of our minds warrants repetition, because it is one of the most treacherous barriers we need to overcome in order to inwardly affirm our position in Christ and enjoy a deeper relationship with Him!

Pray this simple prayer: "Please Father, help me to be transformed by the renewing of my mind, and let this mind be in me which was also in Christ Jesus" (Philippians 2:5). What does this mean, you may ask? Back again to Paul: "but we have the mind of Christ" (1 Corinthians 2:16b). All who come to Jesus Christ by faith can have their mind renewed to become more like Him (Romans 12:2).

How can I switch from my mind to Christ's, when the two are in direct opposition to each other? Switching will not do it; one must die so the other can take over. This is how I prayed: "Father, Your Word tells me that I have the mind of Christ, but I confess that too often I operate with my own mind. Please Lord, crucify my mind and help me to function with Christ's mind; thank You, Father;" Amen. If I told you how often I prayed this, you would probably laugh. Ungodly, impure thoughts must be flushed out of our minds and brought under the obedience of Christ daily. The Holy Spirit will establish in us a new mind pattern, (1 Corinthians. 2:10-12) and give us "the spirit of wisdom and revelation in the knowledge of Him" (Ephesians 1:17b).

This is part of being equipped for service. Likewise, our will and our emotions must be brought under the Spirit's leadership. I did not want it any other way; my will and my feelings had to follow suit. Because; "I delight to do Your will, O my God, and Your law is within my heart" (Psalm 40:8). This hardly leaves any room to pursue my own selfish desires. My pleasure is knowing that; "Christ in you, the hope of glory" (Colossians 1:27b). Do not be discouraged if changes are slow in coming. You will be surprised how other people will notice the changes in you.

Before,...you may have envied other Christians who possess spiritual gifts that you thought were better than yours, but;

Now,...you know that God, who is sovereign, imparts gifts to men as He pleases; and your jealousy will be replaced with the love of Jesus.

Before,... you may have worked hard to appease your conscience before God; but

Now,... you just rest, allowing Jesus to work in and through you. "For it is God who works in you both to will and to do for His good pleasure" (Philippians 2:13).

Before,... you were concerned that you would not be able to satisfy the demands of your fellow Christians; but

Now,... you know that the purpose of your life is to bring glory to God, and not to please men. You will allow the Lord to produce good fruit with the gifts He granted you. This new relationship with the risen Lord will be an exciting experience for you.

Complacency and conformity to a lukewarm spiritual status quo will no longer be your way of life. When you meet Christians who are learning to live in the fullness of Christ, you will rejoice with them. You will learn more about true friendship; your enthusiasm for the Lord will be reflected in your attitude and even on your face.

This may raise "suspicion" among some Christian friends, and some may begin to shun you or even become cold or downright hostile; this will hurt you, because you had never expected this from Christians. Jeanie and I discovered that for every friend we "lost," the Lord brought several new ones into our lives. And then, guess what; some of the "old" ones came back when they heard and saw for themselves what Christ was doing in and through us. Glory to God. If this is happening to you, reflect upon the words of Jesus: "Blessed are you when they revile and persecute you, and say all kinds of evil against you falsely for My sake.

Rejoice and be exceedingly glad, for great is your reward in heaven, for so they persecuted the prophets who were before you" (Matthew 5:11,12).

Real friendship is like a good quality watch. First: it is "waterproof" because it will not be penetrated by the flood of trials and tribulations that enter life's path. Second: real friendship is "rustproof" because, when disrupted for a period of time, for whatever reason, it will be as good as ever when communication is restored. Lastly: it is shock proof because it will endure arguments, misunderstandings and disagreements, always seeking to establish harmony through love and truth. And yet the friendship and love of the Lord Jesus are so much superior; they endure through all eternity. He is your personal Friend. Trust Him with all your heart; and you will love the outcome.

Be alert, Satan is still loose. "Be sober; be vigilant; because your adversary the devil walks about like a roaring lion, seeking whom he may devour. Resist him, steadfast in the faith, knowing that the same sufferings are experienced by your brotherhood in the world" (1 Peter 5:8,9).

The temptation to look down on Christians who are still "feeding on milk" must be countered with zeal to lead them closer to our Savior and Lord. Remember; "By this all will know that you are My disciples, if you have love for one another" (John 13:35). God will resist you if pride enters your heart. "God resists the proud, but gives grace to the humble" (1 Peter 5:5b). And; "Pride goes before destruction, and a haughty spirit before a fall" (Proverbs 16:18).

Your life will be a reflection of what you believe. When people see your Christ-motivated works, they will know something is changing in you. You will have a greater desire to share your experiences with believers and unbelievers alike. You have been chosen for service; the Bible calls you; "a chosen vessel" (Acts 9:15) and you will be a "vessel for honor, sanctified and useful for the Master, prepared for every good work" (2 Timothy 2:21).

In practical terms, you no longer need to imitate other Christians out of envy or for a desire to compete with them, or to appease your conscience before God. You will no longer burn out when you are doing more than most people in your church, or be discouraged when doing less than "expected" by the standards set by others. You will begin to do what God has planned for you.

The Lord will lay a desire upon your heart; you will begin to "see" the assignment, and the Holy Spirit will give you the confirmation and the wisdom to act. Your thoughts, your words and your actions will come into harmony with your faith; in fact, they will be propelled by your increased faith. People will begin to see Jesus in you and even seek counsel from you. This is exciting, because it is true freedom. However, as you begin to touch lives of unbelievers or Christians who have been lulled into complacency by the adversary, you are infringing on his territory. He will try to bring road blocks into your path. Do not be discouraged because: "He who is in you is greater than he (the devil) who is in the world" (1 John 4:4). Keep your focus on the Lord and you will sense His peace.

Chapter Three

The Awesome Power of Jesus Christ

Jesus Christ said: "I Am the way, the truth, and the life. No one comes to the Father except through Me" (John 14:6).

Whether cheered by wise believers or disdained by fools, Jesus Christ's coming into this world marked the greatest event in the history of this universe. After suffering in the hands of wicked men, Jesus died on a cross outside the city of Jerusalem. But the powers of darkness were forced to retreat as the King of Kings came forth from the grave, opening the way for all who are hungry for God, the Creator of all things.

In this chapter I will emphasize the awesome power of our Lord and Savior given to Him by His heavenly Father: "All authority has been given to Me in heaven and on earth. Go therefore and make disciples of all the nations, baptizing them in the name of the Father and of the Son and of the Holy Spirit, teaching them to observe all things that I have commanded you; and lo, I am with you always, even to the end of the age" (Matthew 28:18-20).

From the time of Jesus' birth in Bethlehem, to His glorious return to heaven, Satan, the archenemy of Jesus Christ and His Church, devised incredible ways to destroy Him. In the book of Isaiah chapter 14:12-17 as well as Ezekiel 28:12-19, the Bible gives us some insight why Satan lost his position as one of the archangels, was cast out of heaven and given this earth as his transitional abode. Although in my finite mind I cannot fathom this mystery, I believe with all my heart that Jesus is the reason for my life and that He has given me and all who truly believe in Him, the power to withstand the temptation of the adversary. The unspeakable joy that has filled my heart over the years and decades is my inner assurance that God loves me more than I can ever imagine.

Following are words of the apostle Paul written in his letter to the Colossian church, chapter 1:15-22, through which he conveys to us who Jesus is and that we, who sincerely believe in Him, can enjoy intimacy with the Most High God, through Jesus Christ.

"He is the image of the invisible God, the first-born over all creation. For by Him all things were created that are in heaven and that are on earth, visible and invisible, whether thrones or dominions or principalities or powers. All things were created through Him and for Him. And He is before all things, and in Him all things consist. And He is the head of the body, the church, who is the beginning, the first-born from the dead, that in all things He may have the pre-eminence. For it pleased the Father that in Him all the fullness should dwell, and by Him to reconcile all things to Himself, by Him, whether things on earth or things in heaven, having made peace through the blood of His cross. And you, who once were alienated and enemies in your mind by wicked works, yet now He has reconciled in the body of His flesh through death, to present you holy, and blameless, and above reproach in His sight."

The apostle Paul recorded what was given to him by the Holy Spirit. Overwhelmed by the glorious reality of Jesus Christ in his life, he could not be stopped in his mission to share his joy with the world around him. Through faith in Jesus Christ, the Seed of Life has been planted in our hearts and sealed by the Holy Spirit. It now has the potential to grow into a mighty fruitful tree, limited only by our unwillingness to trust Him with all our heart.

Throughout my life I have met many discouraged Christians who attempted to follow the advice of well meaning church leaders, without success. This has strengthened my resolve to live my life to its fullest God given potential, in order to help those who were left behind.

Only God knows how many years I have left on this earth; but what I do know is that I will continue to offer myself and my time to Jesus Christ, my most faithful Friend, to use me as He pleases, because He is the Way, the Truth, and the Life, and no one can come to the Father God the almighty Creator of all things, except through Him.

Since the fall of man into sin and his subsequent expulsion from paradise, mankind has been blinded to the reality of the only true God. Through his own efforts to reach God, men have only been drawn deeper into the enemy's territory, to whom Adam and Eve had surrendered what God had entrusted unto them; namely, to have dominion over all the earth (Genesis 1:26).

Nothing has changed in man's sinful nature through the centuries. But God, in His love for His creation, has not given up on mankind. Principalities and powers, the rulers of darkness, the spiritual hosts of wickedness in the heavenly places had to retreat as God reached down to select men and women who would keep His testimony in this fallen world alive. Through patriarchs and prophets listed in the Old Testament, God had established a place where men could worship the only true God, and to proclaim and preserve the written word of God. But over and over again, this fledgling nation, Israel, caved in under the furious onslaught of the enemy, who claimed his territory that God had ceded to him as the result of man's disobedience to Him.

Through the prophet Moses, God gave His people a strict code of laws, called the Torah or Pentateuch, in order to provide a way for them to worship their Creator protected from the enemy. The apostle Paul calls this legal code our schoolmaster or tutor (Galatians 3:24,25). Through Abraham and his descendants, God chose for Himself a nation, Israel that was providentially destined to preserve His written word until the coming of the long promised Messiah Jesus. However, the institution of the Torah, which the apostle Paul calls the schoolmaster, though fulfilling a definitive purpose, did not succeed in bringing about free and genuine fellowship of men with God. It demanded strict allegiance to the only true God, and called for the death penalty, when the people of Israel polluted themselves by intermingling with neighboring idol worshipers. This very strict code of moral conduct, with precise instructions for the erection of places of worship, was intended to keep Satan from interfering with Israel's worship of Jehovah.

The casual reader of the Old Testament of the Bible, in his assessment of these accounts, may wonder what benefit he could draw from what appears to him a futile attempt by God to make something work that is already doomed to failure. But the honest seeker of the Truth will find through the books of the Bible that God our Father continued to unfold His eternal redemptive plan for His people. The Old Testament teaches us a lot about the heart and mind of God, the Creator of all things. I believe that Christians are indebted to the Jewish people for preserving the ancient writings in spite of incredible difficulties.

When God's time was fulfilled He established a permanent "Bridgehead," a mighty fortress in the enemy's territory to assure man's access to God by defeating and ultimately banishing Satan and his wicked spirits for all eternity. This Bridgehead is no one but our Lord Jesus Christ, our ROCK, (1 Corinthians 10:4) and perfect SON OF MAN (Acts 7:56). He provided a haven of rest and free and permanent access to our heavenly Father for all who believe in Him. The coming of Jesus was not only prophesied, but over two hundred names are used to describe His power and majesty, leaving no doubt that He is the Messiah.

When Jesus finally came into the world he was rejected by His own people Israel, who were waiting for their promised Messiah. However, Jesus did not fit their description of what they expected from a powerful ruler, who would free them from their Roman oppressors and establish an earthly kingdom. In His divine character, He displayed attributes which made them uncomfortable. To them Jesus was too humble, too gentle, too merciful, too loving and too forgiving—to rule Israel. They were absolutely blinded by Satan, who saw in Jesus the One who would one day "bruise his head," as quoted in Genesis 3:15, referring to Jesus' victory over the enemy.

The words that Jesus spoke should have reminded them of the words of their own prophet Isaiah written hundreds of years before; "The Spirit of God is upon Me, because the Lord has anointed Me to preach good tidings to the poor; He has sent me to heal the brokenhearted, to proclaim liberty to the captives, and the opening of the prison to those who are bound; to proclaim the acceptable year of the Lord, and the day of vengeance of our God; to comfort all who mourn" (Isaiah 61:1,2).

Yes indeed, Jesus came to turn man's perception of God upside down and His Father in heaven confirmed it by His audible words; "This is my BELOVED SON in whom I am well pleased" (Matthew 3:17). The Law has been fulfilled, grace is now freely available and the way to God Jehovah is open through Jesus Christ. No restrictions imposed by man can prevent us from free access to our heavenly Father. Paul, the apostle reassures us of this reality in his epistle to the Galatians 3:13,14; "Christ has redeemed us from the curse of the law, having become a curse for us, (for it is written, 'cursed is everyone who hangs on a tree') that the blessing of Abraham might come upon the Gentiles in Christ Jesus, that we might receive the promise of the Spirit through faith."

Nevertheless, throughout church history, right up to the present time, there are those in the church who take it upon themselves to lay heavy burdens on people which they themselves refuse to accept. I sat under a teacher of religion who said: "Do as I say, but not as I do." As leaders, we must be a reflection of Jesus to those we teach and be willing to address our shortcomings. Jesus had some fitting words for the Pharisees in His time. "For they bind heavy burdens, hard to bear, and lay them on man's shoulders; but they themselves will not move them with one of their fingers" (Matthew 23:4).

They seem to be deaf to the biblical injunctions; "Bear one another's burdens, and so fulfill the law of Christ" (Galatians 6:2). "Come to Me, all you who labor and are heavy laden, and I will give you rest. Take My yoke upon you and learn from Me, for I am gentle and lowly in heart, and you will find rest for your souls. For My yoke is easy and My burden is light" (Matthew 11:28-30). Of course, we must be "full of goodness, filled with all knowledge, able also to admonish one another" (Romans 15:14b).

Our freedom in Christ should never be used as an occasion to sin. Church leaders must counsel those who stray from the faith; but it must be done with their well being in mind and with their hearts filled with the love of God. Legalistic and self-righteous disciplining has driven too many Christians away from churches, becoming easy targets for the enemy.

Praise God for equipping loving Samaritans; loving burden bearers, who are willing to "lay down their lives" to help their hurting friends. They are not afraid of the enemy and will stand in the gap knowing that they can cast all their cares upon the Lord, assured that they will be restored (Ezekiel 22:30). To me, one of the most powerful examples of our Lord's love and compassion is the parable of the prodigal son, recorded in Luke 15:11-32.

Are you one who "fell among the thieves, who stripped him of his clothing, wounded him and departed, leaving him half dead?" (Luke 10:30). Rejoice; our good SHEPHERD, (John 10:11). is ready to rebuild you. Jesus, the "STONE which the builders have rejected, has become the CHIEF CORNERSTONE, and a STONE OF STUMBLING and a ROCK OF OFFENSE" (1 Peter 2:7,8). Jesus is also the HEAD OF THE BODY, THE CHURCH (Colossians 1:18).

Furthermore, He is the HEAD OVER ALL THINGS (Ephesians 1:22). Our Lord has declared before He ascended into heaven; "All power in heaven and on earth is given to Me" (Matthew 28:18). There is no greater joy available to mankind than having Jesus Christ as Lord of their life. If you have not yet done so, I urge you to turn your whole life over to Him who is the ONLY WAY and allow Jesus to become your SAVIOR and LORD.

As the Head of the Body, the Church, Jesus does not run it like the head of a corporation, who bosses his people from the top down. Jesus Christ is "organically" united to each member of His eternal Kingdom, and as such we are receiving our spiritual nourishment from Him; He is the BREAD OF LIFE (John 6:35). Therefore, if we are undernourished we have only ourselves to blame. As the TRUE VINE, (John 15:1) Jesus longs to feed each one of His branches (you and me) until we grow up to the fullness of Christ (Ephesians 4:13).

Jesus also wants to heal you from your physical and emotional hurts, because He is our PHYSICIAN (Luke 4:23). As your GREAT HIGH PRIEST, (Hebrews 4:14), GREAT SHEPHERD (Hebrew 13:20), REDEEMER (Isaiah 59:20), KING ETERNAL (1 Timothy 1:17) and only MEDIATOR between God and Man (1 Timothy 2:5); there isn't anything too small nor too great for Jesus Christ; submit to your GOOD TEACHER (Mark 10:17) and watch Him work in your life. No matter how vile your sins, Jesus wants to cleanse you and deliver you from the power of sin and equip you for His Kingdom. He is even a FRIEND OF TAX COLLECTORS AND SINNERS (Luke 7:34).

You may be beset with the "traditions of your fathers" (Galatians 1:14) that you cannot truly enjoy freedom in Christ. Your family and friends may insist that you keep the church traditions which were passed down to you through generations. If these traditions are not in harmony with the truth of God's Word, the Bible, and you are told that they are required for your salvation in Jesus Christ, you need to ask God to help you settle this matter and you will find true peace. Keep in mind to avoid arguments, but speak the truth in love as the apostle Paul encourages us; "that we should no longer be children, tossed to and fro and carried about with every wind of doctrine, by the trickery of men, in the cunning craftiness by which they lie in wait to deceive, but, speaking the truth in love, may grow up in all things unto Him who is the Head-Christ" (Ephesians 4:14,15). As your DELIVERER (Romans 11:26) Jesus Christ wants to set you free from human demands, so you can enjoy your relationship with the HOLY ONE (1 John 2:20).

Just reflect for a moment; in the book of Hebrews, chapter 11 verse 6 we read: "But without faith it is impossible to please Him, for he who comes to God must believe that He is, and that He is a rewarder of those who diligently seek Him." Every bit of your faith was given to you by the

AUTHOR AND FINISHER of your faith (Hebrews 12:2), and that Jesus Christ as your RANSOM (1 Timothy 2:6) rescued you from the power of Satan and will continue to work in and through you, that which He begun, until you will see Jesus in glory (Philippians 1:6).

JESUS CHRIST OUR LORD (Romans 6:23), as the HOLY AND THE JUST ONE (Acts 3:14), has closed the impassable gap that existed between you and God. As your REFINER AND PURIFIER (Malachi 3:3), He wants to remove every obstacle that hinders your relationship with the Father and the Son and the Holy Spirit.

When I reflect upon my own life, I cannot thank the Lord enough for the many godly men and women who helped me in my relationship with the Lord. The encouragement I received to study and memorize Bible scriptures will never be underestimated. I am deeply indebted to Papa, my father, who would hardly ever begin nor end a day without Bible reading and prayer, often in the company of my mother.

To me my Papa was a reflection of Jesus, my HOPE OF GLORY (Colossians 1:27), THE HOLY SERVANT (Acts 4:27), and my guarantee that I can enjoy a full and victorious life now while on this earth and everlasting life with Jesus Christ, because He is the RESURRECTION AND THE LIFE (John 11:25).

If you lack interest in reading your Bible, ask Jesus to create a thirst for Him and His Word deep inside your heart, and He will answer your prayers, because He is the LIVING WORD (John 1:1-18), the WISDOM OF GOD and the POWER OF GOD (1 Corinthians 1:24,30).

I could list dozens of additional names and titles given to Jesus Christ, but I must move on because I have a lot more to share.

I believe that you have gained a stronger perspective of Jesus' Deity, His humanity, His mission and His character. Is there any wonder why the apostle Paul had such a passion for

Jesus Christ? Nothing could distract him from truly enjoying His abiding presence. Our Lord has much more for you and me; let's not miss anything.

Chapter Four

God Promises to Restore His People

God's promise in the Old Testament:

"Yes, I have loved you with an everlasting love; therefore with lovingkindness I have drawn you. Again I will build you, and you shall be rebuilt" (Jeremiah 31:3,4).

Has been fulfilled in the New Testament by Jesus:

"The Spirit of the Lord is upon Me,
because He has anointed Me to preach the
Gospel to the poor;
He has sent Me to heal the brokenhearted,
to proclaim liberty to the captives
and recovery of sight to the blind,
To set at liberty those who are oppressed;
To proclaim the acceptable year of the Lord"
(Luke 4:18,19).

In the prior chapter we were reminded of Jesus Christ's greatness, and the importance of keeping Him in the center of our lives.

In this chapter we need to be reminded that the Bible gives us many wonderful promises that will enable us to live effective, victorious lives. Through faith in Jesus Christ we entered through the Door, into a new, everlasting life and now we need to establish our feet on a path that will lead us to the most exciting and deeply rewarding journey a human being can ever travel. "And He has delivered us from the power of darkness and translated us into the Kingdom of the Son of His love" (Colossians 1:13). In a biography of a great man of God who lived in the early part of the 20th century, I read an account of a young man that came to him and asked for a promise of God for his life. "Young man, take your Bible and lay it on the floor; now stand on it and claim all the promises therein for yourself;" was the answer of the wise man of God.

The promises of God will certainly not come our way simply because we call ourselves Christians; there is a price to be paid; namely, our obedience to our Lord. It was God's divine purpose, even before He laid the foundation of this universe, for men to enjoy free and loving fellowship with his Creator. The unrestricted flow of God's blessings would continually stir man's heart to glorify the Lord.

However, in exercising his own will, man chose to believe the devil's lies, thus forfeiting his privilege to commune with God. "For you were once darkness..." (Ephesians 5:8a), but God, who in His infinite wisdom knows all things (Psalm 147:5,6), made provisions for sinful men to be reconciled to Him.

The enemy has not disappeared from the scene; neither has he ceased from his wicked schemes to entrap men since the time of Adam and Eve. Unguarded Christians will fall prey to his deception by believing his lies, thus opening themselves to oppression and all kinds of harassment. Our allegiance to Jesus Christ must be total and cannot be shared with the enemy or with anybody or anything else. "No one can serve two masters; for either he will hate the one and love the other, or else he will be loyal to the one and despise the other. You cannot serve God and mammon" (Matthew 6:24).

Although mammon refers to wealth or profit, Jesus means anything that draws us away from Him. We don't really know what goes on in our hearts, sooner or later the Lord will bring something to our memory that may shock us, because He is the only one who truly knows our hearts. His Word says; "The heart is deceitful above all things, and desperately wicked; who can know it? I, the Lord, search the heart, I test the mind, even to give every man according to his ways, according to the fruit of his doings" (Jeremiah 17:9).

It is important to ask the Lord from time to time to search our heart; "Search me, O God, and know my heart; try me, and know my anxieties; and see if there is any wicked way in me, and lead me in the way everlasting" (Psalm 139:23,24). "Purge me with hyssop, and I shall be clean; wash me and I shall be whiter than snow. Create in me a clean heart, O God, and renew a steadfast spirit within me. Restore to me the joy of Your salvation, and uphold me by Your generous Spirit" (Psalm 51:7,10,12).

Most of what the world offers will never satisfy us, it will only make us "sin-sick." If I were to paraphrase the words of Peter I would say; "come here my friend, sit down and enjoy the sumptuous meal. Get to know the Host, you will truly love Him. What He has to offer is far superior to the crumbs the world offers. So don't just stand around munching on snacks, they will ruin your appetite; for the best is yet to come."

In our prayer ministry, we work with brokenhearted people. When they come to us they are often very discouraged and if they know the Lord we tell them that He promised that He will rebuild His people when they come to Him. We will stand in the gap for them until they begin to take hold of God's promises. Many have been lied to and abused in early life; and it takes time before a level of confidence is built into them.

God's Word, the Bible, is our guarantee that:

A. God's Promises are Unfailing:

When we promise something out of the goodness of our heart, we will build a sense of expectation in our friend's mind. If the promise is not fulfilled, our friend will undoubtedly be disappointed. Man's words and actions do not always go hand in hand. God's words and actions are always in harmony. We can build our lives on them. In 1 Kings 8:56 we read: "Blessed be the Lord, who has given rest to His people Israel, according to all that He promised. There has not failed one word of all His good promise, which He promised through His servant Moses."

B. His promises are assured by His ability:

In Romans 4:20-22 Paul writes that: "He (Abraham) did not waver at the promise of God through unbelief, but was strengthened in faith, giving glory to God, and being fully convinced that what He had promised He was also able to perform, and therefore it was counted to him for righteousness."

C. His promises are intended for you and for me:

Continuing in Romans 4:23 and 24, Paul says that what is written in verses 20 to 22 did not only apply to Abraham, but also to you and me who believe in God who raised up Jesus our Lord from the dead. This means that if we act by faith, fully convinced that God's promises are unfailing, and give Him the glory, it will also be counted to us for righteousness.

D. His promises are confirmed by Christ:

2 Corinthians 1:20-22 says that "For all the promises of God in Him (Christ) are Yes, and in Him Amen, to the glory of God through us. Now He who establishes us with you in Christ and has anointed us is God, who has also sealed us and given us the Spirit in our hearts as a guarantee."

His promises are of infinite value, therefore:

A. Our lives will be rebuilt:

"The Lord has appeared of old to me saying; yes, I have loved you with an everlasting love; therefore with lovingkindness I have drawn you. Again I will build you, and you shall be rebuilt" (Jeremiah 31:3).

B. We can rest in God, fully confident that Jesus is in control:

"Come to Me, all you who labor and are heavily laden, and I will give you rest" (Matthew 11:28). "Be still, and know that I am God" (Psalm 46:10), "And

God said; My presence will go with you, and I will give you rest" (Exodus 33:14).

C. New things will be revealed to us:

"Call to Me, and I will answer you, and show you great and mighty things, which you do not know" (Jeremiah 33:3). "Blessed be the God and Father of our Lord Jesus Christ, who has blessed us with every spiritual blessing in the heavenly places in Christ, just as He chose us in Him before the foundation of the world, that we should be holy and without blame before Him in love" (Ephesians 1:3,4).

D. God's promises help us in time of trouble:

"Fear not, for I am with you; be not dismayed, for I am your God. I will strengthen you, yes, I will help you, I will uphold you with My righteous right hand" (Isaiah 41:10). "Casting all your care upon Him, for He cares for you" (1 Peter 5:7). "The righteous cry out, and the Lord hears, and delivers them out of all their troubles" (Psalm 34:17). "Many are the afflictions of the righteous, but the Lord delivers him out of them all" (Psalm 34:19,20). "One thing I have desired of the Lord, that will I seek: that I may dwell in the house of the Lord all the days of my life, to behold the beauty of the Lord, and to inquire in His temple. For in the time of trouble He shall hide me in His pavilion; in the secret place of His tabernacle He shall hide me; he shall set me high upon a rock" (Psalm 27:4,5).

E. God's promises assure us that our trials will bring us closer to Jesus:

"In this you greatly rejoice, though now for a little while, if need be, you have been grieved by various trials, that the genuineness of your faith, being much more precious than gold that perishes, though it is tested by fire, may be found to praise, honor and glory at the revelation of Jesus Christ whom having not seen you love, though now you do not see Him, yet believing, you rejoice with joy inexpressible and full of glory, receiving the end of your faith—the salvation of your souls" (1 Peter 1:6-9). "And suddenly, a woman who had a flow of blood for twelve years came from behind and touched the hem of His garment. For she said to herself, 'if only I may touch His garment, I shall be made well;' but Jesus turned around, and when He saw her He said, 'Be of good cheer, daughter; your faith has made you well' and the woman was made well from that hour" (Matthew 9:20-26).

F. The Scriptures give us promises for victorious living:

From the time of our new birth in Christ, we are transformed into His likeness by the Holy Spirit (2 Corinthians 3:18). This is the process of sanctification to which every born again believer should obediently submit in order to enjoy victory in Christ.

Following are Scripture promises that assure us:

A. Spiritual fullness:

"The thief (Satan) does not come, except to steal, and to kill, and to destroy. I (Jesus) have come that they may have life, and that they may have it more abundantly" (John 10:10). The enemy is determined to rob you of everything he can in order to make you ineffective for the Kingdom of God. Jesus wants to deliver you from the intrusion of the enemy into your life (Matthew 6:13); and fill you with the power of the Holy Spirit. In John 7:37,38 we hear it more clearly: "If anyone thirsts, let him come to Me and drink. He who believes in Me, as the Scripture has said, out of his heart will flow rivers of living water." This means that the Holy Spirit will activate you into living a joyful and powerful life that will affect people around you.

B. Fullness of joy:

"These things I have spoken to you, that my joy may remain in you, and that your joy may be full" (John 15:11).

C. Victory over the world:

"For whatever is born of God overcomes the world. And this is the victory that has overcome the world— our faith. Who is he who overcomes the world, but he who believes that Jesus is the Son of God" (1 John 5:4,5).

D. Answers to our prayers:

"If you abide in Me, and My words abide in you, you will ask what you desire, and it shall be done for you" (John 15:7). "Now this is the confidence that we have in Him, (Jesus) that if we ask anything according to His will, He hears us. And if we know that He hears us, whatever we ask, we know that we have the petitions that we have asked of Him" (1 John 5:14,15).

E. A faith that dares the impossible:

In Mark 9:17-29, we are told about a man coming to Jesus asking help for his son who was possessed by a mute spirit since childhood. The disciples of Jesus tried to cast out the evil spirit but could not; Jesus had to teach them how they would be able to do it. The father described how terribly his son was tormented by that spirit. Then Jesus said these words: "If you can believe, all things are possible to him who believes"(vs. 23). Immediately the father of the child cried out and said with tears. "Lord, I believe; help my unbelief!" (vs. 24) Then Jesus rebuked the unclean spirit, saying to it: "Deaf and dumb spirit, I command you, come out of him, and enter him no more!" (vs. 25)

My point is that faith can move mountains because all things are possible to him who believes. To this day, unbelief blocks the way for God to perform His mighty works through you and me. Unbelief also prevents God from increasing our faith; Satan pumps up our unbelief so he can keep our hands tied to our backs. Countless Christians claim that they believe in the Holy Spirit, but in reality, pay Him only lip service; their powerless lives are a testimony of this fact. It is up to us to change this. Jesus promises us that: "Most assuredly, I say to you, He who believes in Me, the works that I do he will do also; and greater works than these he will do, because I go to My Father" (John 14:12).

How can this be possible? Again, all things are possible to him who believes. The enemy will whisper into our ears: "Don't believe it; doubt it; don't believe it; doubt it..." and soon we will believe his wicked lies, and disbelieve the Lord. You see, the breakthrough into victorious living cannot fully come about, until we are willing to take that insidious bunch, "unbelief and doubt" to the cross, and ask Jesus to slay it and wash us clean. And thank God, He will.

"Please Father, eradicate doubt and unbelief from my heart; I hate it, I want to get rid of them, I reject them and refuse to let them cripple me any longer; I truly desire to live in victory. Come Holy Spirit, fill me to overflowing with love, joy, and peace, and empower me to triumph over my flesh, over the world, and over Satan and his minions. In Jesus' name" Amen. And then say with Paul: "I can do all things through Christ who strengthens me" (Philippians 4:13). Say it out loud, confess with your mouth, so the devil can hear you and leave you alone.

This victorious faith is a gift from God to His obedient child and is maintained:

A. By our intimate union with Christ:

Jesus answered and said to him: "If anyone loves Me, he will keep My word; and My Father will love him, and We will come to him and make Our home with him" (John 14:23). "Behold, I stand at the door and knock. If anyone hears My voice and opens the door, I will come in to him and dine with him, and he with Me" (Revelation 3:20). This is intimate fellowship with the Lord, available to everyone who is willing to obey Him.

These and many more promises of our Lord, that were confirmed later by the coming of the Holy Spirit at Pentecost, speak of a rich and intimate fellowship of the believer with the Father, the Son, and the Holy Spirit, available to all who sincerely believe!

Why run your own life when the Lord can do a much more excellent job? Surrender fully to him; spirit, soul, and body; don't wait until tomorrow; you will be wasting precious time. By procrastinating you will usually play into Satan's hand.

B. By our inner assimilation of the Truth of God's Word:

"I delight to do your will, O my God, and Your law is within my heart" (Psalm 40:8). "You will keep him in perfect peace, whose mind is stayed on You, because he trusts in You" (Isaiah 26:3).

In the next chapter, I will outline practical steps to show you how you can appropriate God's promises and begin to see your life transformed.

Chapter Five

God's Promises are for You, Take Hold of Them

How can I know which of the many promises in the Bible are meant for me? You may ask. If they are for me; how will I be able to see them become reality in my life, and know that the Lord is pleased with me? These and other questions will be at the heart of this lesson. We learned that our obedience to the Lord will always be followed by the release of His blessings.

Our dependence upon Jesus must be total; in other words we must realize that "for without Me, you can do nothing," as Jesus tells us (John 15:5). This means we cannot do anything of eternal value without Jesus Christ leading and empowering us.

"Now may the God of peace Himself sanctify you completely; and may your whole spirit, soul, and body be preserved blameless at the coming of our Lord Jesus Christ. He who calls you is faithful, who also will do it" (1 Thessalonians 5:23,24). Just as Jesus saved you from eternal separation from God when you accepted Him into your life, so He wants to give you the power to live above sin, free from the dominion of sin over you. "That you may walk worthy of the Lord, fully pleasing Him, being fruitful in every good work and increasing in the knowledge of God; strengthened with all might, according to His glorious power, for all patience and long-suffering with joy; giving thanks to the Father, who has qualified us to be partakers of the inheritance of the saints in the light" (Colossians 1:10-12). Total freedom from sin will only be attained after we leave this body to be with our Lord. Thank God that when we fall into sin we have Jesus, our advocate, to forgive us the moment we confess our trespasses.

Promise after promise flow from God's Word into the life of an obedient Christian. Only spiritually shortsighted and complacent Christians will fail to appropriate the promises that will enable them to finish the work that our Lord has assigned to them. I say it again; in order to receive and enjoy spiritual abundance, you must relinquish control of your life and turn it over to the Lord. He is the only One who will impart the right instructions to get you out from under your circumstances, and lead you into victory. This is my experience; and I truly desire it for you, my fellow pilgrim.

You may see something in Christians that makes you wonder what you are missing. Remember, you are precious in God's sight; He loves you dearly and has only your best in mind. Every individual Christian is as clay in the Potter's hand; He molds and forms us as He pleases. He is not bound to time; we are. On your knees, with outstretched arms, ask your best Friend that you truly desire more of Him and less of the old you. He is waiting for you to plead with Him and He loves to answer your heart's cry.

D. L. Moody, the great evangelist once said: "Receive the promises of God from Genesis to Revelation, that He made to Abraham, to Isaac, to Jacob, to the Jewish people and to the Gentiles, and to all His people around the world, and spend a whole month feeding upon them; you cannot help but to lift up your face to God in praise and thanksgiving." I totally agree.

Please understand that your willingness to have God help you brings great joy to the heart of the Lord; He is always ready to help you, no matter how often you may fail.

"For a righteous man may fall seven times and rise again, but the wicked shall fall by calamity" (Proverbs 24:16). As loving parents, we will certainly be there for our frustrated children through all their pitfalls and help them.

Assume you give your child an erector set for his birthday. He sees beautiful pictures on the box and can't wait to start putting pieces together. After he opens the box and sees hundreds of pieces fall out, his heart begins to sink. Then he looks at the instruction book and the first tears begin to appear. I don't have to ask you whether you are ready to help him at this point; of course you will; it is your child and as his father, you want his best. When the job is completed he will thank you and tell his friends what a great daddy he has.

"If you then, being evil, know how to give good gifts to your children, how much more will your Father who is in heaven give good things to those who ask Him!" (Matthew 7:11) However, the Holy Spirit, your Helper, needs your cooperation in order to transform you and bring the promises of God to fulfillment in your life; He will not circumvent your will. You need to:

1. Understand the Scripture's urging for holiness.

2. Yield to the Holy Spirit's work of sanctification.

3. Submit to the cleansing of your "temple," the inner man; and you will begin to enjoy victory in your life.

1.Understanding the Scripture's urging for Holiness:

By understanding, I mean to "comprehend;" to perceive in your mind and receive in your heart, with genuine intent to submit to God's truth and a willingness to act upon it. It is the kind of understanding that moves your heart to be obedient to what God wants to reveal to you through the Holy Spirit. God will only reveal as much truth as you are ready to digest. He will not choke you with more than what you are able to assimilate. Your hunger for more will continue the flow of the Lord's blessings. "The entrance of Your Words gives light; it gives understanding to the simple" (Psalm 119:130). As you give to others, the flow will intensify. When you study God's Word reverently, with your heart wide open, His promises will begin to come alive in you. This was, is, and will be my experience until I see my blessed and faithful Shepherd face to face.

Not much will happen if you read the Word while holding preconceived notions in your heart, which are not in harmony with it. Mixing opinions and traditions of men with the pure Truth will leave you spiritually impoverished. God will not allow His Word to be diluted by man's opinions.

In Proverbs 30:5,6 we read: "Every word of God is pure; He is a shield to those who put their trust in Him. Do not add to His words, lest He rebuke you, and you be found a liar." The Church needs more Christians who, in regard to the Bible declare with inner conviction; "God said it, I believe it, and this is sufficient for me to submit myself obediently to His teaching, and act upon it." As a Christian believer, you have access to the mind and heart of God your Father, as revealed through Jesus Christ. This is very important; you need to keep this firmly in your mind and heart as we consider another form of understanding.

We live in an era of rapid scientific and technological progress. The mind of man is achieving great advances in the area of communication that are even helping the Church in its monumental task of evangelizing the world. But man without God cannot gain spiritual insight into His oracles because his mind is obscured by sin, and will remain this way, until he is regenerated by spiritual birth.

Paul says: "But the natural man does not receive the things of the Spirit of God, for they are foolishness to him; nor can he know them, because they are spiritually discerned" (1 Corinthians 2:14). For a Christian who walks in righteousness, this is a settled fact; he believes what his Father tells him in His Word. However, far too many Christians think and reason with their carnal minds that "filter out" truth. Our carnal mind is saturated with unbelief, doubt, and all sorts of humanistic thinking. "For to be carnally minded is death, but to be spiritually minded is life and peace. Because the carnal mind is enmity against God; for it is not subject to the law of God, nor indeed can be, so then, those who are in the flesh cannot please God" (Romans 8:6,7,8). Our carnal minds must die at the Cross, so we can operate with the mind of Christ.

So, when men and women use their un-redeemed intellect to "discern and exposit" the Bible, we must be on the alert. Human intellectualism usually rejects anything that cannot be proven scientifically, and will therefore question the Word of God and its supernatural power. Where this form of understanding the Bible has infiltrated the Church, it must be rejected no matter how "godly" the instructor may seem. You should not be surprised to find so much teaching of the letter of the Word without the Spirit of the Word. As the apostle Paul said: "Not of the letter but of the Spirit; for the letter kills, but the Spirit gives life" (2 Corinthians 3:6b). Jesus said: "It is the Spirit who gives life; the flesh profits nothing. The words that I speak to you are spirit, and they are life" (John 6:63).

Someone who reads the Bible "picking and choosing" what is convenient will finally suffer spiritual malnutrition. Stay in the pure and full Word of God; it will safeguard you against any "strange voices," audible or inaudible. "How sweet are Your words to my taste, sweeter than honey to my mouth! Through Your precepts I get understanding; therefore I hate every false way" (Psalm 119:103,104). The proper understanding of the Word is essential because the Bible tells us: "Beloved, do not believe every spirit, but test the spirits, whether they are of God; because many false prophets have gone out into the world" (1 John 4:1). Blessed are you when you proceed in your life in accordance with the instruction of God's Word. I am excited that, since my conversion to Jesus Christ, in November 1943, I am still digging up precious nuggets that I didn't know were in the Bible for me. The Gospel of Jesus Christ affects both, the mind and the heart of people. If it only penetrates the mind and not the heart, the individual will remain in his sins, and thus cannot enjoy the Kingdom of God. "Blessed are the pure in heart, for they shall see God" (Matthew 5:8). I believe that the widespread lack of properly understanding the urging of the Word to be filled with the power of the Holy Spirit, is one of the principal reasons for so much apathy in the Church today. The enemy has clouded the minds of Christians; and consequently their hearts are insensitive to the voice of the Shepherd. Verbal confession and heart belief must go together.

In his letter to the Roman church, chapter 10 verses 9 and 10 the apostle Paul writes: "If you confess with your mouth the Lord Jesus and believe in your heart that God has raised Him from the dead, you will be saved. For with the heart one believes unto righteousness, and with the mouth confession is made unto salvation."

I recognize that other factors contribute to the lack of proper understanding of the Truth. In some cases it may be the lack of proper teaching. However, as Jeanie and I have often experienced, there are many sincere Christians who, as a result of hurtful experiences during their childhood, have erected inner protective barriers which keep them imprisoned. In their subconscious fear of ever being hurt again, they have become impervious to the truth that will ultimately set them free. Praise God that their captive spirit can be awakened and set free through genuine Christian love in action. Jesus will never abandon those who are called and chosen to be members of His Body. You and I have been planted in His vineyard in a specific place and for a specific task. It is therefore God's divine purpose and absolute prerogative to mold us into the likeness of His beloved Son. Having the proper understanding of the need for holiness is essential for the next step in your spiritual growth:

2. Yielding to the Holy Spirit's Work of Sanctification in our lives:

This will undoubtedly bring about the God intended fruit bearing. Our obedient submission to God's Spirit, will enable Him to engraft the truth into our spirit and soul and strengthen our will power to live and walk in the Spirit.

The apostle Paul who was so committed to Jesus Christ, always ready to lay down his life for his friends, was upset when he learned that the Christians in Galatia had fallen back to the works of the law. The apostle states: "This only I want to learn from you; did you receive the Spirit by the works of the law, or by the hearing of faith? Are you so foolish? Having begun in the Spirit, are you now being made perfect by the flesh?" (Galatians 3:2,3). And then Paul said; "Walk in the Spirit, and you shall not fulfill the lust of the flesh" (Galatians 5:16).

How applicable these words are to the church today! Unfortunately, many Christians commit their lives to Jesus, which opens them to the work of the Holy Spirit and, for one reason or another, fail to move into a deeper spiritual dimension, which the apostle describes as "walking in the Spirit." Paul's injunction in Ephesians 5:18b to "be filled with the Holy Spirit," means nothing less than being immersed deeper and deeper into His supernatural power, so that Christ can be "formed in you" (Galatians 4:19b). This should be the normal lifestyle for every born-again Christian. Many useless things must be purged out of our lives if Jesus Christ is to rule supreme in our hearts and minds. "How much more shall the Blood of Christ, who through the Eternal Spirit offered Himself without spot to God, cleanse your conscience from dead works to serve the living God? (Hebrews 9:14).

Paul, the great apostle to the Gentiles, did not hesitate to submit to the sanctification process of the Holy Spirit, in order to become a vessel for honor and bring glory to Christ. His words in 2 Corinthians 4:2 have helped me to lay every sinful thing that the Holy Spirit brought to my attention, to the feet of Jesus and verbally renounce its roots. "But we have renounced the hidden things of shame, not walking in craftiness nor handling the Word of God deceitfully, but by manifestation of the truth commending ourselves to every man's conscience in the sight of God." It is the mission of the Spirit of God to glorify Jesus Christ even through us. However, we are preventing the Holy Spirit from doing His work in us, and then through us, if we refuse to yield to Him.

It is certainly not left to our discretion to be or not to be empowered by the Holy Spirit; in fact, a willful refusal to submit will cause us to grieve, quench, resist, and even rebel against Him. Paul says:

A. "Do not grieve the Holy Spirit of God, by whom you were sealed for the day of redemption" (Ephesians 4:30).

The dictionary defines "to grieve:" to be saddened, even to the point of pain. We can only grieve someone who loves us. When we refuse to do something the boss told us to do, we will not grieve him, we will infuriate him and he may fire us. Neither will we grieve the authorities when we break the law, they will fine us or even arrest us.

When we are disobedient to the Holy Spirit, whom Jesus sent to sanctify us, we will grieve the heart of our Lord, who wants us to do His works on this earth. Jesus loves you more than you will ever be able to comprehend. He desires the very best for you. He wants to strengthen your faith so that you can overcome the world and the enemy who is controlling it, and move into deeper mysteries of the Gospel of Jesus Christ. Is it any wonder that Satan uses all resources available to him to keep us from yielding to the Holy Spirit's power? The Bible warns clearly not to stand in the way of the Spirit of God. God's warnings are not suggestions; they have consequences if willfully ignored.

B. Do not quench the Spirit (1 Thessalonians 5:19). This means we can restrict the flow of the Holy Spirit's power; it is as if one throws a blanket over the fire until it is extinguished. Why is there such a low percentage of Christians enjoying intimacy with God? It is available to every redeemed child of God. "Oh, taste and see that the Lord is good; blessed is the man who trusts in Him" (Psalm 34:8).

C. Do not resist the Holy Spirit; "You stiff-necked and uncircumcised in heart and ears! You always resist the Holy Spirit; as your fathers did, so do you" (Acts 7:51).

D. Do not rebel against the Holy Spirit; "In all their affliction He was afflicted, and the Angel of His Presence saved them; in His love and His pity he redeemed them; and He bore them and carried them all the days of old. But they rebelled and grieved His Holy Spirit; so He turned Himself against them as an enemy, and He fought against them" (Isaiah 63:9,10).

With these four stages; grieving, quenching, resisting, rebelling, we have a picture of the gradual hardening of the heart of a believer. The Comforter and Helper came to abide with the disciples of Christ. For a believer to claim that he is in-filled with the Holy Spirit, while preventing Him from performing God's sanctification work in him, is not aware of the Spirit's mission in the world. Jesus said: "I will pray the Father, and He will give you another Helper, that He may abide with you forever. But the Helper, the Holy Spirit, whom the Father will send in My name, He will teach you all things, and bring to your remembrance all things that I said to you" (John 14:16,26).

He wants to permeate your entire being; give Him permission and let Him do it. Invite Him with these simple words: "Come Holy Spirit, fill me to overflowing, take over every area of my life; I am tired of living a dull, un-excited life; I need a radical change. Thank You, Lord Jesus." Amen

Following are some of many titles and assignments of the Holy Spirit;

The Spirit of God (Genesis 1:2)
The Spirit of Holiness (Romans 1:4)
The Spirit of Glory and of God (1 Peter 4: 14)
He speaks (Acts 28:25)
He teaches (John 14:26)
He helps our weaknesses (Romans 8:26)
He convicts men of sin (John 16:8-11)
He performs miracles (Matthew 12:28)

Now that you know that the Holy Spirit is a Person and speaks, you may begin to realize that this "small voice" from inside your heart is His prompting to obedience. Jesus said very emphatically: "My sheep hear My voice, and I know them, and they follow Me. And I give them eternal life, and they shall never perish; neither shall anyone snatch them out of My hand" (John 10:27,28). When the Lord's prompting in my heart becomes intense, I often feel sorry that I ignored the Holy Spirit's first signal; He is the One who does the work of the Father and of the Son on earth.

You see, it is when we ask God to cleanse our hearts that we will be able to hear the Shepherd's voice with our spiritual ears more clearly. At times when I ignored Him, it was usually because the Holy Spirit was making me aware of sin, and I was not ready to give it up.

The enemy wanted me to believe that it was my imagination playing tricks on me; so he whispered; "don't worry about it, move on, you are doing great, don't become a fanatic. Look around and watch other, more mature Christians." It saddens me, even to this day, when I remember watching Christian friends doing what I was doing, while thinking it was alright; when in fact it was not.

Over time, my perception of the Spirit's prompting was refined to the point that I took immediate action. If sin was involved, I quickly addressed it by taking it to the cross of Jesus for its cancellation by the Blood of the Lamb, and peace and joy filled my heart. I enjoyed it because it was setting me free to live according to the Lord's will; and from the depth of my heart I asked God let me be "a vessel for honor, sanctified and fit for the Master, (my Lord Jesus Christ) prepared for every good work" (From 2 Timothy 2:21). The taste of true freedom in Christ will make us crave for more of Him. I admit there are sinful habits, even compulsions to commit sins that are difficult to give up.

At this point, some readers may think that the direction I am moving in my relationship with the Lord will land me in some place of solitary confinement. Nothing can be further from the truth. Jeanie and I are having a great time rejoicing in the Lord our God, while enjoying ourselves in the company of our families and many friends of all ages and walks of life.

Let me encourage you to ask God to help you take an inventory of your heart; you cannot hide anything from the penetrating, yet loving eyes of the Almighty. He knows you from the inside out. There may be pride, resentment, hatred, envy, strife, unforgiveness, covetousness, evil temper, bitterness, fear; did I miss anything? Now that you know that the Holy Spirit is dynamic and His mission is to act and perform in you what the Father and the Son have sent Him to do in your life, let Him do it; you will never regret having taken this step. Your heart will become more susceptible to God's love which will affect your whole disposition.

You may still be hesitant or perhaps even a bit afraid to fully surrender to the Holy Spirit's sanctification. Allow Him to soften your heart so He can get in there and deliver you from all that "ugly stuff" that is keeping Him out. Perhaps you never heard so much talk about the Holy Spirit. I spent years among Christians who avoided conversations about the Holy Spirit; and what was the result? Their lives were spiritually powerless. Many of their conversations were centered on themselves and trivial things of the world. Sharing my excitement in the Lord and His Kingdom was often not the "right subject" to bring up in their company; I could see it on their faces.

However, people continued to invite Jeanie and me; I know they loved us and we loved them, and still love them today. At times, someone in the group would dare to ask us questions; perhaps they saw that we were not faking and that our joy was real.

I mention these experiences, not to judge other Christians, but simply to share with you how tremendously important it is to yield to the Holy Spirit's process of sanctification. Is our sanctification not really God's will? Yes indeed it is. "For this is the will of God, your sanctification" (1 Thessalonians 4:3). We are all guilty of speaking idle words; "For we all stumble in many things. If anyone does not stumble in word, he is a perfect man, able to bridle the whole body" (James.3:2). Trying to bridle a stubborn donkey is no easy task. I have compassion for Christians who live in spiritual poverty because of their limited knowledge of God's Word; but it agitates me when otherwise mature Christians, resist scriptural truth that would enrich their relationship with God. When sinful habits become compulsions that drive us to commit certain sins over and over again, we need to know that we have opened doors to the enemy. He will not hesitate to harass or even torment us. Failing to confess sin will give him legal rights to torment us.

Jesus tells us through His parable in Matthew 18, verses 21 to 35, what will happen to us when we fail to forgive those who trespass against us. He will turn us over to the tormentors, which are evil spirits. We hold the key to our heart for God to unleash tremendous blessings upon us; the choice is ours. I pray that you will heed the apostle Paul's urging:

"I beseech you therefore, brethren, by the mercies of God, that you present your bodies a living sacrifice, holy, acceptable to God, which is your reasonable service. And do not be conformed to this world, but be transformed by the renewing of your mind, that you may prove what is that good and acceptable and perfect will of God" (Romans 12:1,2).

I admit that I have belabored this subject, perhaps to the point of tiring you out. I would not have done this, unless I was convinced that this is an area of great need within the Body of Christ. Searching our hearts and admitting our need for help is a dreadful thought for most of us. So we rather continue hiding our hurts, by putting up a good front, until we lose control and fall flat on our face. Praise God that He is still there ready to pick us up.

The following personal experience may help you think about addressing the skeletons in your closet. A pamphlet, announcing a Healing Ministry seminar came into our possession. Jeanie suggested that we attend this seminar in order to update our ministry skills. The conference was to be held in Western Canada; which I thought was far enough from our home base to address some personal issues.

So, off to Canada we went and after many interesting stops on the way we arrived at the great province of Saskatchewan. At the end of the first day we were handed a tag with the room number we were to gather for small group sessions. Each room had five chairs in it, indicating that each group consisted of five participants. I found my room and was the first to take a seat. I wondered when the remaining four guys would walk in. Soon the next person walked in; a woman; followed by three more friendly ladies. They seemed pleasantly surprised that they had to contend with only one guy. I fully intended to share my heart with a group of men. Obviously, the Lord had other plans.

As our session began to unfold, it was decided that the four ladies would have their turn on Monday through Thursday, leaving me for Friday. Against all expectations it was a great experience for all of us, and we returned home tremendously relieved and set free from needless stuff.

Jesus came to do the will of His Father; He was absolutely and totally obedient to Him. Likewise, you and I should be obedient to our Lord and do what He tells us. It does not come easily; it takes an act of our will, but the reward is immense.

The following graph will help illustrate my point:

I. The Man without Christ:	**II. The Man in Christ:**
Needs Justification (Salvation)	Needs Sanctification (Holiness)
"By Him (Jesus) everyone who believes is Justified" (Acts 13:39).	"For this is the will of God your sanctification" (1 Thessalonians 4:3).
A. He hears the Gospel of Jesus Christ	A. He hears about sanctification
B. He understands that he must believe in Jesus Christ to be saved from his sins	B. He understands that he must yield to the Holy Spirit.
C. Believes and is justified	C. Yields obediently to the Holy Spirit
D. Confesses Jesus publicly	D. Lives victoriously by trusting Jesus

In steps A and B, a person hears and understands; the message of the Truth has entered through his ears into his mind; whereas steps C and D demand a heart-action in order to receive the blessings God has planned for his or her life.

1. If an unbeliever, after hearing the message of salvation does not act by receiving Jesus into his heart, he will remain separated from God.
2. If a believer hears and reads in the Word that God calls him to sanctification, yet refuses to yield to the Holy Spirit's ministry, he will forfeit great blessings that the Lord has in store for him, now in this life. And when he stands before Jesus Christ he will be rewarded according to what he has gathered for himself in

heaven while on earth. The apostle Paul tells us that; "For we must all appear before the judgment seat of Christ, that each one may receive the things done while in the body, according to what he has done, whether good or bad" (2 Corinthians 5:1).

Jesus said: "Lay up for yourselves treasures in heaven, where neither moth nor rust destroys and where thieves do not break in and steal. For where your treasure is, there your heart will be also" (Matthew 6:20,21) (Read also 1 Corinthians 3:11-17).

To expect God's unending blessings without yielding to the Holy Spirit's lifelong transforming work, is an unbiblical shortcut that will not work. "Mushroom faith" grows overnight but is quickly spoiled. We need "oak tree faith" that is developed over many years of learning in the school of Jesus Christ; it has been tempered through trials and all sorts of tribulations. Its roots have grown deep into good soil and can therefore withstand the strongest tempests. The world around us needs to see the character of Christ in us; this takes a lot of uncompromising discipline. God is not glorified by showing off our own works, but by His works in and through us. I am not referring to monastic mysticism but practical, joyful Christian living.

Reflecting on my own life, I can't help but see the wonderful hand of the Lord; the Potter, molding the clay in His hand. I can hardly remember a time that I was not aware of the presence of Jesus in my life; I always loved and adored Him. However, there were times when I could not freely commune with God because of sin that needed to be confessed.

In His infinite love and unending grace, He made me aware of a specific sin and through His Spirit prompted me to repent and be cleansed. I am aware that I grieved the heart of the Lord many times; yet He never gave up on me, but continued to draw me closer to Him. This overwhelming love and compassion of our Shepherd intensified my inner quest for more of Him.

During the darkest time in my life, I learned that there was nothing more magnificent; nothing more desirable for me than to worship and praise God the Father and the Lord Jesus Christ, who so freely offers to satisfy our hunger with the Bread of Life and quench our thirst with the Living Water.

"Was I losing my sanity and slowly turning into a mystic recluse who sought to escape the filth of this world?"- You may wonder. Not so; I was genuinely enjoying God's powerful anointing. Others may think of us, who have a passion for Jesus Christ, as "strangely religious" or "irrational fanatics." I simply wanted Jesus to take all of me, and give me all of Him.

With this new enthusiasm for the Lord came an increased commitment to my family, church, job, and to hurting people. Everything took on a new dimension, and the love of Jesus flooded my innermost being. I became aware that Jesus Christ, in His infinite love and mercy, surrounded me all my life, ever since I was conceived in my mother's womb. It was His purpose since I was chosen by God long before my birth, to live a life in the fullness of Christ. This is a promise to all who live for Jesus Christ.

With this change in my life came the realization that very few of my Christian friends shared this excitement for the Lord. I had to be cautious, in not judging them for their relationship with Christ; too often I was not. I had much to learn about my critical spirit. Judgments had to be brought to the cross, one by one, with no exceptions. My compassion for them and for those who did not know the Savior increased, and sharing the Gospel of Jesus Christ became a top priority. Without Him, men will be eternally separated from God; we need to keep this in mind when we mingle with those who don't know Him and be loving encouragers.

In giving the apostle Peter instructions about forgiveness, Jesus likens the kingdom of heaven to a certain king who wanted to settle accounts with his servants (Matthew 18:21-35). At the end of this illustration (vs. 35) Jesus pronounces these powerful words: "So My heavenly Father also will do to you if each of you, from his heart, does not forgive his brother his trespasses." (Let me suggest again that the torturers mentioned in verse 34 are forces of darkness.) In another chapter I will share interesting demonic activities I was confronted with early in my life in Argentina, as well as in our ministry to the brokenhearted.

Let me continue to encourage you in your quest for more of God with the words of the apostle Paul: "Therefore I also, after I heard of your faith in the Lord Jesus and your love for all the saints, do not cease to give thanks for you, making mention of you in my prayers: That the God of our Lord Jesus Christ, the Father of glory, may give to you the spirit of wisdom and revelation in the knowledge of Him, the eyes of your understanding being enlightened; that you may know what is the hope of His calling, what are the riches of the glory of His inheritance in the saints, and what is the exceeding greatness of His power towards us who believe, according to the working of His mighty power which He worked in Christ when He raised Him from the dead and seated Him at His right hand in the heavenly places, far above all principality and power and might and dominion, and every name that is named, not only in this age but also in that which is to come. And He put all things under His feet and gave Him to be head over all things to the church, which is His body, the fullness of Him who fills all in all" (Ephesians 1:15-23).

Throughout the Old Testament, we find that the place where God manifested His glory had to be very specifically prepared and thoroughly cleansed. God Himself instructed His chosen leaders among the people of Israel to follow strict directions in the erection of the Tabernacle and later the Temple.

Nothing that was defiled in any way was to enter the Holy Place. In the New Testament we learn that born-again Christians are the temple of the Holy Spirit. (See 1 Corinthians 6:19) Therefore, our hearts must be cleansed for God to manifest His glory in and through us. This brings us to our next step in our spiritual growth:

3. Cleansing of our "Temple" for the Manifestation of God's Glory:

The Holy Spirit, through the Word of God, carries out the cleansing of Christ's Church. No member of His Body is excluded. In Ephesians 5:25-27, Paul says: "Husbands, love your wives, just as Christ also loved the church and gave Himself for her, that He might sanctify and cleanse her with the washing of water by the Word, that He might present her to Himself a glorious church, not having spot or wrinkle, or any such thing, but that she should be holy and without blemish."

Naturally, the cleansing process is not pleasant. In fact, at times it may be very painful. If Christ is to reign as King of our lives, we must open every chamber of our inner being and let His light reveal that which must be relinquished. He knows what is hidden in those secret places. Jesus was there when we did it. He heard us when we said it; in fact, He even knows our thoughts.

"The Lord knows the thoughts of the wise, that they are futile" (1 Corinthians 3:20).

"But Jesus, knowing their thoughts, said; why do you think evil in your hearts?" (Matthew 9:4).

Jesus will not be shocked when you confess your sins; in fact, ever since you committed that sin, He was ready to forgive you and take you into His arms to let you know how much He loves you. Don't let Satan talk you into putting it off; procrastination is a mighty tool in his hand to frustrate you and impede your spiritual growth. We may fool others into thinking that we are wonderful Christians by wearing a mask, but we cannot hide from God, He sees us exactly as we are: "Do not be deceived, God is not mocked; for whatever a man sows, that he will also reap" (Galatians 6:7). The Word of God will reveal every secret in our heart, because; "Is not My Word like a fire?" says the Lord, "And like a hammer that breaks the rock in pieces?" (Jeremiah 23:29).

"For the Word of God is living and powerful, and sharper than any two-edged sword, piercing even to the division of soul and spirit, and of joints and marrow, and is a discerner of the thoughts and intents of the heart. And there is no creature hidden from His sight, but all things are naked and open to the eyes of Him (Jesus) to whom we must give account" (Hebrews 4:12, 13).

Breaking the commandments of God triggers a cycle of sowing and reaping with painful consequences and, unless the sin is confessed and brought to the Cross in repentance, it will stay alive and haunt us. Generally, it seems easier for us to confess our sins to God than confessing them to one another; which requires a lot more courage. If we want things to go well with us, we must confess to others our trespasses, as well as forgiving those who sin against us.

"Confess your trespasses (sins) to one another, and pray for one another, that you may be healed" (James 5:16a). Jesus taught us to pray; "And forgive us our debts, as we forgive our debtors" (Matthew 6:12). Unforgiveness says: "You owe me something."

It is therapeutic to admit our shortcomings to one another and share our blessings. Granted, it may not be the norm in most churches to become transparent and open our hearts to one another. However, we need to begin doing it, even at the risk of dropping the masks we wear; it will set us on the road to true freedom. When we risk becoming vulnerable, particularly in a small group, we may quickly see others follow our example, and we will begin to open our hearts to the love of our Father. This was Jesus' prayer to His Father for the Church as recorded in the Gospel of John, chapter seventeen.

Jeanie and I experienced in several Bible study groups, after we dared to share personal shortcomings in our walk with the Lord that others began to risk sharing their own, personal prayer requests. It wasn't long before our fellowship became increasingly animated and relational.

Jeanie was ahead of me in this matter of admitting our shortcomings. Perhaps the reason for this might be that, embedded in my German heritage, there is the expression; "It is hard to be humble when you are the best." This thought pattern had to be dismantled and taken to the cross of Jesus. I was comforted when I learned that the apostle Paul struggled with the matter of pride. Then I was reminded through God's Word—it was because of pride that Satan lost his position in heaven. Wow; haughtiness is certainly a negative character trait that, if not properly addressed will bring ruin.

As important as it is to confess our sins to one another (James 5:16), we must use discretion when sharing very personal matters that should only be disclosed to someone with a loving and caring heart. Jeanie and I experienced many opportunities to help Christians in their inner anguish while sitting beside their deathbed. The ensuing freedom and deep joy is well worth any amount of time and effort.

Freedom is granted us through Jesus Christ, who is the Truth; "And you shall know the Truth, and the Truth shall set you free....Therefore if the Son makes you free, you shall be free indeed" (John 8:32,36). The old sinful nature in us does not want to die; our mind keeps telling it to stay alive so we can do what we please, failing to realize that it is by doing what is pleasing to the Lord that we will truly be content and enjoy His promises. But, as I have repeatedly mentioned in this book, the center of the battlefield is the mind. Through our reborn spirits comes the Truth from the Lord, our un-renewed mind picks it up and the battle rages. The mind says; "I don't think so," the will says; "I don't want to," and the feelings and emotions agree; "we don't feel like." All this goes on in our soul, which is still controlled by that insidious sinful mind.

It doesn't profit us anything if the mind understands the Truth, while our will is still stubbornly in opposition. The nature and the character of Jesus Christ must displace our sinful nature and be firmly implanted in us, so we can be effective disciples. "For we are to God the fragrance of Christ among those who are being saved and among those who are perishing" (2 Corinthians 2:15).

Recently, early one morning, while in prayer and preparation for my writing, I perceived the voice of my Shepherd relative to a three phase process of sanctification, that His followers are taken through:

a. Pharisaic

b. Brokenness

c. The Outflow of the Father's Love

The Pharisaic Phase (a) is usually the period after our conversion when we think we know it all, making sure that everybody around us is aware of it. In my case, it took years, if not decades, before I was led into phase b. I do not suggest that the Pharisees were all evil men. They were the learned among the people of Israel. The apostle Paul is a formidable example of a sanctimonious Pharisee, before his dramatic conversion at the gate of the city of Damascus. From his own pen we read about his testimony as he spoke to an angry crowd who saw him as a renegade from Judaism;

"Brethren and fathers, hear my defense before you now."And when they heard that he spoke to them in the Hebrew language, they kept all the more silent. Then he said: "I am indeed a Jew born in Tarsus of Cilicia, but brought up in this city at the feet of Gamaliel, (a Pharisee and celebrated doctor of the Law), taught according to the strictness of our fathers' law, and was zealous toward God as you all are today" (Acts 22:1-3).

His brokenness, phase (b) began after Jesus Christ spoke to him from heaven with a thunderous voice, bringing his violent persecution of Christian believers to a sudden stop. His strong resolution and zeal to pursue what he now believed was true, was now transformed into complete surrender and obedience to his new Master and Lord Jesus Christ. From phase (A) this prominent Pharisee was moved into phase (B) by the providential hand of the Almighty, when he was transformed into a mighty apostle to the Gentiles. As a loving, spiritual father, Paul spent the rest of his earthly life firmly grounded in;

The Outflow of the Father's love, phase (c),.and so can we as we continue to submit to the renewing power of the Holy Spirit.

Reading the Book of Acts became instrumental in my leap into a deep commitment to the Father, the Son, Jesus Christ and the Holy Spirit.

Mediocre Christianity draws unbelievers into religious cults; it opens the church to the sinful practices of the world, it ceases to be light and salt, and most of what remains is as "sounding brass or a clanging cymbal" (1 Corinthians 13:1).

That old sinful nature that is still on the throne in complacent Christians, keeps them in the company of levelheaded and popularly accepted brands of Christianity.

This is not the direction you want to follow; you would not be reading this book if you didn't have a desire to grow in the Lord. But, you may feel that you're sitting on a seesaw. On one hand you perceive that you want to do God's will, but on the other you sense a pull to do your own thing. Your confusion is shared by millions of Christians. The sad reality is, too many follow their own desires and instincts, while missing the wonderful promises of God. Bring that sin that is drawing you into defeat to the Cross; then you will enjoy victory. The enemy loses his hold and will depart.

We need to hear the Word of God over and over again, in order to have the truth firmly implanted in our minds and hearts. The crucifying process is accomplished in us by the Lord Jesus who gave Himself to be crucified for you and me. We died with Him on that Cross; spiritually our old nature died with Him, and thus our heavenly Father sees us perfect through His Son.

"This I say, therefore, and testify in the Lord, that you should no longer walk as the rest of the Gentiles walk, in the futility of their mind, having their understanding darkened, being alienated from the life of God, because of the ignorance that is in them, because of the blindness of their heart" (Ephesians 4:17,18). Then the apostle encourages us to put off the old man who grows corrupt according to the deceitful lusts and be renewed in the spirit of our mind and to put on the new man who was created according to God in righteousness and true holiness.

In his letter to the Colossians chapter three, verses 1-4 and 14-17, Paul writes: "If then you were raised with Christ, seek those things which are above, where Christ is, sitting at the right hand of God. Set your mind on things above, not on things on the earth. For you died and your life is hidden with Christ in God. When Christ who is our life appears, then you will also appear with Him in glory. But above all these things, put on love, which is the bond of perfection. And let the peace of God rule in your hearts, to which also you were called in one body; and be thankful. Let the Word of Christ dwell in you richly, in all wisdom, teaching and admonishing one another in psalms and hymns and spiritual songs, singing with grace in your hearts to the Lord. And whatever you do in word or deed, do all in the name of the Lord Jesus, giving thanks to God the Father through Him."

The richness of God's Word overwhelms me; it challenges me to move to even higher grounds. You are not alone in this often very frustrating struggle; countless fellow Christians are engaged in the same battle. We are all going through the same process, except that we have attained different levels of growth. Let me encourage you to press in; do not despair; be persistent, Jesus is with you helping you through every step of the way.

Neither self cleansing nor self sanctification; neither mortification nor mutilation will accomplish anything of eternal value, because it has selfish roots. Let me illustrate with a process in nature: In Autumn, the leaves of an oak tree, as most trees, begin to turn brown. Some of its leaves will drop off; however, a good number of them will remain on the tree and refuse to fall off, even through fierce storms. Then, upon arrival of spring, they gradually begin to drop off as new leaves break out. Old, sinful habits and compulsions will be brought to the surface by the Holy Spirit and we can, in prayer, take them to the Cross for its cancellation.

One day, after discussing this subject with Jeanie, she called me into the kitchen to show me something in the chicken soup she was cooking. She lifted up the lid and, on top of the soup, was this brown scum; "this stuff floating on top reminds me of our sins coming out from our hearts, when the Holy Spirit convicts us" Jeanie said with a smile. Then she turned up the heat and quite a bit more floated to the surface of the soup. With a smile Jeanie said; "Notice what happens when the Lord turns up the heat?" He truly knows our heart. After scooping off the scum, the soup was clear. This illustration should in no way diminish the seriousness of sin; it is never to be taken lightly. This is simply a visual picture depicting the necessity to "cleanse our temples."

It is not until we yield to the Holy Spirit, that real cleansing can take hold. He will lead us into the Scriptures and convict us of sin. After we repent and confess them, we will obtain freedom from those insidious, sinful compulsions. You see, sanctification is not only the will of God; it is also the work of God.

As the Living Water runs through the vessel, (you and me) all kinds of impurities break loose from our hearts, and are brought to our attention. As quickly as we confess them, they will be removed through the Blood of Jesus and the heart is cleansed. The Bible also calls this process the purging away of dross (Isaiah 1:25).

"But who can endure the day of His coming? And who can stand when He appears? For He is like a refiner's fire and like launderers' soap. He will sit as a refiner and a purifier of silver; He will purify the sons of Levi, and purge them as gold and silver, that they may offer to the Lord an offering in righteousness" (Malachi 3:2,3).

Just before Jesus' ministry, His forerunner, John the Baptizer said of Him: "I indeed baptize you with water unto repentance, but He who is coming after me is mightier than I, whose sandals I am not worthy to carry. He will baptize you with the Holy Spirit and fire. His winnowing fan is in His hand, and He will thoroughly clean out His threshing floor, and gather His wheat into the barn; but He will burn up the chaff with unquenchable fire" (Matthew 3:11).

Believe me, or better yet, believe the Scriptures, that when these things happen in your relationship with Jesus, you will not only begin to understand the reality of God's promises; you will take hold of them and enjoy them. Jeanie and I are blessed with testimonies from Christians who, after breaking through walls of frustration, are now truly enjoying their fellowship with the Lord. You too, will enter into a new dimension of faith, which is the victory that conquers the world.

Chapter Six

Our Faith, the Victory that has Overcome the World

"For whatever is born of God overcomes the world. And this is the victory that has overcome the world — our faith" (1 John 5:4). Spiritual maturity is the fruit of intimacy with God; Father, Son, and Holy Spirit, rather than the product of time since our conversion. Many Christians are still in their spiritual infancy, literally struggling to survive. Others, on the other hand, receive Christ and are radically transformed. They are willing to give up all of self and seek all of Jesus.

According to the above mentioned words by the apostle John, it is obvious that there is no stagnation in a Christian's life! Our intimate union with our Lord provides the necessary faith-power for our ever-ascending move toward our heavenly goal. Aware of the reality that this is a narrow and often rugged path and not a wide open freeway, we can rest assured that our heavenly Father, who predestined and even loved us before we were born, will also provide the wherewithal to reach our God-given destiny.

The never-ending hunger for more of God will increase our faith to become overcomers. Are you determined to live your life as an overcomer? As a young Christian I looked up to brothers and sisters in the Lord who rarely complained or murmured; they seemed to have their mind set on the positive side of life. Circumstances did not hold them down, because they lived above them. They exuded peace and joy and when engaged in conversations I usually walked away uplifted. Upon closer observation of their lifestyle, I determined that, with God's help, I will be an overcomer.

Overcomers do not only read the Word, they believe it, speak it, and act upon it. The full armor of God is their strong weapon against the forces of evil; they put it on every day. Infilled with the Holy Spirit, covered with the Blood of Jesus, and surrounded with His mighty angels, they march through each day trusting their heavenly Father. When difficulties come their way, they keep their eyes on Jesus with full confidence that He will lead them through.

They also carefully watch their tongues, they yield that evil little thing to the control of the Holy Spirit, because they know that; "Even so the tongue is a little member and boasts great things. See how great a forest a little fire kindles! And the tongue is a fire, a world of iniquity. The tongue is so set among our members that it defiles the whole body, and sets on fire the course of nature; and is set on fire by hell. But no man can tame the tongue. It is an unruly evil, full of deadly poison (James 3:5,6,8). "Death and life are in the power of the tongue, and those who love it will eat its fruit" (Proverbs 18:21). "For by your words you will be justified; and by your words you will be condemned" (Matthew 12:37).

Job's words illustrate the above verse: "As long as my breath is in me, and the breath of God in my nostrils, my lips will not speak wickedness, nor my tongue utter deceit" (Job 27:3,4). Mature Christians are living in the fullness of Christ; they are no longer children tossed to and fro and carried about with every wind of doctrine, by the trickery of men, in the cunning craftiness by which they lie in wait to deceive; from Ephesians chapter four. Their lives are marked by many of the following character traits; they:

Recognize their shortcomings, trusting Christ in every situation, because they know that: "Without Me you can do nothing" (John 15:5b).

Are diligent in Bible study and prayer; "I delight to do your will, O my God, and Your law is within my heart" (Psalm 40:8).

Truly enjoy their communion with God; "When I remember You on my bed, I meditate on You in the night watches. Because You have been my help, therefore in the shadow of Your wings I will rejoice" (Psalm 63:6,7).

Possess a supernatural inner peace; "The peace of God, which surpasses all understanding, will guard your hearts and minds through Christ Jesus" (Philippians 4:7).

Are content in any situation; "I have learned to be content, in whatever state I am in; because I can do all things through Christ who strengthens me" (Philippians 4:11,13).

Nourish themselves on solid food, because they are no longer babies; "Solid food belongs to those who are of full age, that is, those who by reason of use have their senses exercised to discern both good and evil. For everyone who partakes only of milk is unskilled in the Word of righteousness, for he is a babe" (Hebrews 5:13,14).

Live fruitful lives, because; "The fruit of the Spirit is love, joy, peace, long-suffering, kindness, goodness, faithfulness, gentleness, self-control. Against as such there is no law. If we live in the Spirit, let us also walk in the Spirit" (Galatians 5:22,23,25).

Hear the voice of their Shepherd, and follow Him; "My sheep hear My voice, and I know them, and they follow Me" (John 10:27).

Receive answers to their prayers; "If you abide in me, and My words abide in you, you will ask what you desire, and it shall be done for you" (John 15:7).

Reflect the love of God in all their relationships; "Beloved, if God so loved us we also ought to love one another" (1 John 4:11).

Speak the truth with love; "Speaking the truth in love, may grow up in all things into Him who is the head—Christ—" (Ephesians 4:15).

Bridles his tongue; "If anyone among you thinks he is religious, and does not bridle his tongue but deceives his own heart, this one's religion is useless" (James 1:26).

Join a local body of believers; "Not forsaking the assembling of ourselves together, as is the manner of some, but exhorting one another, and so much the more as you see the Day approaching" (Hebrews 10:25).

Edify other members in the fellowship; "for the equipping of the saints for the work of ministry, for the edifying of the body of Christ" (Ephesians 4:12).

Give cheerfully and sacrificially of the means God provides; "he who sows sparingly will also reap sparingly, and he who sows bountifully will also reap bountifully. So let each one give as he purposes in his heart, not grudgingly or of necessity; for God loves a cheerful giver" (2 Corinthians 9:6,7).

Seek prosperity for their city, "…and seek the peace of the city…" (Jeremiah 29:7a).

Pray for their government; "Therefore I exhort first of all that supplications, prayers, intercession, and giving of thanks be made for all men, for kings and all who are in authority, that we may lead a quiet and peaceable life in all godliness and reverence" (1 Timothy 2:1).

Show compassion for the less fortunate; "Blessed is he who considers the poor; the Lord will deliver him in time of trouble" (Psalm 41:1).

Are always prepared for every good work; "He will be a vessel for honor, sanctified and useful for the Master, prepared for every good work" (2 Timothy 2:21).

Are sober and well equipped to fend off the enemy; "Be sober and vigilant; because your adversary the devil walks about like a roaring lion, seeking whom he may devour" (1 Peter 5:8).

Maintain their vessel clean, by regularly confessing their sins; "Therefore, having these promises, beloved, let us cleanse ourselves from all filthiness of the flesh and spirit, perfecting holiness in the fear of God" (2 Corinthians 7:1).

Believe in the manifestation of all the Gifts of the Spirit for the edification of the Body; "Now concerning spiritual gifts, brethren, I do not want you to be ignorant. The manifestation of the Spirit is given to each one for the profit of all" (Taken from 1 Corinthians chapter twelve, verses 1 and 7). Jesus has won the victory over the flesh, over the world, and over Satan for you and me. He died for every human affliction in soul, spirit, and body.

The victory celebration, while battles are still raging, is a privilege that is enjoyed only by the members of the heavenly King's army.

If you are presently in a difficult predicament, keep trusting your faithful Lord. Soon you will be out of that valley, and you will begin to understand that you spent time in the Master's workshop; the darkness that you experienced was the shadow of His mighty arm. The promises of God that seemed to elude you while in the valley will begin to become reality.

The first thing I do when I open my eyes in the morning is to thank the Lord for another day and then I praise and worship Him. I need God's direction for every day; and so the first couple of hours are spent mostly in conversational prayer and Scripture reading. I don't have to worry about a thing; because I know God is in charge. This may sound too simplistic or sanctimonious. So be it. I have tried other ways to start my day; but this method beats them all.

There was a time when I thought that this victorious life was the privilege of only a few select Christians; not anymore. This is for you and me. I am well aware of what the Lord did while in my valleys of brokenness. My will was broken, my spiritual ears unplugged, my pharisaic mind crucified, my spiritual eyesight cleared up, and my spirit sensitized to the ugliness of sin. For some of us it took a "whip and a bull horn" to bring us to our senses. As I came out of the darkest valley of my life, I looked into a brand new sunrise; the green pasture looked so beautiful with sheep peaceably feeding on it. I began to sense real joy again. "Weeping may endure for a night, but joy comes in the morning" (Psalm 30:5b).

Martha, my first wife, had gone home to be with the Lord, after a six year battle against an ugly disease in February 1983, at age fifty. I learned how beautifully the Shepherd cares for His sheep; how much He loves them, and how well He knows every detail of their lives. Absolutely nothing escapes His attention. There is no suffering that you and I will ever endure that Jesus had not suffered in His own spirit, soul, and body for us.

The ever abiding presence of Jesus will become your blessed experience. You will begin to "see" the Shepherd caring for His flock; your ears and your heart will be sensitized to His voice. You will no longer get upset when you hear other Christians tell you; "the Lord spoke to me" or "the Lord told me." He had spoken to you too; you just didn't know how to familiarize yourself with His voice. Ask Jesus to teach you and pay close attention.

When the Lord speaks to me, I have no doubt who it is. I used to think that it was my mind playing tricks on me; not anymore. If I ignore His prompting, my heart will begin to throb. At times, when trying to do something which in the past seemed all right because I saw other Christians do it, I "felt" some kind of a physical sensation, and I knew it was high time to obey.

If this has become your experience, look up and praise God. Pay close attention to the Holy Spirit's prompting. If you abide in the Word of God, and ask the Holy Spirit to discern it for you, you will have the assurance that the prompting comes from Him.

Do not fear what men can do to you or think of you. Seek advice from men and women who walk in obedience, wholly committed to Christ and who walk in love and truth; and then check it with the Word of God.

At times you may receive counsel from wise Christians that will hurt you. Don't walk away from them too quickly, they may have been directed by the Holy Spirit to confront sin in you. Continue to seek their help until that sin is properly addressed. Sometimes, confrontation is needed to redirect us from negative choices we make. True, "agape" love hurts at times; and that is alright. I learned many years ago that love without the truth is not God's love, but human love, which is sentimentalism. This kind of love, emerging from man's sinful nature, will not lead you into God's truth, neither will it bring true repentance.

On the other hand, telling someone the truth without the love of God is brutal; it often causes great damage, and the person may "run away" from God with a bitter taste in his mouth. Too much of that kind of correction is experienced in some churches. Truth and love must go hand in hand. Paul says: "Speaking the truth in love" (Ephesians 4:15). Keep trusting the Lord; He promised to give you rest. "Come to Me, all you who labor and are heavy laden, and I will give you rest" (Matthew 11:28).

One day, while still in my mid-teens, my uncle Erich, the leading elder in my home church in Buenos Aires, told me to refrain from taking Holy Communion until I confessed a sin that I was convinced would not become public knowledge; but it did. I knew in my heart that my uncle truly loved me; but some voice inside me said; "Never mind; just forget it and move on." Well, that strategy didn't work. In my youthful daring mind I thought I could get away with it; not so. I found no peace until the matter was properly addressed. I learned a powerful lesson, the result of which is still active in my life today; namely, confessing my sins before participating in Holy Communion.

All the fretting about those endless, messy situations that I attempted to resolve in my own strength, only led me into the next one; valuable time and effort was wasted, and my heart did not find the rest that I needed. Praise God for not ceasing to pursue me at a time when I thought I knew better than anyone else what was best for me.

As you move deeper in your relationship with Jesus Christ, you will begin to experience His working in and through you affecting people around you. The "passion for Jesus" that you may have heard Christians refer to, will no longer be "fanaticism" to you; it will become your way of life. You will be excited for the Lord and the things of His Kingdom, without those constant ups and downs. All enticing things you thought you could never relinquish will begin to fall away with no regrets. God has blessed you with so many new things far beyond anything the world can offer you. Your utmost desire will be to please the Lord and do what He lays upon your heart.

However, at times, the old nature will "raise its ugly head;" don't be discouraged, it will only be short-lived, because you hate it. You have your loving heavenly Father who enables you to take "that thing" to the Cross where it belongs. The Bible tells us very simply, that if we ask anything in Jesus' name, God will hear us and undoubtedly respond in ways that are best for each of His children.

Your whole decision making process will be transformed. Your vision was blurred to spiritual realities and you made decisions based upon your emotions or feelings, often with disastrous consequences. The Lord had to help you out of your predicament; and He did. But now you are aware that: "We who worship God in the Spirit, rejoice in Christ Jesus, and have no confidence in the flesh," writes the apostle Paul in his letter to the Philippians 3:3. As he continues in his message he writes; "But what things were gain to me, these I have counted loss for Christ. But indeed I also count all things loss for the excellence of the knowledge of Christ Jesus my Lord, for whom I have suffered the loss of all things, and count them as rubbish that I may gain Christ... that I may know Him and the power of His resurrection and the fellowship of His suffering, being conformed to His death" (Philippians 3:7,8,10).

This portion of Scripture became an intense and effective tool used by the Holy Spirit to set me free from a lot of rubbish that I was carrying around in "my service for the Lord." In retrospect, I find it hard to believe, that I had so many preconceived notions and personal opinions of how other Christians are supposed to live their lives. I realize now that God wanted me to let go of many things that were hindering the Holy Spirit from filling me to overflowing.

At times, you'll be surprised how quickly man's law seeks to overrule God's grace in our relationship with people. The law demands but grace gives freely. Our tongues can be perpetrators of great harm.

We must be cautious in the use of our words. Satan uses every possible means to entrap us. Words are powerful; they can be like projectiles. We desperately need God's wisdom in our everyday interactions with people; "Be wise as serpents and harmless as doves;" the Lord cautions us. (Matthew 10:16) I absolutely love the wisdom that Jesus was anointed with. People around Him were awed, yes they were mesmerized. They had never heard anyone speak like Him.

Legalism is an insidious weapon at Satan's disposal; he uses it to destroy relationships. Our old, sinful nature, often seeks to cram our opinions down someone else's throat. We should live together as Christians; at times just "agreeing to disagree," letting the Lord iron out the differences. From the apostle Paul we read the following; "Let your speech always be with grace, seasoned with salt, that you may know how you ought to answer each one" (Colossians 4:6).

Jesus said; "It is the Spirit who gives life; the flesh profits nothing. The words that I speak to you are spirit, and they are life" (John 6:63). As followers of Christ we need to take an ongoing inventory of the words that issue from our mouths. Are they blessings or curses; positive or negative words? Do they build up or tear down those we communicate with?

Who has not been tempted to join the "crusade against the infidel," believing that we were called to judge our brother or sister in the Lord for something we believed they were in error, only to find out later that we had misjudged the whole situation. This may lead to enmity against our brother, unless properly addressed through repentance, followed by full restoration.

Some of our Lord's disciples were no different when it came to judging people too hastily, as illustrated in the following event; "Lord, do You want us to command fire to come down from heaven and consume them, just as Elijah did. But He turned and rebuked them, and said, "You do not know what manner of Spirit you are of. For the Son of Man did not come to destroy men's lives, but to save them" (Luke 9:54-56).

Our faith, which is the victory that conquers the world around us, is granted us by Jesus. The Bible declares in Hebrews 12:2, that He is the author and finisher of our faith. This powerful faith in us provides the way and the means for us to act. "Now faith is the substance of things hoped for, the evidence of things not seen" (Hebrews 11:1). The gradual increase of our faith dispels doubt, unbelief, and skepticism.

If you continue to press into what God has for your life, you will be a lighthouse in your community, a mighty witness for Jesus Christ. He will fill you with so much love and joy, and equip you with power that you will be able to disregard the criticism of believers and unbelievers alike, and move on with the Lord. Your family, the Church, and the world need you; there is unbelievable pain, frustration, desperation, fear, and confusion; far too many people, including a lot of Christians are in captivity, craving for freedom.

Only Jesus can demolish prison walls and set the captives free; He is the One sent by God (Luke 4:18), and when He returned to His Father, He assigned the job to the Church. We, as believers in Christ, have been given the Word of God, the power of the Blood of the Lamb and the Holy Spirit, the mightiest credentials known to the world, in order to resist the powers of darkness and command them to flee. Jeanie and I are very grateful that God has entrusted us with a prayer ministry to brokenhearted people. Being able to lead someone to a personal relationship with Jesus Christ, and then seeing them freed from bondage, is a most rewarding and joyful experience in this life; in fact, even heaven rejoices with us. Jesus said so: "Likewise, I say to you, there is joy in the presence of the angels of God over one sinner who repents" (Luke 15:10).

In the parable of the Prodigal Son, quoted from Luke, chapter 15; Jesus reminds us how patiently our heavenly Father waits for us to return home to Him when we find ourselves lost in the wilderness of this world. In our shame we are hesitant even to look up; and then, to our great surprise our eyes are opened and we see our Father waiting to receive us with open arms. This undeserving love is overwhelming, and falling on our face we cry out; "Father, I have sinned against heaven and in your sight and am no longer worthy to be called your son. Make me one of your hired servants. And he arose and came to his father. But when he was still a great way off, his father saw him and had compassion, and ran and fell on his neck and kissed him."

Our heavenly Father waits patiently for His lost sheep to come to Him; He is ready, to restore us to an exciting, living relationship with Him, through Jesus Christ, His Son. He has chosen us to go and bear fruit: "You did not choose Me but I chose you and appointed you that you should go and bear fruit, and that your fruit should remain, that whatever you ask the Father in My name He may give you" (John 15:16). Is there a price to be paid? Yes indeed—but it is worth it.

> "If the world hates you, you know that it hated Me before it hated you. If you were of the world, the world would love its own. Yet because you are not of the world, but I chose you out of the world, therefore the world hates you. Remember the word that I said to you, 'A servant is not greater than his master.' If they persecuted Me, they will also persecute you. If they kept My word, they will keep yours also. But all these things they will do to you for My name's sake, because they do not know Him who sent Me" (John 15:18-20).

Chapter Seven

The "Roaring Lion" on the Attack

In this chapter I'll share some of the wicked tactics the devil and his evil minions use to attack believers in Jesus Christ, and mention some of the powerful weapons that are at their disposal to resist him. When you disregard the reality of Satan and his evil spirits, you will be deceived and become a victim of his destructive schemes. We may think that we can simply ignore him and things will be fine; the devil will certainly agree with this thought. Before continuing with this very important subject, I believe that certain points I focused on in this book, warrant repetition. Our battle as Christians in this world is not against flesh and blood; meaning human beings; but against powers of darkness, which are the devil and his wicked demons, as Paul states in Ephesians 6:10-18.

Old testament believers were not aware that all their various enemies' strategies were schemed by the master deceiver, the devil. I'd like to direct your attention to the Old Testament prophetic book of Zechariah. The prophet was heavily burdened by Israel's rejection of the Messiah. They rejected the call of God to repentance and kept fighting the visible enemies, totally unaware that the invisible enemies used their disobedience to divert their attention from God and His promises for future blessings. Jesus wants our heart commitment to Him and this includes that we walk circumspectly—not as fools but as wise; stated by the apostle Paul in Ephesians 5:15-17.

The following Scripture verses will strengthen our resolve to be fine tuned to our Shepherd's voice to avoid unnecessary pitfalls along the way.

"For your obedience has become known to all. Therefore I am glad in your behalf; but I want you to be wise in what is good, and simple concerning evil. And the God of peace will crush Satan under your feet shortly. The grace of our Lord Jesus Christ be with you all. Amen." (Romans 16:19,20).

"Above all, taking the shield of faith with which you will be able to quench all the fiery darts of the wicked one" (Ephesians 6:16). These eye opening words spoken by Christ's apostle are as valid and powerful for us today as they were in his time.

Though winning some battles, Satan lost the war. He is doomed to the everlasting fire at a time God has determined. He received his death blow at the Cross of Calvary, where Jesus of Nazareth, the Son of God shed His precious Blood to save us from our sins. At the empty tomb, where the power of God brought back to life His beloved Son, Satan's fate was sealed forever.

"Then He will also say to those on the left hand, 'Depart from me, you cursed, into the everlasting fire prepared for the devil and his angels'" (Matthew 25:41).

This is also the destiny of the Antichrist and his helper, the false prophet, after they have finished their great deception of mankind, and Israel and the Church in particular.

"Then the beast was captured, and with him the false prophet who worked signs in his presence, by which he deceived those who received the mark of the beast and those who worshipped his image. These two were cast alive into the lake of fire burning with brimstone" (Revelation 19:20). As I mentioned elsewhere, I do not concentrate on the chronological order of the end time events as given to us in the prophets, by Jesus Christ in the Gospels and by our Lord through His beloved apostle John in the book of Revelation. However, I believe that all still unfulfilled prophesies recorded in the Bible, will come to pass.

"Then I saw an angel coming down from heaven, having the key to the bottomless pit and a great chain in his hand. He laid hold of the dragon, that serpent of old, who is the Devil and Satan, and bound him for a thousand years; and he cast him into the bottomless pit, and shut him up, and set a seal on him, so that he should deceive the nations no more till the thousand years were finished. But after these things he must be released for a little while" (Revelation 20:1-3).

Praise God that we who believe in Jesus Christ His beloved Son, will be with Him at the heavenly celebration of the eternal union of Christ, the Groom with His bride, the Church.

The Bible calls this feast the Marriage Supper of the Lamb; "Then he said to me, 'write: Blessed are those who are called to the marriage supper of the Lamb!' And he said to me, 'These are the true sayings of God'" (Revelation 19:9).

As Christian believers, we have the privilege to claim the protection of Jesus' Blood over our lives, so we can resist the evil one and reclaim what he has stolen from us. Earlier, I shared the sad reality that Satan has succeeded in removing the mention of the blood of the Lamb from many hymn books, sermons and prayers, thereby contributing to the complacency found in too many churches. At the same time, the enemy has convinced many Christians, that he is either a figment of someone's imagination or he should just be ignored.

Perhaps the fact that I was born and raised in Argentina, where, like in many other countries, the devil found more freedom of action, has equipped me to be less ignorant of his wicked devices. In 2 Corinthians 2:11 the apostle Paul, after mentioning our need to forgive says; "lest Satan should take advantage of us; for we are not ignorant of his devices."

Jesus said; "The thief does not come except to steal, and to kill, and to destroy. I have come that they may have life, and that they may have it more abundantly" (John 10:10).

"And they overcame him, by the Blood of the Lamb and by the word of their testimony, and they did not love their lives to the death" (Revelation 12:11). It is imperative that we keep our minds and hearts upon Jesus and His Word, and not on the enemy; we resist him and command that he depart from us, in Jesus' name. The devil is afraid of Jesus and his powerful blood and he will take off when His followers call upon Jesus' mighty name. Satan cannot prevail against true believers in Jesus Christ because: "The gates of Hades shall not prevail against it" (Matthew 16:18). The word "it" refers to the Church, the universal Body of Christ, those redeemed with His Blood, and not to an institution. We must understand that though Satan's power is controlled and his freedom limited by God, he should not be ignored or underestimated. The pressure that he exercises upon believers and the damage he often inflicts upon them, is cause for concern.

Unwary believers often fail to recognize the devil's cunning schemes and, as a result, fall into his traps. Keeping

Christians in a lifelong state of spiritual infancy seems to be one of his favorite and most successful tactics. Having lost them to Jesus, he is now determined to keep them on "baby food," crying for milk. "For everyone who partakes only of milk is unskilled in the word of righteousness, for he is a babe" (Hebrews 5:13).

The devil attempts to keep Christians in a cradle, rather than see them out in the battlefield winning people for Christ. A house full of babies or sleeping giants are favorite targets for prowlers. Powerless churches give the devil a chance to steal, to kill, and to destroy, as mentioned above.

As a young Christian, I criticized churches that invited the Holy Spirit to manifest God's power. I admit that at times I was hesitant to separate hearsay from facts. Obviously there was also fear of being scorned by friends. With preconceived notions of how a "decent and orderly" service should be conducted, I often brushed aside what was indeed from the Spirit of God.

"God is a God of order and not of confusion;" I used to hear Christians say and I just repeated after them, without realizing that it was a misquotation of Scripture, which says; "God is not the author of confusion but of peace, as in all the churches of the saints" (1 Corinthians 14:33).

The next verse I quoted in order to exclude any form of Christian service conducted contrary to the traditionally established and orderly form, is found in 1 Corinthians 14:40; "Let all things be done decently and in order." I combined both verses into one, and this made me feel "smug" in what I considered an orderly traditional Christian church service.

Again and again, I carefully and devotionally read the entire chapter fourteen, in addition to chapters twelve and thirteen, with an open heart and mind, while asking God to grant me discernment. What was the result? I was reminded to continue reading God's Word, believing its truth and acting upon it. "Teachings of men" had again prevented the free flow of God's transforming power. The ensuing freedom and joy brought me into new heights and taught me to be more careful and loving, lest I judge something that is from the Holy Spirit. Of course, as shared in this book, I have received wonderful healing from our Lord and caring Christians, helping me to renounce what prevented the free flow of our Father's love!

I understand that a member of a denominational tradition, who believes in the cessation of the power gifts of the Holy Spirit, will be confused by what he observes in more contemporary worship services. It is so far out from what he is used to, that he begins to look for the door. Thank God that the Holy Spirit is not limited by our rational thinking in His plan to touch those who are seeking the deeper things of the Kingdom of God.

If you are in any way like me, you may come to a point of deciding to stay put and ride out the storm while attending a spiritual renewal service. If your whispering prayer for help in this very unfamiliar service is sincere, your spiritual eyes will be opened to something that will touch your heart. You will slowly stop judging what you observe and receive revelation that you had missed before. We need to remember that the sanctification process of the Holy Spirit varies from one Christian to another and cannot be judged by simple observation. The conduct of the Corinthian church in their expression of the power gifts of the Holy Spirit, demanded clarification on the part of the apostle Paul. It helps us understand that it was not the use but the misuse of the spiritual gifts that triggered confusion.

I cannot draw any conclusions from chapters 12-14 of first Corinthians; neither can I find any reference in the New Testament that would lead me to believe that these effective spiritual gifts have ceased. Satan is a liar and a thief, and it is sad that through Christians' apathy and ignorance he has been permitted to impoverish many churches. It is important to withhold judgment on something we do not understand, lest we resist the Holy Spirit. As the redeemed of the Lord, we are assured protection from the evil one. However, through our disobedience and stubbornness, we give Satan an opportunity to harass us (see Ephesians 4:27). He is a legalist and knows that the presence of sin will grant him "landing rights." By the way, he has been around longer than you and I and he knows quite a bit about our generational background. He is still the "ruler of this world," as Jesus calls him (John 14:30).

We have no reason to succumb to the trickery of Satan, who seeks to destroy us. There is no need to retreat or run from him, absolutely no reason to fear him, and no biblical instruction to ignore him. We have a God who made us; "The Spirit of God has made me, and the breath of the Almighty gives me life" (Job 33:4), and He has the whole universe in His hand. God says: "Everything under heaven is Mine" (Job 41:11b).

He sent His precious Son, the Lord Jesus Christ, to rescue us from the grip of Satan, and give us victory over him. "He has delivered us from the power of darkness and conveyed us into the Kingdom of the Son of His love" (Colossians 1:13). He also gave us clear instructions in His holy Word what we must do, and keep doing, to remain free from the enemy's intrusion into our lives.

"We know that whoever is born of God does not sin; but he who has been born of God keeps himself, and the wicked one does not touch him" (1 John 5:18b). The question is: Are we guarded against the enemy? Or are we opening doors for him to harass us, through unconfessed sins, beginning with our words?

Jeanie and I submit ourselves daily to our heavenly Father. We ask Him to cover us, our loved ones and our homes, as well all other life's areas, with the precious Blood of Jesus Christ, the Lamb of God. We pray that the Almighty God of Abraham, Isaac, and Jacob give his holy angels charge to protect us in all our ways, (read Psalm 91:11 and Psalm 103:20,21). In addition, and fully aware of our enemy's attempts to attack us, we quote Ephesians 6:10-17, believing that our real enemies can only be "seen" through trained spiritual eyes.

In the Old Testament, God emphatically instructed the Israelites to keep any defiled thing out of their camp. His precise instructions in building their places of worship and His demand for holiness on the part of those assigned to perform the ceremonies had to be strictly obeyed. God was angered when any defilement came into His house. His people paid stiff penalties for disobedience, because Satan would immediately use this as an opportunity to destroy God's people.

Praise God, Jesus paid the full penalty for our sins, so we can live under the protection of His shed Blood. Giving Jesus full reign of our lives will keep Satan away from us. Mere human sentiments and believing Satan's lies, constitute fertile ground for the enemy's attacks.

The apostle Paul attributes discord among brethren, such as; envy, strife, reviling, evil suspicions, disputes and arguments, to ungodliness, disobedience and teaching that is not consistent with the words of Jesus (1 Timothy 6:3,5). The devastation that bitterness and resentment brings into the lives of countless Christians and entire church congregations cannot be measured. If bitterness and resentment are not properly addressed, it will bring ruin to the Christian's testimony and many will be defiled. (Hebrews 12:15). Usually one can observe a four "R" process;

Resentment + Resistance + Revenge = Ruin.

It usually begins with:

Resentment; often for trivial things. We decide to dig-in our heels and criticize the person that offended us, thus allowing the bitter root inside our heart to defile us.

The next time we see the person we will:

Resist him; by just ignoring him, and soon we begin to seek:

Revenge; "I must get even." "I will show him." But God says: "Vengeance is Mine, I will repay. Therefore 'If your enemy is hungry, feed him; if he is thirsty, give him a drink; for in so doing you will heap coals of fire on his head. Do not be overcome by evil, but overcome evil with good.'" (Romans 12:19,20). "No way," you may think; "I will show him who is right!" But the accumulated hatred and anger will escalate to such a point that I will end up in;

Ruin; "lest any root of bitterness springing up cause trouble, and by this many become defiled" (Hebrews 12:15). Unless we address the conflict, we will become so bitter that we cannot experience God's love, peace and joy. We may even begin to scheme ugly things against that person, not realizing that we have already "swallowed the devil's bait, hook, line and sinker;" and as a result we will begin to get sick; first emotionally, spiritually and eventually also physically. Had we followed the conviction of the Holy Spirit right away, and taken that "thing" to the cross, regardless of who was right or wrong, we could have been free.

Praise God, for the absolute reality that our precious Lord and Shepherd Jesus Christ was and is always there, closer than any friend, ready to reconcile us with our fellow men and to Himself!

If we think that we can start our day without putting on the full armor of God, we are deceiving ourselves and the enemy will take advantage of us. Do not be fooled into thinking that the presence of the devil, with his wicked minions, is the product of some fanatic's imagination or a fairy tale carried over from the Dark Ages. Don't be deluded in thinking you can sail through the day unnoticed by him, thinking; "if I ignore him he will leave me alone." There is no such thing.

You may have been told by friends that some Christians "see" a demon under every stone. I heard that statement so many times that I believe those who think so, don't see a demon anywhere. Christians who are involved in prayer ministries and spiritual warfare, have learned their lessons and are more determined than ever to wrestle precious brothers and sisters from the enemy's control. Too many Christians live in self-made prisons; they are literally held in captivity. They are not willing to be set free, perhaps for fear of being polluted by the devil, when in reality he has already blinded them.

At times, Jeanie and I pray with Christians who are so defeated they can hardly keep their head above water. They need to be delivered; but they must be willing to reach out and submit to the Lord. Our Father wants to restore what the "thief" has stolen from them.

In Ezekiel 28:12-19, God revealed to the prophet that "You were the seal of perfection, full of wisdom and perfect in beauty. You were in Eden, the garden of God;...you were the anointed cherub...You were perfect in your ways...since the day you were created, till iniquity was found in you."

Satan's rebellion and fall is further mentioned by the prophet Isaiah 14:12,13; "How you are fallen from heaven, O Lucifer, son of the morning! How you are cut down to the ground, you who weakened the nations. For you have said in your heart: I will ascend into heaven, I will exalt my throne above the stars of God."

Jesus said; "I saw Satan fall like lightning from heaven" (Luke 10:18). Since that time, those who exalted themselves were humiliated by God. Pride still destroys many lives today. In spite of the fact that Satan was cast out of heaven, he still seems to be able to approach God. In Zechariah 3:1,2, we read that Satan was standing at the right hand of the Angel of the Lord and the Lord said to him: "The Lord rebuke you, Satan."

Following are some additional names given to Satan in the Bible:

The devil or the adversary; (enemy) 1 Peter 5:8
God of this age; 2 Corinthians 4:4
Tempter; Matthew 4:3
Prince of power of the air; Ephesians 2:2
Accuser; Revelation 12:10
Murderer and liar; John 8:44
Ruler of this world; John 12:31

As long as we live in this body we are prone to attacks from the enemy. If he tempts us, we can only blame ourselves when we fall into his temptations. "Let no one say when he is tempted: 'I am tempted by God;' for God cannot be tempted by evil, nor does He Himself tempt anyone. But each one is tempted, when he is drawn away by his own desires and enticed" (James 1:13, 14,). And verse15 says: "Then, when desire has conceived, it gives birth to sin; and sin, when it is full grown, brings forth death." Here we have a step by step description how our thoughts can become sin, and eventually strongholds for Satan.

When thoughts are mulled over and over in our minds, we are producing all kinds of imaginations, and imaginations build strongholds, and strongholds provide "open doors" for the enemy. We must bring every thought and everything that elevates itself against our deeper knowledge of God, into submission to Christ, before we become polluted by them (read 2 Corinthians 10:3-6). Before temptation comes to us,

God has already made provisions for us to escape before sin is conceived.

> "No temptation has overtaken you except such as is common to man; but God is faithful, who will not allow you to be tempted beyond what you are able, but with the temptation will also make a way of escape, so that you may be able to bear it" (1 Corinthians 10:13).

God wants to set us free from all sorts of compulsions, hang-ups, and from whatever else leads us into sinning, so that the adversary has nothing to accuse us before Him. "Then they cried out to the Lord in their trouble, and He saved them out of their distresses. He sent His Word and healed them and delivered them from their destructions. Oh, that man would give thanks to the Lord for His goodness, and for His wonderful works to the children of men" (Psalm 107:19-21).

Jesus' relationship with His Father was so close and intimate, that everything He said and did was sanctioned by His Father; "Do you not believe that I am in the Father, and the Father in Me? The words that I speak to you, I do not speak in My own authority; but the Father who dwells in Me does the works" (John 14:10).

Satan also attacks us through the sinful world system to which we are exposed. As the deceiver, he attempts to draw us away from God, into a system that is under his control. "We know that we are of God, and the whole world lies under the sway of the wicked one" (1 John 5:19). This world, as we know it, will pass away. "And the world is passing away, and the lust of it; but he who does the will of God abides forever" (1 John 2:17).

"And do not be conformed to this world, but be transformed by the renewing of your mind, that you may prove what is that good and acceptable and perfect will of God" (Romans 12:2). By befriending ourselves with sinful things of this world while compromising our faith in Christ, we separate ourselves from our heavenly Father, who wants us to fully enjoy Him. "Do not love the world or the things in the world. If anyone loves the world, the love of the Father is not in him. For all that is in the world—the lust of the flesh, the lust of the eyes, and the pride of life— is not of the Father but is of the world" (1 John 2:15,16).

The strength of our intimate relationship with the Lord, is our most powerful protection from the enemy. "Because you are strong, and the Word of God abides in you, and you have overcome the wicked one" (1 John 2:14b).

Unfortunately, Satan has ensnared many Christians into believing that they can enjoy both, the sinful things of the world and the Kingdom of God. This is a terrible deception, a fast and sure way into lukewarm Christianity at best. Is it any wonder that all kinds of philosophies and worldly teachings have infiltrated the Church and watered down the Gospel of Jesus Christ? This is the spirit of the antichrist. There is no power in an adulterated Gospel; what is offered is only a form of godliness. This kind of Gospel will not and cannot confront sin; in fact, it will justify sin as human weakness and call for understanding that "things will get better."

"But know this, that in the last days perilous times will come: for men will be lovers of themselves, lovers of money, boasters, proud, blasphemers, disobedient to parents, unthankful, unholy, unloving, unforgiving, slanderers, without self-control, brutal, despisers of good, traitors, headstrong, haughty, lovers of pleasure rather than lovers of God, having a form of godliness but denying its power. And from such turn away" (2 Timothy 3:1-5).

In such an environment, the truth of Christ's deity will be questioned if not denied. Satan will not spare any effort to confound the minds of men in regard to Jesus Christ. When the foundation is washed away it will not take long for the building to collapse. "For no other foundation can anyone lay than that which is laid, which is Jesus Christ" (1 Corinthians 3:11). Man may try many paths to reach God, but he cannot have fellowship with the Almighty God, until he finds and accepts the only and true Mediator who will lead him to His Father; namely, Jesus Christ.

"For there is one God and one Mediator between God and men, the Man Jesus Christ" (1 Timothy 2:5). Jesus unequivocally said that: "I am the Way, the Truth, and the Life, no one comes to the Father but by Me" (John 14:6).

Christian fellowship that enjoys intimate communion with the Father, the Son Jesus Christ and the Holy Spirit is a bulwark, a strong fortress against the onslaught of Satan. It will provide a safe haven for the unprotected and a mighty healing center for the deeply hurting; a refreshing brook for the spiritually thirsty, and a guidepost for the seeker of the Truth. God's pleasure with such a gathering of believers can best be expressed in the words of the Psalmist as recorded in Psalm 91:7-11, and by the Lord Himself in Isaiah 54:17; "A thousand may fall at your side, and ten thousand at your right hand; but it shall not come near you. Only with your eyes shall you look, and see the reward of the wicked. Because you have made the Lord, who is my refuge, even the Most High, your dwelling place, no evil shall befall you, nor shall any plague come near your dwelling; for He shall give His angels charge over you to keep you in all your ways."

"No weapon formed against you shall prosper, and every tongue which rises against you in judgment you shall condemn. This is the heritage of the servants of the Lord, and their righteousness is from Me, says the Lord" (Isaiah 54:17). It overwhelms me when I read the many promises the Lord has given His children for their protection, when obediently obeying His instructions.

In addition to doubt, unbelief, and skepticism, Satan knows that through pride he has another powerful weapon to trip Christians and make them fall. This was at the root of his own fall from God's presence.

Self-exaltation and pride caused him to be cast out from heaven; and since misery seeks company, he tries to ensnare Christians to become victims of this treacherous character trait. The dictionary defines this form of pride as arrogant behavior or conduct, conceit, egotism, vanity. This provides fertile ground for the enemy to plant his wicked seed. Scripture teaches when pride enters our heart, God will resist us. "God resists the proud, but gives grace to the humble" (1 Peter 5:5b). "Pride goes before destruction and a haughty spirit before a fall" (Proverbs 16:18).

As the pure Word of God enters our heart it ministers to our motives and purifies our thoughts, words, and actions. "For the Word of God is living and powerful, and sharper than any two-edged sword, piercing even to the division of soul and spirit, and of joints and marrow, and is a discerner of the thoughts and intents of the heart. And there is no creature hidden from His sight, but all things are naked and open to the eyes of Him to whom we must give account" (Hebrews 4:12,13).

Another tactic the enemy uses to discourage Christians is to dig up old sins that were confessed and washed with the Blood of the Lamb. He delights to annoy us and attempts to steal what is rightfully ours. God does not remember sin that has been confessed and forgiven. "I, even I Am He who blots out your transgressions for My own sake; and I will not remember your sins" (Isaiah 43:25). In fact, they are cast into the sea. "You will cast all our sins into the depths of the sea" (Micah 7:19b).

If you are presently plagued by any kind of disruption in your life that dampens your joy in the Lord, call out to Jesus and He will intervene in your behalf. You must ask, seek, and knock, in order to receive; all three are actions; we must engage our will and act. Ask the Father in Jesus' name and He will hear you:

"Dear heavenly Father; in the name of Your Son Jesus Christ, I ask that You help me to live in victory over my flesh, the world, and Satan and all his wicked minions. I refuse to believe the devil's lies and choose to believe Your Word and live in Your Truth. I commit myself totally to You, my Father; spirit, soul, and body and offer myself as a living sacrifice. Remind me of any unconfessed sins, so I can bring them to the Cross and be washed in the Blood of Jesus. Protect me from the adversary when he falsely accuses me. Please help me to be a vessel for honor, sanctified and fit for the Master, and prepare me for every good work. In Jesus' exalted and holy name I pray;" Amen.

Submission to God, causes Satan to flee: "Submit to God. Resist the devil and he will flee from you" (James 4:7). We must speak the Word of Truth, from our hearts and minds.

It is important to make it a practice to not only read the Scriptures visually, but to engage our vocal cords, so that we can hear God's Word which will increase our faith. The Bible says that faith comes by hearing the Word of God (Romans 10:17).

"And they (believers) overcame him (Satan) by the Blood of the Lamb and by the word of their testi-

mony, and they did not love their lives to death"
(Revelation 12:11).

A Christian, who lives in bondage to sinful habits and
compulsions, needs to be delivered from demonic oppression. Through disobedience to God's Word, he has opened
himself to demonic intrusion, and the enemy will not leave
until the person is willing to confess his sins and ready to
change his ways. The enemy must be told that; "He who is
in you, is greater than he who is in the world" (1 John 4:4b).
Other areas of attack are anxiety, fear, and insecurity about
tomorrow. Through them, the enemy can blind us to the point
of panic; we must "cast all our cares upon the Lord" (1 Peter
5:7). When I feel discouraged, I shout to the enemy:

"I am a child of God, called according to my Father's
purpose, redeemed with the Blood of Jesus Christ, the Son,
sealed and filled with the Holy Spirit and my name is written
in the Lamb's Book of Life. In the Name of Jesus Christ and
by the power of His shed Blood, I command that you, devil
and all your evil spirits depart from me now. I choose to live
in the light of my Lord Jesus Christ, and reject anything that
comes from you. I renounce all works of Satan in my life and
any agreements that I may have made with powers of darkness; whether conscious or unconscious and command any
attached demons to flee from me now. You were defeated
by the Blood of Jesus Christ the Lamb of God. Lord, please
grant me Your peace and joy; help me to bring glory to Your
name."

The apostle Paul gives us great encouragement; "Be
anxious for nothing, but in everything by prayer and supplica-
tion, with thanksgiving, let your requests be made known to
God;" (Philippians 4:6). Believe that God hears your prayers
and thank Him every day for His answers; be assured that
your heavenly Father will honor your obedience. To possess
the inner assurance that Jesus loves us and wants our best,

will equip us to handle every situation in life, even those that seem insurmountable.

"The Lord is my light and my salvation; whom shall I fear? The Lord is the strength of my life; of whom shall I be afraid?" (Psalm 27:1). How often do we wake up in the morning after a day of worrying, being able to breathe, watch the sun rise, sit down for breakfast, and then realize that "this is the day I was so worried about yesterday; O Lord, please forgive me for my little faith."

Aware of our weaknesses, Jesus tells us: "Therefore I say to you: do not worry about your life, what you will eat... or drink...or clothe...Is life not more than food and the body more than clothing? Look at the birds...your heavenly Father feeds them. Are you not of more value than they? Consider the lilies of the field, how they grow: they neither toil nor spin and yet I say to you that even Solomon in all his glory was not arrayed like one of these. Now if God so clothes the grass of the field...will He not much more clothe you, O you of little faith?.Therefore do not worry, saying, 'What shall we eat?' or 'What shall we drink?' or 'What shall we wear?' For after all these things the Gentiles seek. For your heavenly Father knows that you need all these things. But seek first the Kingdom of God and His righteousness, and all these things shall be added to you. Therefore do not worry about tomorrow, for tomorrow will worry about its own things. Sufficient for the day is its own trouble" (Taken from Matthew 6:25-34).

It absolutely amazes me; that so much is at our disposal to live a victorious life. Will we finally realize the urgent need to get the Word of God into our minds and hearts?

Christians should be the most pleasant people on earth. They should be the best workers, the best managers, the best citizens, the best parents, the best communicators and so much more. A Christian should be an asset to his community no matter what situation he or she may encounter. "For we are to God the fragrance of Christ among those who are being saved and among those who are perishing" (2 Corinthians 2:15). "Let your speech always be with grace, seasoned with salt, that you may know how you ought to answer each one" (Colossians 4:6).

Jesus' triumph over sin, death, and Satan, has opened the way for us Christians to live in the fullness of Christ, free from the enslavement of sin and oppression of darkness.

He has risen from the dead and lives forever, and so shall we.

Chapter Eight

Peacekeeper or Peacemaker

Jesus said:
"Blessed are the Peacemakers, for they shall be called
sons of God" (Matthew 5:9).

A quick definition of what I believe to be Peacekeepers
and Peacemakers in the Kingdom of God, will not
satisfy my desire to help believers in Jesus Christ in their
quest for greater spiritual maturity. I understand from God's
Word that a peacemaker is also a peace giver and must
therefore undergo a radical transformation through the Holy
Spirit's sanctification process.

Our Lord speaks of two kinds of peace; His peace as
opposed to the peace the world offers. "Peace I leave with
you, My peace I give to you; not as the world gives do I give
to you. Let not your heart be troubled, neither let it be afraid"
(John 14:27).

I love Jesus' Sermon on the Mount in Matthew chapters
5, 6 & 7. I read these words of Jesus Christ many times in
my youth. I committed verses to memory, in German, then
in Spanish, and later in English. However, decades passed
before I more fully understood and experienced the meaning

of this great, life-changing sermon, delivered by Jesus Christ

"Blessed are the peacemakers, for they shall be called sons of God." I believe that a disciple of Jesus Christ cannot become an effective peacemaker unless he obediently submits to the pruning knife of His Master, until he finds his way home in his heavenly Father's heart.

Our society has suffered a major breakdown in morality, and it is often difficult for Christians to determine what is really evil. Statistics also prove that immorality has flooded the Church of Jesus Christ with devastating consequences. Indifference toward biblical standards of holiness makes it easier for Christians to justify sinful behavior; "other Christians are doing it, so why can't I?"— seems to be the excuse.

However, the Holy Scriptures' injunction for purity hasn't changed. "Blessed are the pure in heart, for they shall see God" (Matthew 5:8). As our heart is purified and healed, our ability to perceive the Shepherd's voice will be intensified; God's love will flow into and through us more freely "as rivers of living water" and our deep gratitude will find its expression in praise and adoration of our heavenly Father.

Our Father wants His beloved Son's disciples to be peacemakers. He wants to transform every peacekeeper to become a peacemaker.

Let me describe what I believe is a Peacekeeper:

He usually seeks his own interest; what can I gain from it?

He is not willing to lay down his life for his friends. Since peace as he understands it is his goal, he will maintain the "status quo" at any cost; don't rock the boat, is his motto.

He makes decisions on outward appearance.

He seeks to please his superiors for personal gain.

He denies the presence of conflict for fear of losing control.

He wants to look "spiritual" to be admired by others.

He is more of a "hireling" than a true shepherd.

Since control is his real goal, he needs to push out the troublemakers, who are often peacemakers.

His unhealed heart is not "in it" as he performs to please, and is therefore doomed to failure.

Performance orientation is an indication of a wounded heart. John Sandford, of Elijah House, defines it as:

"The constant tendency of the born anew Christian is to fall back into striving by human effort. Our minds and spirits know the free gift of salvation, but our hearts retain their habits to earn love by performing. We live unaware that motives other than God's love have begun to corrupt our serving through striving, tension, and fear. Performance orientation is a term, which refers neither to the work we do nor the things we accomplish, but to the false motives which impel us. After we bring performance orientation to death, we may do exactly the same work in much the same way, but from an entirely different intent in the heart. By offering Christ's unconditional love and acceptance we can bring healing to those in this wounding."

Jeanie and I had the privilege to attend three courses of Elijah House training for the Ministry of Prayer Counseling. Their excellent training provided an important building block for our Ministry; in fact I received a fresh understanding of the operation of God's laws of the universe.

I saw God's love in the life of my earthly father whom I called Papa. He had undergone "intense surgery" in the school of his Master. He had a track record of one who found his place of rest in his Father's heart, because he experienced that: "There remains therefore a rest for the people of God" (Hebrews 4:9).

His character was refined through the heat of adversity and his trust and heart allegiance in the God of Abraham, Isaac, and Jacob, was affirmed by his absolute confidence that Jesus Christ cannot fail him, nor will He ever forsake His elect.

When in his presence, one could not ignore the love, joy, and peace that exuded from Papa's heart. I knew this was the "Fruit of the Spirit" as listed in Galatians 5:22. Of course he had his shortcomings, but whatever these may have been, they never hindered my quest for more of God. Papa left this earth after he had a vision of Jesus Christ holding His arms open to receive His son. "Come home Ludwig," he heard His precious Lord calling out. I was sitting at his bedside as he opened his eyes and shared his exciting experience.

These godly characteristics cannot be inherited; they must be developed in one's own walk with the Lord. I cannot deny the fact that my Christian forefathers definitely opened channels of generational blessings, making it less painful for me to find rest in my Father's heart.

The making of a Peacemaker is first and foremost the transforming work of the Holy Spirit with the Lord Jesus Christ as our model. By the grace of God and our obedience to Him the "Fruit of the Spirit" (Galatians 5:22-25) will become evident as people "see your good works and glorify your Father in heaven" (Matthew 5:16).

A Peacemaker is distinguished by many of these characteristics:

He is not ignorant of Satan's devices; therefore he is clad from head to toe with the full Armor of God, holding up the Sword of the Spirit (2 Corinthians 2:11; Ephesians 6:10-18).

He knows that he is "in process" and not a "finished product" (Philippians 1:6 and 3:12).

He is diligent in prayer and the study of the Holy Scriptures (Psalms 40:8, and 2 Timothy 3:15).

He recognizes his shortcomings and runs to the Cross for daily cleansing (John 1:9).

He bridles his tongue and seeks to speak the truth in love (James 1:26; Ephesians 4:15).

He is willing to receive instruction and correction when needed (2 Timothy 3:16,17).

He abhors what is evil (Romans 12:9).

He submits to God in all situations and resists the devil, knowing he will flee from him (James 4:7).

He asks God for wisdom daily and in all situations (James 1:5).

He enjoys intimate communion with his heavenly Father (Psalm 63:6,7).

He enjoys supernatural inner peace (Philippians 4:7).

He believes and flows in the Gifts of the Holy Spirit (1Corinthians 12:4-11).

He is learning to be content in any situation (Philippians 4:11,13).

He nourishes himself with "solid spiritual food" (Hebrews 5:14).

He hears the voice of his Shepherd and follows obediently (John 10:27).

He edifies others (Ephesians 4:12).

He shows compassion for the less fortunate (Psalm 41:1).

He freely gives of himself and his means as directed by his Lord (Matthew 10:8).

He does not fear conflict but seeks to resolve it, while esteeming others higher than himself (1 Corinthians 6:5; Romans 14:19).

He is also a peace giver, giving what he receives from the Prince of Peace (John 14:27; Ephesians 2:13,14).

He is not deceived by outside appearance but looks at the heart, because he keeps his own heart open (1 Samuel 16:7; John 7:24).

Well aware of my own shortcomings, I cling to Jesus Christ, from whose grace and mercy I draw my daily strength. The inner peace and unspeakable joy that fills my heart through every day is, as I understand it, my Fathers pleasure in His son.

Chapter Nine

Unless You are Converted and Become as Little Children ...

The purpose of this chapter is to share some practical experiences from our healing prayer ministry, hoping it will shed some light into what seems a mystery to many earnestly seeking believers in Jesus Christ; namely, how can my heart become more Christ like? Jesus did not leave us a legacy of mysteries without providing the necessary wisdom to understand and properly apply His words.

I will set the stage by first quoting an account recorded in the Gospel of Mark 9:33-35, followed by Matthew 18:1-6:

Then Jesus came to Capernaum. And when He was in the house He asked them; (His disciples) "What was it you disputed among yourselves on the road? But they kept silent, for on the road they had disputed among themselves who would be the greatest. And He sat down and, called the twelve and said to them; "If anyone desires to be first, he shall be last of all and servant of all."

"At that time the disciples came to Jesus, saying, 'Who then is greatest in the kingdom heaven?' Then Jesus called a little child to Him, set him in the midst of them and said: "Assuredly, I say to you unless you are converted and become as little Children, you will by no means enter the kingdom of heaven. Therefore whoever humbles himself as this little child is the greatest in the kingdom of heaven. And whoever receives one little child like this in My name receives Me. But whoever causes one of these little ones who believe in Me to sin, it would be better for him if a millstone were hung around his neck, and he were drowned in the depth of the sea."

The disciples of our Lord Jesus Christ are about to learn another powerful lesson in humility.

The backdrop of this event is just another relaxed occasion our Lord Jesus uses to convey crucial truths about the kingdom of heaven, not only to the apostles, but also to all those who will believe in Him.

A most familiar situation emerges as the disciples try to define their "business position" in their Lord's company. Since they anticipated the imminent establishment of God's kingdom on earth, they wanted Jesus to assign their job descriptions.

Is this a matter only a few of us struggle with? Over the years I've learned that true humility is not passed on to us by our forefathers. The Word of God and experience teach us that often the path to humility leads through humiliation, if we insist having our own way.

Pride is dismantled, and with our face on the ground, we will inhale the proper ingredients for humility to germinate. I believe the path of a follower of Christ is twofold; one leading upward closer to Jesus and the other downward, often through dark valleys. The path to humility will provide the foundation for the ascending path to spiritual maturity. Without this foundation we will be frustrated and, as is often the case, suffer spiritual shipwreck. It is during our walk through trials and tribulations that we acquire the spiritual tenacity, so essential for the overcomer.

When we read the Book of the Acts, we will notice how the Holy Spirit begins to transform God's servants by renewing their ways of thinking. And then later in the Epistles; what amazing wisdom and knowledge emerges from its pages. Not only did the disciples ask for more of God, but also received and faithfully applied the Lord's instructions while still learning even more through difficult experiences. Their willingness to put off the old and put on the new is the only path to true change of heart. God delights to speak to tender hearts.

"What was it you discussed among yourselves on the road?"- Jesus asked them. But they kept silent; sounds familiar? It is amazing how Jesus could read their thoughts, and knew the intents of their hearts. Wow; our Lord knows every thought that occupies our minds. How often are we truly aware of this sobering reality? I often willfully ignored my parents' wise counsel: "Remember boy, your heavenly Father watches over you, He sees and hears everything you do, speak, and even knows your thoughts." In my more adventurous years I often thought God is too busy elsewhere; so, go ahead do it; besides, other Christian friends do it too.

Praise God, He knows how to grab His boy's ears and take him back into His arms. But, how did my parents find out? Well, "For My thoughts are not your thoughts, nor are your ways My ways," says the Lord (Isaiah 55:8). That settled it. I was reminded that I was raised; "On the knees of a godly mother and across the knees of a godly father;" they truly knew how and when to administer proper discipline.

My wife Jeanie and I learned from ministering God's love and healing power to many wounded Christians, that it is through child-like simplicity that Jesus wants us to under-stand our Father's heart in order to more fully enjoy Him and His Kingdom.

The object lesson is given to Christ's disciples through a child whom Jesus sat in the midst of them and spoke these most profound words that are worth repeating; "Assuredly, I say to you, unless you are converted and become as little children, you will by no means enter the kingdom of heaven. Therefore whoever humbles himself, as this little child is the greatest in the kingdom of heaven. And whoever receives one little child like this in My name receives Me. But whoever causes one of these little ones who believe in Me to sin, it would be better for him if a millstone were hung around his neck, and he were drowned in the depth of the sea" (Matthew 18:3-6).

These words often alarmed me; and they still deeply concern me today when I see the consequences in the lives of those who carelessly neglect Jesus' injunction.

If access into the kingdom of heaven can only be enjoyed by child-like faith; then, I believe the answer to our quest for more of Him and His kingdom, must be found in God's desire that we become more Christ-like. In other words, it is really about character building or what the apostle Paul calls "For this is God's will, your sanctification" (1 Thessalonians 4:3a).

How do I become more child-like? Taking this question deeper it will sound like; how can my inner child, the real me, the one that God created, and knew everything about, even while in my mother's womb, come into full freedom and become what God purposed me to be? These questions point right to the heart, the mind, and the need for healing and renewing.

At this point, I can visualize some "raised eyebrows." That's all right; I don't blame you. It took me about three years to come to grips with the term Inner Healing. With my devout Christian background I was not ready to believe that "my child" needed healing. I grew up in the Holy Scriptures, the Bible; and if sixty-six books couldn't persuade me of my need for inner healing, who or what in the world could? Furthermore, the Word of God tells me: "Therefore, if anyone is in Christ, he is a new creation; old things have passed away; behold all things have become new" (2 Corinthians 5:17).

Most of my contemporaries during the fifties and sixties would flash this Scripture into the face of anyone who dared to suggest that a born-again believer needs inner healing or perhaps even freedom from generational curses. Today, I am saddened that these words are like red flags that frequently conjure up the specter of "New Age," "another Gospel" or similar phantoms.

In Psalm 51, 5-13, King David, after he was deeply convicted by the prophet Nathan for his sexual sin, wrote; "Behold I was brought forth in iniquity, and in sin my mother conceived me. Behold, You desire truth in the inward parts, and in the hidden part You will make me to know wisdom. Purge me with hyssop, and I shall be clean; wash me and I shall be whiter than snow. Make me to hear joy and gladness, that the bones You have broken may rejoice. Hide Your face from my sins, and blot out all my iniquities."

"Create in me a clean heart, O God, and renew a steadfast spirit within me. Do not cast me away from Your presence, and do not take Your Holy Spirit from me. Restore to me the joy of Your salvation, and uphold me by Your generous Spirit. Then I will teach transgressors Your ways, and sinners shall be converted to You."

These and other Scripture references clearly indicate the need for the cleansing and restoration of our hearts, the most profound area of our inner being. No doubt that the deep roots of our iniquities, which are flaws in our character, have their origin in the genesis of our being and were therefore passed down from our forefathers. Biblically addressing these issues will undoubtedly lead to true freedom. Whatever has been brought to the Cross of Christ and washed with His Blood is out of our Father's mind, because He said; "For I will forgive their iniquity, and their sin I will remember no more" (Jeremiah 31:34b).

Sin may taste sweet as honey, but when it is swallowed it stings like a bee.

Praise God that after twenty years of ministering to God' people, Jeanie and I have seen and rejoiced over the many who found freedom in Christ and healing for their hearts and souls. Several of them who still call us Mom and Dad have become spiritual pillars in God's kingdom.

True inner freedom from brokenness, enriched by our enjoyment of intimacy with our heavenly Father, can only be attained by our willingness to become childlike; which is contrary to childishness. A childlike heart in a mature Christian provides a haven of rest for the brokenhearted. Caring for a wounded child of God, and seeing his or her gradual healing, is an experience that neither I nor Jeanie would ever trade for any other occupation.

In the first part of this book I mentioned Mary, our first spiritual daughter, and how wonderfully God healed this child of His.

I need to share another experience as to how our Lord is using her as an intercessory prayer warrior. It was on October 14th 2008; I had an appointment at the local hospital for a specific in-depth physical examination. Just before the doctor administered the anesthesia, he had me sign a form that I was unable to read without my eyeglasses. I guessed where I was to sign and handed back the form and committed myself to my heavenly Father. At about 8:30 AM, after I came back to reality, I heard the nurse ask me how I felt, and I responded; "great; while I was out, I saw myself enjoying a prime rib dinner," which quickly changed the somber atmosphere into laughter.

The next day, Mary, who lives in the Midwest, called and asked: "Mom, what happened to Dad? Around 8:30 my phone rang, and on the caller ID I saw the words urgent message. I picked up the phone and no one answered. Then a message came to my heart; 'Pray for Harold.'" Now, Mary had no clue regarding the medical procedure but, as a powerful and obedient prayer intercessor spending many night hours praying for those who need help, she received a message from the Lord to pray for her spiritual Dad. This and many other similar answers to Mary's intercessory prayers, not only emphasizes the importance of our need to intercede for one other, but it has brought great joy to Jeanie and me for God's awesome love and grace demonstrated in Mary's transformation from a literal outcast to a mighty prayer warrior!

After experiencing many miracles, we are convinced that bodiless beings, angels and demons alike are actively involved in human affairs. "Are they (angels) not all ministering spirits sent forth to minister for those who will inherit salvation?" (Hebrews 1:14).

Chapter Ten

The Law of Sowing and Reaping and the Law of Increase

One very important reality that I missed in my quest for a better understanding of my sanctification was the process of sowing and reaping, so obviously visible in the lives of biblical characters, specifically in the Old Testament. This discovery not only caught my attention but triggered months of intense study of the Bible and all kinds of related resources. I remembered my mother's frequent references to her father as she "saw him in me." I perceived she was pleased about it, and so I went along with the spiel.

According to mother's description, my grandfather was a strong and devout believer in Christ. I never knew him, as grandpa lived in Germany while I was born and raised in Argentina. After moving to the United States, I began to take a greater interest in my ancestors. I had the opportunity to visit one of my mother's older sisters, who had fled Communist East Germany before the infamous separation wall was built, to settle in Canada. What I heard was not entirely what I was led to believe by my well-meaning Mama. She was the youngest of twelve siblings and was separated from her father and her sisters since age nineteen.

While conversing with my aunt, I had another confirmation that I was born into a family line of many believers in Christ. However, I also realized that with the good there were also some bad traits that were still active in me. Consequently, I was now convinced that renouncing my ancestor's iniquities and all resulting curses had to be given top priority in my life.

Of course, I am grateful for the wonderful blessings passed down to me from my forefathers. However, sowing and reaping of blessings and curses as outlined in the Bible, must be a daily reminder for the way I speak and act in every situation. Jesus said; "By your words you will be justified, and by your words you will be condemned" (Matthew 12:37). Our position in Christ and eternal life are God's gifts to every born-again believer, but unless we "walk in newness of life," according to Romans 6:4b, we will hardly experience real transformation.

Have you ever seen yourself in your children and didn't like it? Or have you become like your father or mother in areas where you determined, even early in life, that you will never be like them? Did you marry someone and found out later that your spouse is like your dad or your mom? Though I wondered why I acted and spoke in ways I disliked, I did not realize that I inherited negative traits from my forefathers. Later in my life, after receiving wonderful teaching from various ministries and reading pertinent books, my eyes were opened in totally new ways to the operation of the universal laws of God and how they affect Christians and non-Christians alike.

What you see in your family are the laws of God in operation. Cause and effect, action and reaction, sowing and reaping will happen no matter what age, nationality, whether Christian or pagan. The seed that falls into the ground will bring forth fruit after its kind.

Having been raised in the German and Argentinean cultures I had the opportunity to collect a vast array of folksy expressions; obviously not all of them were virtuous when held against God's standards. Unfortunately, the ones of lesser value were tossed into the same memory bank with the good ones, which required careful mental scrutiny on my part before letting the wrong ones slip out of my mouth.

As a major metropolis, Buenos Aires is, in my opinion a great city with an incredible variety of things to enjoy. However, similar to New York, one must be attentive not to be trampled underfoot by the crowd. My relationship with my heavenly Father was my best standard to stay on top of many unpleasant situations. I figured, if I am in a right relationship with Him I do not have to fear what men would do to me. Those who came up against me had to answer my Lord and Master who said: "Vengeance is Mine, I will repay;" says the Lord, (Romans 12:19b); and indeed, God will repay in ways and within a time frame that is not necessarily revealed to us. What we do know is that; "If God is for us, who can be against us?" (Romans 8:31b).

"Befriend yourself with the judge in town, for it is good to have a stake on which to scratch your back." This Argentinean expression had its origin when horses were more commonplace. I cannot recount the many situations I was favored over others, knowing that God was involved and I often saw opportunities to help others. Of course, there is the other side to this expression; namely, taking advantage of a situation for dishonest purposes. In these situations my mother would say: "Harold, remember; God's mills may grind slow but they will grind very fine; nothing escapes God's attention." And the Word of God tells us: "Do not be deceived God is not mocked; for whatever a man sows, that he will also reap" (Galatians 6:7).

Praise God that the Cross and Blood of Jesus Christ the Lamb of God will cancel out the consequences of our transgressions and, by humbly appropriating its power through repentance, we will be forgiven and set free, and "Therefore if the Son makes you free, you shall be free indeed" (John 8:36).

I cannot overemphasize our need to address inner issues before our sunset years arrive. Our frequent visits to nursing homes and hospitals are often sad experiences when interacting with dear people, non-Christians and Christians alike. Their attitude toward other patients, as well as nurses and doctors, is often horrendous. Even family members are often stunned by what they hear and experience while visiting their loved ones. One may wonder whether health institutions "teach" their patients nasty manners and foul words that can hardly be observed elsewhere.

Jeanie and I have decided that our ministry must be presented to God's people through cleansed vessels. In 2 Corinthians 4:2 the apostle Paul tells us what he did in regard to his inner "stuff." "But we have renounced the hidden things of shame, not walking in craftiness nor handling the Word of God deceitfully, but by manifestation of the truth commending ourselves to every man's conscience in the sight of God." Words that issue from our mouth are tainted by the stuff in our hearts.

Genuine child-likeness, as Jesus refers to, cannot be play-acted; it must flow from the heart under the guidance of the Holy Spirit. A believer in Christ, who has been rejected or abused in words or actions as a child, has repressed painful memories that are affecting his or her present behavior. Ministering to severely abused Christians for over twenty years, Jeanie and I believe that, unless the pain of the past is healed by our Lord Jesus Christ, and by the in-grafting of God's truth, the believer cannot live and walk in genuine freedom. The adult, whose heart has been deeply wounded in childhood, is unable to properly "absorb" the seed of God's Word.

Few of us, if any, are free from memories such as: "Children must be seen, not heard; leave me alone; I am busy; not now; you are really bad; you are the wrong sex; you will never amount to anything; do what I say and I will love you; you were born at the wrong time; go to..., I wish you were..." Emotional signals emitted by these repressed memories will cause us to overreact to present situations. In a marriage relationship we blame our spouse for carelessly hurting or offending us, when in reality we are subconsciously reacting to our childhood perpetrators.

Many Christians are literally encumbered in their walk with the Lord, fearful to admit it, lest they forfeit their good standing in the church. They move along in life carefully guarding their walled-in child, thus keeping everyone out. But, when the sunset years of our earthly walk begin to arrive, we wonder what God's inventory of our lives will reveal, perhaps wishing we had cleaned house a lot earlier. A weakening of our minds is often a byproduct of aging; consequently, "play-acting" becomes more difficult.

Jeanie and I had the privilege to minister to my mother at age 91. A wonderful prayer warrior, mother had issues that were never addressed. She had allowed the sun to set many times over troubles that affected her relationships. Before we left her bedside on one of our last trips to Milwaukee, Wisconsin, mother pressed my face into her hands and after kissing me said: "My son, I have never felt so free in my life." Mother was glad to leave her stuff behind when she went home to meet her Lord and Savior.

The painful memories of his parents will make it difficult for the adult to relate to his heavenly Father, who is subconsciously perceived as someone who hurt him. Consequently, the false personality, hiding behind a mask, has to play-act in order to "look and act godly," hoping that someday things will get better, and he no longer needs to look at "the great ones" in the Kingdom of Heaven, wishing it was him.

Thank God for Paul's words: "And yet, I show you a more excellent way" (1 Corinthians 12:31b). How deeply rewarding when we observe the healing work of Jesus Christ, our blessed Lord, Shepherd and Redeemer in the lives of precious sons and daughters of God in their gratitude expressed through praise and adoration to Him.

Paraphrasing selected verses from Isaiah 61, we learn what was later confirmed by Jesus in the Gospel of Luke, chapter 4; that—the brokenhearted are healed, the captives are liberated, prisons are opened to those who were bound, the mourning are comforted, and our Father gives them beauty for ashes, the oil of joy for mourning, the garment of praise for the spirit of heaviness; that they may be called trees of righteousness; the planting of the Lord, that He may be glorified.

What about the child in you? Are you truly connected to yourself, reconciled to the real you, God's creation? Can you say that the seed of God's Word is falling on "good ground yielding a crop; some a hundredfold, some sixty, some thirty?" Or do you begin to realize that when you hear God's Word, for some reason it does not produce the expected fruit in your life?" (Read the Parable of the soils, Mark chapter 4 or Luke chapter 8)

Jesus always aims for the spiritual heart, the core of the person. He seeks to shine His light into the dark heart of men. If someone who watched you on Sunday were to stop at your home or place of work on Monday; would he be surprised to "see someone else?"

When you read this very important parable and do not truly understand it; don't be surprised; Jesus' disciples didn't either (Mark 4:13). "And Jesus said to them, 'Do you not understand this parable? How then will you understand all the parables?'" Are you perplexed by these questions? If so, be assured, you have a lot of company. The Lord is not done with my heart either.

Let me invite you to pray the following words in your time with God; He loves to see us come to Him and ask what is on our hearts that displeases Him; it will surprise you to learn that Jesus is more willing to answer your prayers than you ever imagined.

"Abba, dear heavenly Father, I open my heart for Jesus Christ to search me and make me aware of every sin. Help me to truly repent from my words, thoughts, and actions that are encumbering my fellowship with You. Burn them out with the fire of Your Holy Spirit; wash me with the Blood of Jesus Christ the Lamb of God, and please let me know the names of those I need to forgive. Help me to renounce every ungodly belief and set me free from all the consequences of my forefathers' iniquities that are affecting my life and the lives of my descendants. I sincerely desire to know your loving heart so I can receive all the blessings you have provided for me and my descendants. I thank you that Jesus Christ, your only begotten Son, shed His precious Blood to save me from all my sins, granting me eternal life; I pray in Jesus' name;" Amen.

I have frequently uttered these words from the depth of my heart with overwhelming results. He has heard me and He will most certainly hear your sincere prayer.

Now back to the heart/ soul/ mind, whatever you choose to call it. It is the area of ourselves that needs to be renewed in order for us to be transformed. We should never underestimate the need for a strong and sound human nature; by this I mean a Christ-like character. Jesus is our model for this inner process. It took thirty years for Jesus to reach full human adulthood when He was ready to receive His Father's anointing for His ministry. Introducing His Son to the world He said: "This is my Beloved Son, in whom I am well pleased" (Matthew 3:17).

It is so rewarding when we perceive our Shepherd's voice telling us that He is pleased with us, in addition to other words of encouragement. Intimacy with our heavenly Father and knowing deep in our heart that He truly loves us, is indescribable; there is nothing in this life that comes even close to this inner assurance. And let me tell you; it is all available to you!

How often do we find ourselves caught in a situation we sincerely believed was God's will and later find out it was not His appointed time, because some things had to change in us first. We see in our Lord's life that genuine, Holy Spirit created spirituality produces the richest fruit when built upon a sound character/personality, our redeemed humanness. By the transforming power of Jesus' words, combined with His pure love and deep compassion, Jesus attracted people from all walks of life. While the spiritually hungry were fed by the Bread of Life, the critics plotted to kill Him. We also observe this transformation in Christ's disciples; specifically through the Acts of the Apostles and the Epistles. How can anyone deny this gradual, yet deep transformation and the resulting blessings flowing into-and through them?

The absence of true inner transformation, either through unwillingness or ignorance of the Word of God, is hardly more obvious than during spiritual revivals with supernatural manifestations. When the critical eye sees "weird" human behavior, he walks away from the meeting, disgusted by what he attributes to the devil, while missing what could have been a blessing for him. This has been, and unfortunately will continue to be, the human byproduct of our Lord's work on earth; even more so as His return draws near. Healed humanness combined with spiritual maturity will present a more dignified sight to the puzzled observer. However, it may not change the mind of those with preconceived notions about the supernatural; but this is not for me to resolve.

Jesus wants us to be child-like; this implies that our hearts and minds must be receptive and ready to receive the truth. A deeply hurting heart is afraid to open. It is unsafe out there—the child believes. Early in life he or she made an inner vow never to trust, never to become vulnerable and be hurt again. Transferring this concept to the mind, I would define it as subconscious denial. This later becomes a barrier to the flow of the Holy Spirit. I can best picture this as a partition between the spirit and soul of the person or between the conscious and subconscious mind, if you will. The living Word of God, taught under the anointing of the Holy Spirit, has the power to heal this condition. Remember the following scripture: "For the Word of God is living and powerful, and sharper than any two-edged sword, piercing even to the division of soul and spirit, and of joints and marrow, and is a discerner of the thoughts and intents of the heart" (Hebrews 4:12).

What keeps me from overcoming this situation on my own?...you may wonder. I have learned through the years that most of the hurts of our past can be addressed between God and us. However, we must ask our Lord for help, because: "I, the Lord, search the heart, I test the mind, even to give every man according to his ways, according to the fruit of his ways, according to the fruit of his doings" (Jeremiah 17:10).

We need to read what King David prayed; "Search me, O God, and know my heart, try me, and know my anxieties; and see if there is any wicked way in me, and lead me in the way everlasting" (Psalm 139:23,24), Our Father loves to hear us quote His Word back to Him.

God will bring people and situations to your remembrance, but it is your responsibility to clean house. At times we may blame the devil for lying to us when in reality the Lord is bringing up stuff from deep inside us.

When the deep motives and intentions of our heart are scrutinized by the Holy Spirit, and if we are willing to obediently follow His instructions, we will begin to enjoy the fruit of His cleansing. Our faith will increase and we become more sensitive to the voice of our Shepherd. The child in us; the inner man, will become a lot more trusting without fear of being hurt, because the Lord God Almighty is our Defender and those who dare come up against us will have to answer to our Lord and King Jesus Christ. This is awesome, to say the least. Many things will begin to change, in-and outside of us. People and situations around us will be affected supernaturally, as angels of the Lord will become more active in their service to us.

As "children," even while taking our position as adult sons and daughters of our heavenly Father, we will be privileged to know and experience that: "…their angels always see the face of My Father who is in heaven" (Matthew 18:10b). There are many references in the Bible of angels ministering to God's children. Jeanie and I have experienced on more than one occasion how heavenly messengers intervene in our behalf.

We have seen how carefully our Lord Jesus Christ protects his precious Lambs who are willing to receive His restoration work. In the beginning stages of their healing/sanctification journey we encounter deep anxiety and distrust and other negative emotions. We know that we first have to earn their trust.

The "more excellent way" that Paul mentions in 1 Corinthians 12:31 and then explains in chapter thirteen, is LOVE, which never ends. This love does not have its source in us. It emanates from our heavenly Father's heart and, as a result, we become channels of "living water." This indeed is the greatest healing power in the universe, because it became flesh in the Person of our Lord Jesus Christ.

Chapter Eleven

The Overcomer's Inheritance

"He who overcomes shall inherit all things, and I will be his God and he shall be My son" (Revelation 21:7).

It is good to give thanks to You LORD,
And to sing praises to Your name, O Most High!
To declare Your loving-kindness in the morning,
And Your faithfulness every night.
For You, LORD, have made me glad through
Your work;
I will triumph in the works of Your hands.
O Lord, how great are Your works!
Your thoughts are very deep.
A senseless man does not know.
Nor does a fool understand this.
When the wicked spring up like grass,
And when all the workers of iniquity flourish,
It is that they may be destroyed forever.
But You, LORD, are on high for evermore.
The righteous shall flourish like a palm tree,
He shall grow like a cedar in Lebanon.

Those who are planted in the house of the LORD
Shall flourish in the courts of our God.
They shall still bear fruit in old age;
They shall be fresh and flourishing,
To declare that the LORD is upright.
He is my rock, and there is no unrighteousness
in Him.
(Excerpts from Psalm 92)

What a great way to wake up in the morning, ready to receive and act out what our Father has planned for us! If God is with us; who in the visible or invisible world can be against us?

In my teenage years, my Papa gave me a German study book about the Bible's Book of Revelation. Fascinated by this powerful message of Jesus Christ to His beloved disciple John, I developed an interest in reading and studying the Holy Scriptures, specifically the book of Revelation. This was the risen Savior speaking to His faithful follower John, after His return to heaven! The apostle John represents to me the loving personality of Jesus Christ. His obedience to His Lord and his willingness to allow Him to transform John from a "son of thunder," (Mark 3:17) to His beloved apostle (John 21:20), is a clear example of an overcomer worthy to be trusted.

The apostle Paul, though blessed with a very different personality than John, is certainly the most notorious over-comer in the early Church. His radical transformation from a raging enemy of the fledgling Church to a passionate follower of Jesus Christ has been a lifelong inspiration in my walk with the Lord.

No matter how many "shrouded mysteries" the reader may encounter in the book of Revelation, one cannot help but be gripped by what a believer in Christ can understand. Even while writing this article, I am overcome with joy, anticipating Christ's glorious return, in order to assume His reign over our Father's entire creation.

In the book of Revelation of Jesus Christ, our Lord stated eight times that those who overcome shall receive an inheritance.

The first three chapters give us an introduction of how this prophetic message came to the apostle John, with specific instructions to the leaders of seven churches in Asia Minor. Under the power of the Holy Spirit John writes, beginning with chapter one, verses four through twenty:

"John, to the seven churches which are in Asia: Grace to you and peace from Him who is and who was and who is to come, and from the seven Spirits who are before His throne, and from Jesus Christ, the faithful witness, the firstborn from the dead, and the ruler over the kings of the earth. To Him who loved us and washed us from our sins in His own blood, and has made us kings and priests to His God and Father, to Him be glory and dominion forever and ever. Amen.

"Behold, He is coming with clouds, and every eye will see Him, even they who pierced Him. And all the tribes of the earth will mourn because of Him. Even so, Amen.

"I am the Alpha and the Omega, the Beginning and the End," says the Lord, "who is and who was and who is to come, the Almighty."

"I, John, both your brother and companion in the tribulation and kingdom and patience of Jesus Christ, was on the island that is called Patmos (Greece) for the Word of God and for the testimony of Jesus Christ. I was in the Spirit on the Lord's Day, and I heard behind me a loud voice, as of a trumpet, saying, "I am the Alpha and the Omega, the First and the Last," and, "What you see, write in a book and send it to the seven churches which are in Asia: to Ephesus, to Smyrna, to Pergamos, to Thyatira, to Sardis, to Philadelphia, and to Laodicea."

"Then I turned to see the voice that spoke with me. And having turned I saw seven golden lampstands, and in the midst of the seven lampstands One like the Son of Man, clothed with a garment down to the feet and girded about the chest with a golden band. His head and hair were as white like wool, as white as snow, and His eyes like a flame of fire; His feet were like fine brass, as if refined in a furnace, and His voice as the sound of many waters; He had in His right hand seven stars, out of His mouth went a sharp two-edged sword, and His countenance was like the sun shining in its strength."

"And when I saw Him, I fell at His feet as dead. But He laid His right hand on me, saying to me, Do not be afraid; I am the First and the Last. I am He who lives, and was dead, and behold, I am alive forevermore. Amen. And I have the keys of Hades and of Death. Write the things which you have seen, and the things which are, and the things which will take place after this. The mystery of the seven stars which you saw in My right hand, and the seven golden lamp-stands: The seven stars are the angels (leaders) of the seven churches, and the seven lampstands which you saw are the seven churches."

Not only the introduction but also the conclusion of this powerful book fills one's heart with living hope. Listen to what Jesus says recorded in chapter twenty-two:

"And behold, I am coming quickly, and My reward is with Me, to give to every one according to his work. "Blessed is he who keeps the words of the prophesy of this book. I am the Alpha and the Omega, the Beginning and the End, the First and the Last.

"Blessed are those who do His commandments that they may have the right to the Tree of Life, and may enter through the gates of the City. But outside are the dogs, those who practice magic arts, the sexually immoral, the murderers and idolaters and those who practice falsehood. I, Jesus have sent My angel to testify to you these things in the churches. I am the Root and the Offspring of David, the Bright and Morning Star.

"And the Spirit and the Bride say, 'Come.' And let him who hears say, 'Come.' And let him who thirsts come. And whoever desires let him take the Water of Life freely." (Selected verses from Revelation 22)

As followers of Jesus Christ, we can look ahead with joy knowing that our Lord will establish a new world order, far above and beyond of what Satan is presently planning. Christ's return will usher in a Kingdom of Peace of unimaginable proportions, when all the nations will become the Lord's.

The Book of Revelation has been a source of hope and inspiration since my commitment to follow Jesus Christ. The awesome revelation of our resurrected Lord Jesus Christ, the Head of the true Church, who will soon return to establish His Kingdom and rule over all things, has ignited deep within me an unquenchable desire to pursue God. I believe that the words of our Lord are a message to His Church today, and a call to action to every follower of Christ; Jew and Gentile. Present-day events are daily reminders for us to be aware of the fulfillment of what our Father has spoken through His prophets, with the assurance that our Lord Jesus Christ will never, ever leave us nor forsake us.

The avid seeker of intimacy with his heavenly Father will find comfort and strength in the book of Revelation, resulting in his ability to overcome life's hardships. However, lasting joy and deep inner contentment will not become an abiding experience without a radical change of heart. We must be willing to open every "hidden chamber" of our heart that has not been penetrated by the light of Christ, and we will begin to truly enjoy God. "Taste and see that the Lord is good; blessed is the man who trusts in Him" (Psalm 34:8).

The apostle John writes in his first letter chapter 5:4: "For whatever is born of God overcomes the world. And this is the victory that has overcome the world-our faith;" which means nothing less than to trust and obey our Lord, for there is indeed no other way to true freedom and victory. Unfortunately, we often find ourselves kicking and screaming in order to have our own way. Let me illustrate with my experience with horses:

The Bible tells us: "Do not be like the horse or like the mule, which have no understanding, which must be harnessed with bit and bridle, else they will not come near you" (Psalm 32:9). During my European trip I was amazed at the amount of effort and dogged perseverance required in training a horse to properly jump over a hurdle. However, at times, to the horror of the rider, a horse would suddenly stop before the hurdle, sending him flying through the air.

In Revelation chapters two and three we have the content of the individual messages to the seven churches. After the Lord Jesus Christ evaluates their "state of affairs," He gives them a "report card." The grades range from "A to F;" a stern reminder for those who are living in sinful complacency. However, He promises an inheritance to all who are faithful in their walk with Christ. Following are the closing words spoken by Jesus Christ to the seven churches:

Ephesus: "To him who overcomes I will give to eat from the Tree of Life which is in the midst of the Paradise of God."

Smyrna: "He who overcomes shall not be hurt by the second death."

Pergamos: "To him who overcomes I will give some of the hidden manna to eat. And I will give him a white stone, and on the stone a new name written which no one knows except him who receives it."

Thyatira: "He who overcomes, and keeps My works until the end, to him I will give power over the nations."

Sardis: "He who overcomes shall be clothed in white garments, and I will not blot out his name from the Book of Life; but I will confess his name before My Father and before His angels."

Philadelphia: "He who overcomes I will make him a pillar in the temple of My God and he shall go out no more. And I will write on him the name of My God and the name of the city of My God, the New Jerusalem, which came down out of heaven from My God. And I will write on him My new name."

Laodicea: "To him who overcomes I will grant to sit with Me on My throne, as I also overcame and sat down with My Father on His throne."

Surprisingly, Jesus has words of encouragement even for a church that teeters on the brink of being spewed out of His mouth; granted that they repent and follow Jesus' injunction; as recorded in Revelation 3:18,19.

What an exciting future awaits those who love the Lord. Paul expresses it in 1 Corinthians 2:9; "Eye has not seen, nor ear heard, nor have entered into the heart of man, the things which God has prepared for those who love Him."

The book of Revelation is, in my opinion, no longer a "sealed book." The meaning of Christ's message; "What will be hereafter" is unfolding around us today. The discerning Christian cannot fail to see end-time events as foretold by Jesus in the Gospels and in the letters of His apostles. As born-again believers we have Christ in us by the power of the Holy Spirit, who reveals and confirms God's written words. "My little children, for whom I labor in birth again until Christ is formed in you" (Galatians 4:19). These touching words of the apostle Paul, show us how deeply committed he was to exemplify the Lord Jesus Christ. As a loving spiritual father, he not only led many to Christ, but was also willing to face any hardship, even physical death, for the sake of his beloved fellow Christians. He so desperately wanted them to experience the presence of God and truly enjoy Him.

I get excited when I meditate upon all these powerful words of Scripture that speak of Christ's coming to rescue His followers from this chaotic world system into the glorious presence of our heavenly Father. Witnessing my Papa's glorious departure from his earthly body and Martha's home-going while rejoicing in Christ her Lord, plus many other dear friends and family members, increased my excitement about our eternal future. Therefore, I refuse to waste time listening to doom-sayers.

My forefathers spoke with such conviction about the return of Christ with His Bride, the church, that it became an essential ingredient of my spiritual make-up. Regardless what happens in this world, politically, socially or financially, I know without any doubt where those who believe in Jesus Christ will spend eternity. This does not mean that I do not care about earthly matters; of course I want to be a good steward of what God has entrusted to me. However, I will not allow these fleeting things to distract me from keeping my eyes and heart anchored in the Lord!

Jesus' comforting words as recorded in John 14:1-4 provide the assurance of the believer's immediate and future destiny;

"Let not your hearts be troubled; you believe in God, believe also in Me. In My Father's house are many mansions. If it were not so; I would have told you, I go to prepare a place for you. And if I go and prepare a place for you; I will come again and receive you to Myself that where I am, there you may be also. And where I go you know, and the way you know."

After Paul's dramatic encounter with the risen Christ on the road to Damascus as an enemy of His followers, Paul became the most powerful apostle to the Gentiles. His zeal for Christ and His church never diminished until His blessed Lord called him into His presence. May God grant this zeal to Christ's followers today.

I believe that there are many who crave for intimacy with God, whether within or without the Church. He is also preparing true shepherds who are willing to lay down their lives for His flock and bring in those who are still "outside."

Jesus Christ is returning soon to receive His Church to Himself; "That He might sanctify and cleanse it with the washing of water by His word, that He might present it to Himself a glorious Church, not having spot or wrinkle or any such thing, but that it should be holy and without blemish" (Ephesians 5:25-27).

What is the state of His Church today? I do not have the proper answer to this question, nor do I want to judge those who Jesus Christ loves so much that He shed His precious Blood to redeem them from the power of darkness. Only God knows the hearts of His children. However, I would like to share some experiences that I picked up along my walk with the Lord.

As a result of several geographical moves in my life, first from Buenos Aires, Argentina, to the USA, and then across several states, I was a member of seven churches affiliated with different Christian denominations, holding leadership positions, for a period of sixty years.

On this journey I witnessed practically everything Jesus had against the churches in Asia Minor. But upon self-examination, I found that my own heart needed not only an "adjustment" and "fine-tuning" to be able to hear my Shepherd's voice, but a radical cleansing of my entire "temple" for greater fruit bearing. "Just hanging in there," was never good enough for me.

The casual reader of Paul's Epistles may think of him as a zealot, a man without real joy, who recklessly pursued unattainable goals. "I press toward the goal for the prize of the upward call of God in Christ Jesus" (Philippians 3:14). "I have fought the good fight, I have finished the race, I have kept the faith" (2 Timothy 4:7). "Do you not know that those who run in a race all run, but one receives the prize? Run in such a way that you may obtain it. And everyone who competes for the prize exercises self-control in all things. Now they do it to obtain an earthly crown, but we for a heavenly crown" (1 Corinthians 9:24,25).

However, as we get to know God's mighty apostle Paul, we learn that he knew deep within his heart, that the grace of our Lord Jesus Christ, the love of God our Father, and the fellowship of the Holy Spirit, was all he needed to overcome. His heart was full of thanksgiving as he wrote to the church in Corinth: "Blessed be the God and Father of our Lord Jesus Christ, the Father of mercies and God of all comfort, who comforts us in all our tribulation, that we may be able to comfort those who are in any trouble, with the comfort with which we ourselves are comforted by God. For as the sufferings of Christ abound in us, so our consolation also abounds through Christ" (2 Corinthians 1:3-5).

As a spiritual father to many of his contemporaries, he warms my heart as he writes: "For though you might have ten thousands instructors in Christ, yet you do not have many fathers; for in Christ Jesus I have birthed you through the Gospel. Therefore I urge you to imitate me"
(1 Corinthians 4:15,16).

Many of us have succumbed under the weight of adversity, trying to imitate Paul, not realizing that our fallen nature is unable to attain anything of eternal value, unless Christ is allowed to perform it in and through us. This was Paul's own experience as he writes to the Roman church: "For I know that in me (that is in my flesh) nothing good dwells; for to will is present with me, but how to perform what is good I do not find. For the good I will to do, I do not do; for the evil I will not to do, that I practice" (Romans 7:18,19). He was plagued with self-condemnation until the truth of God's Word illumined his mind and he understood that victory comes to those who live and walk in the power of the Holy Spirit. "There is therefore no condemnation to those who are in Christ Jesus, who do not walk according to the flesh, but according to the Spirit" (Romans 8:1).

For the rest of my life I will be grateful that I was raised by Christian parents who knew in their heart, and reflected in their lives that Jesus Christ is who He claims to be. They believed that He is the only Son of God, not created but begotten; one with God the Father; perfect Man and perfect God. They possessed that faith that overcomes; no matter what difficulties they encountered in their lives. When I heard them share their faith with love and kindness, it sounded so convincing, so reassuring that I decided to take it to heart and pursue Christ Jesus, my Lord.

Because of this blessed heritage I am ever so aware of my indebtedness to Jesus Christ and His Church. Freely I have received this gift from the Lord and therefore I have committed myself to freely give of my time and effort to God's brokenhearted children.

I don't know where you presently are in your walk with Christ. Whatever your circumstances, let me bless you with the apostle Peter's words: "May the God of all grace, who called us to His eternal glory by Christ Jesus, after you have suffered a while, perfect, establish, strengthen, and settle you. To Him be all glory and the dominion forever and ever. Amen" (1 Peter 5:10,11).

You may be discouraged by what you see around you, wondering about your place in God's Kingdom. Perhaps you wandered from church to church and have still not found the "right one." You may have tried everything you heard a good Christian must do to please God. Perhaps you had personal counseling, attended seminars, retreats, and conferences, and purchased every tape or book available to the point of running out of energy and money, and still found no lasting peace and rest.

Be assured, you are not alone in your desperate quest for God's love. Countless Christians are disappointed in their search for the "right" church. I was one of them, until God's truth caught up with me. It was not so much about cold churches or uncaring pastors; it was about the Lord Jesus Christ and my relationship with Him. He wanted my heart; all of it, period. I was also reminded of the words of Jesus in regard to end of the age; "Because lawlessness will abound, the love of many will grow cold" (Matthew 24:12).

The heart of man is God's target. He will not let go of us. When He truly has our heart, we can stop "play-acting" and just rest in Him. He instills in us the will and the strength to do what He has planned for us, but also the wherewithal to do it. "For it is God who works in you both to will and to do for His good pleasure" (Philippians 2:13). In other words, Jesus is always the initiator in everything He has planned for us. Of course, lip service or waiting for someone else to do it for us, certainly will not accomplish much of anything. Our loving and caring "Abba Father" knows all our needs even before we ask Him. He waits for us to kneel before Him and surrender our heart and tell Him; "here is my heart Lord, have Your way in me."

In the Old Testament we read over and over again how our Father was "tired" of His peoples' empty words and constant disobedience; He wanted their hearts. In the New Testament we read about Christ's warning to a lukewarm church (Revelation 3:16).

If you gave your heart to Jesus, He gave you His gift of eternal life. Now, reflect for a moment; did you really open every area of your life to Him? Only God is able to see our hearts; we can only "see" what our five senses perceive. My heart had to be transformed from a heart of stone to a heart of flesh. Too often I found myself criticizing and judging others by their appearance, expecting them to conform to my understanding of God's Word.

God will perform His work in you; He will uphold you with His righteous Spirit while helping you overcome every difficulty. Remember, and be encouraged by the words of Moses to Joshua: "And the Lord, He is the One who goes before you. He will be with you; He will not leave you nor forsake you; do not fear nor be dismayed" (Deuteronomy 31:8).

No matter what church you attend, you will soon discover that you are surrounded by Christians who wonder if this is all there is about their faith. You will also discover that your continued growth in the Lord Jesus Christ does not come without strange inner tensions.

Along with your desire to become more like Jesus, you will find that another force is pulling you in the opposite direction. This is what someone called "sin-energy." Let me assure you; this tug of war will intensify. You are also dealing with the enemy of your soul. After he lost you to Jesus, Satan will spare no effort to tie your hands to your back. His plan is to lead you into such frustration and ultimately into depression that you will find yourself in a rut. He will attempt to convince you that you only need a "face-lift," and that's all right with him, because people usually look at the outside anyway. Not so. He is a liar and a thief; Jesus said so; and as such he wants to keep you from revealing your heart.

If you think you can hide from the Lord, listen to King David, as he wrote Psalm 139:

O LORD, You have searched me and known me.
You know my sitting down and my rising up;
You understand my thoughts from afar off.
You comprehend my path and my lying down;
You know all my ways.
There is not a word on my tongue;
Behold, O LORD, You know it altogether.
You have guarded me from all sides, and laid Your
hand upon me.
Such knowledge is too wonderful for me;
It is so high, I cannot comprehend it.
Where can I go from Your Spirit?
Or where can I flee from Your presence?
You have formed my inward parts;
You have covered me in my mother's womb.
I will praise You, for I am fearfully and wonderfully
made;
How precious are Your thoughts to me, O God.
They are so manifold that if I were to count them,
They would be more in number than the sand.
When I awake I am still with You.
Search me, O God, and know my heart;
Try me and know my anxieties;
And see if there is any wicked way in me,
And lead me on Your everlasting way

Do you feel caught with no way out? If so, that's okay. This may result in a true and awesome encounter with your heavenly Father, who is looking for "failures," in order to begin something new and absolutely exciting. "But how in the world can I even think of overcoming when in reality I am up to my chin in a miry pit?"

Those who claim to be your friends also wonder; except with a different motive. You may notice them whispering behind your back. However, in reality they are as stuck as you are, except that they are in denial. Unaware of the desperate state of their hearts, they function under the cover of well-tailored masks; and by putting someone else down they are lifting themselves up. Gossiping can be juicy entertainment; but God hates it.

Is there a way out of my predicament? Is there a way of escape? The answer is an absolute; yes. It's all about Jesus Christ, your Redeemer, your Protector, your Defender, your Deliverer, your Healer and your Provider. If you seek to do what pleases Him, He will be your very best Friend; because He loves you more than you can imagine. He is the only path to true freedom. As the "Lifter of your head," Jesus will help you overcome all obstacles in your path. This is the Holy Spirit's process of sanctification. This is true freedom; freedom from legalism which is the devil's brand of Christianity. He convinced the Pharisees in Jesus' time that Jesus Christ was not the Messiah prophesied by the Prophets of old. They swallowed his bait and missed the freedom that the apostle Paul enjoyed after his miraculous encounter with the Lord. "Therefore if the Son makes you free, you shall be free indeed" (John 8:36).

While sharing my heart with you, I'm aware that there are many dear people who struggled all their lives in an attempt to reach their calling in life, only to land in another miry pit. Jeanie and I have ministered to many hopeless people. With little or no self-esteem they wandered through life to the point of utter frustration.

While watching news reports about the world in general, and Christianity in particular, we can easily be discouraged about the future. Listen to what the prophet Isaiah writes:

> "Fear not for I have redeemed you,
> I have called you by your name;
> You are Mine.

> When you pass through the waters, I will be
> with you;
> And through the rivers, they shall not overflow you.
> When you walk through the fire, you shall
> not be burned,
> Nor shall the flame scorch you.
> For I am the Lord your God. (Excerpts from
> Isaiah 43)

God's Word is awesome and I am so encouraged when words like these touch my heart. I cannot count the many times this Scripture portion has encouraged me to push on in my commitment to Jesus Christ. If you desire to live your life as an overcomer, please know that according to Jesus' words; "All things are possible to him who believes" (Mark 9:23).

It would not be scriptural if I told you that the path of an obedient Christian, who seeks to trust and obey the Lord, is a rosy one. What I will tell you is that the Lord will equip you to more fully walk in God's anointing for your life. When in the midst of a trial, your mind is so preoccupied that you are unable to "see" what transpires in the spiritual realm. Be reassured that, no matter how difficult the situation, your faithful Shepherd is aware of every detail in your life. He knows your name, hears the faintest cry, your desperate responses, every complaint or accusation and the most exasperated call for help. He is aware of the perceived silence that often follows your prayers. He is all knowing, ever-present, all-powerful, and never-changing. He will not only help you to overcome, but will reward you afterwards.

There is a desire, lodged deep within my heart that is greater than me. I know it is the joy of the Lord and the compassion for those who do not know Him. Over the years I have learned to be careful in not pushing the Gospel onto somebody who was not ready to receive it. I like to wait for the Holy Spirit's inner signal. However, when meeting with fellow Christians who lost their hope in Christ, my excitement concerning our eternal future with Christ, begins to flow out of my heart!

Unfortunately, the enemy has infiltrated the Church of Jesus Christ, deluding its testimony as a transforming power in the world. When Jesus entered the world scene as the promised Messiah to redeem Israel, He found a people in disarray. As sheep scattered by ravenous wolves, they desperately needed a true Shepherd. Crippled by spiritual blindness they were as salt trampled underfoot, even by their own leaders. Those who sincerely waited for His arrival and accepted what Jesus offered them, found true rest for their souls. Spiritual apathy and emotional hardness were dispelled by the power of the Holy Spirit that fell upon Christ's followers on the day of Pentecost. Endued with power from above, they mightily proclaimed the Gospel of Jesus Christ that changed the world.

As countless world events signal the return of our Redeemer, we need to awaken from our sinful complacency. While nations are raging against God's people, seeking to build weapons of mass destruction and vying for world domination, we need to use our spiritual weapons and stand fast in the liberty by which Christ has made us free. (Galatians 5:1) Not in our strength as crusaders who seek to impose their own opinions, but as faithful disciples full of the Holy Spirit and the love of God, because it is: "Not by might, nor by power, but by My Spirit, says the Lord of Hosts" (Zechariah 4:6b).

Chapter Twelve

A Strange Dream

Now, in my sunset years, I begin to share my dreams more freely. The prophet Joel in chapter 2:28 says: "Your old men shall dream dreams." In the past, I would not remember most dreams or quickly disregard them as meaningless. However now I am experiencing more meaningful dreams. At the same time I am discovering that the Holy Spirit will reveal the meaning of a godly dream without seeking the opinions of others.

On the night of November 13th to the 14th, 2008, I had a dream with such a sense of reality that it could have been more like a vision. Contrary to dreams in the past, this one I was unable to brush aside. It deeply impressed, even shocked me for days. The Lord's revelation came and the meaning of the dream began to unfold.

I saw before me what appeared to be a picture of mankind. At first it looked like mass confusion; people were running to and fro, seemingly without direction. In the midst of it all I began to perceive a stronghold of oppression; some higher power seemed to be in control of everything and everyone as far as I could see. Then the crowd began to close in on me, while shouting accusing words at me. I felt motionless, downright paralyzed. I desperately wanted to shout that I am a child of the Most High God; but my jaw was frozen. I had heard several accounts of Christians' dreams about life after death and even of hell; but this dream was about people in their present lives.

I realized that I "saw" a picture of the unfolding of the reign of the Antichrist. Everything around me was under his very tight control. In my great distress, deep within me, I wanted to cry out for Jesus, but was unable. My jaw was numbed and I thought if I could only shout out the name of Jesus. Immediately, right over my head I saw, in gigantic letters, the words; ONLY JESUS; and I woke up immensely relieved.

Slowly, the meaning of my terrible sense of imprisonment began to unfold: "My Church is in captivity, and I will heal My people and give rest to their souls." There was more in that dream related to the present spiritual state of Christianity. It was regarding Jesus' displeasure as expressed in His messages to the seven churches in Asia Minor. After sharing this dream with Jeanie, we were encouraged to proceed in our rewarding prayer ministry.

As time advances we will see more end-time events that Jesus spoke about in the Gospel of Matthew, chapters 24 and 25. Some will cause great fear among the people on the earth. Just as we see nations moving closer to one another for global agreements on one hand, we will see rogue nations banding together bringing fear to those who feel threatened. But those who trust in the Lord with all their hearts are encouraged to; "Let us hold fast the confession of our hope without wavering, for He who has promised is faithful" (Hebrews 10:23).

As Christians we may disagree on the chronological order of end-time events; however we can surely agree that our future will indeed be glorious, knowing without any doubt that our heavenly Father will fulfill the plan for His creation.

May the following words recorded by Christ's apostle John as His Lord showed him the masterwork of His new creation, stimulate our trust in Him:

"And I saw a new heaven and a new earth, for the first heaven and the first earth had passed away. Also there was no more sea. Then I, John, saw the holy city, New Jerusalem, coming down out of heaven from God, prepared as a bride adorned for her husband. And I heard a loud voice from heaven saying, 'Behold, the tabernacle of God is with men, and He will dwell with them, and they shall be His people. God Himself will be with them and be their God. And God will wipe away every tear from their eyes; there shall be no more death, nor sorrow, nor crying. There shall be no more pain, for the former things have passed away.'"

Then He who sat on the throne said, "Behold, I make all things new." And He said to me, "Write, for these words are true and faithful." And He said to me, "It is done! I Am the Alpha and the Omega, the Beginning and the End. I will give of the fountain of the water of life freely to him who thirsts. He who overcomes shall inherit all things, and I will be his God and he shall be My son" (Revelation 21:1-7).

> "Blessed and holy is he who has part in the first resur-
> rection. Over such the second death has no power,
> but they shall be priests of God and of Christ, and
> shall reign with Him a thousand years" (Revelation
> 20:6).

You may wonder how it could ever be possible to keep the hope of a glorious future alive, while surrounded from all sides with not much more than pessimism and hopelessness. You may have been raised in a family that only occasionally went to church and to speak about the future, as described in the Bible, was just like a "pipe dream." Someone may have led you to Jesus Christ and you decided to attend a church where the Gospel is taught, but you did not hear much about the Book of Revelation.

I believe our Lord is not pleased with the spiritual state of some churches. The overemphasis on material possessions and the moral decay in our society have penetrated some churches which were called to be salt on earth and light to the world. Aware of Jesus' injunction as recorded in Matthew 24:12; "And because lawlessness will abound, the love of many will grow cold." This increases our determination to pray for a mighty outpouring of the Holy Spirit over our land.

Chapter Thirteen

Fear not Little Flock,

Jesus said; "Do not fear, little flock, for it is your Father's good pleasure to give you the Kingdom" (Luke 12:32).

Fear scatters the sheep and prevents them from enjoying the green pasture that their shepherd has provided for them.

If it is our heavenly Father's good pleasure to give His kingdom to those who follow the Chief Shepherd, our Lord Jesus Christ, why then are so many Christians hesitant to take their rightful positions in His kingdom on earth? Why, instead of feasting on God's unending blessings which He so freely and abundantly offers to His children, do we seek to quench our thirst and satisfy our hunger with things that last for only a season, while ignoring an inner craving for intimate relationship with our heavenly Father?

Fear is one of the greatest obstacles to a Christian's victory in Christ. He cannot fully develop into spiritual maturity when crippled by fear. The voice of the Shepherd is imperceptible to him. Sometimes we hear well-meaning church leaders tell their people to pull themselves together and march as soldiers of the Lord to the beat of His drum, claiming Paul's words; "I can do all things through Christ who strengthens me" (Philippians 4:13), when in reality they can hardly muster enough strength for each day. They need to be reminded that in verses 11 and 12 the apostle states that he had learned to be content in whatever situation he experienced.

Praise God for those who lovingly care for the ones hardly able to walk, much less run the race. Some time ago, I received a call from a pastor asking if I would minister to a woman who needed heavy maintenance. It saddened me because too many precious Christians are falling through the cracks—while churches are busy with their programs.

Jesus, our blessed Shepherd never overlooked those calling out for help as He came close to them. The disciples attempted to get Jesus away from the "heavy maintenance" ones and urged Him to move on to more important matters. He received His directions from His Father and was unaffected by what He knew came out of selfish hearts.

"He will feed His flock like a Shepherd; He will gather the lambs with His arm, and carry them in His bosom, and gently lead those who are with young" (Isaiah 40:11). Our Lord Jesus wants us, His followers to do likewise. He wants to heal our hearts so that we remain intimately united to Him and not miss what our Father has preordained for us. Jesus promised that He will reward even the smallest deed done in His name. "For whoever gives you a cup of water to drink in My name, because you belong to Christ, assuredly, I say to you, he will by no means lose his reward" (Mark 9:41).

I believe that the time of Christ's return is closer than most of us realize. I pray for America every day, especially during this present period of political and financial uncertainty. Our nation is shaken by fear about the future. My fervent prayer is that the church of Jesus Christ will be shaken out of her spiritual complacency by a powerful move of the Holy Spirit. I ask that restricting denominational barriers will fall, for the Body of Christ to become united by the Father's love which is the bond of perfection, ready to meet Jesus. It was our

Lord's Prayer for His disciples and for all those who would believe in Him through their testimony.

Jesus spoke these words, lifted up His eyes to heaven, and said: "Father, the hour has come. Glorify Your Son, that Your Son also may glorify You. As You have given Him authority over all flesh, that He should give eternal life to as many as You have given Him. And this is eternal life, that they may know You, the only true God, and Jesus Christ whom You have sent. I have glorified You on the earth, I have finished the work You have given Me to do. And now, O Father, glorify Me together with Yourself, with the Glory which I had with You before the world was.

"I have manifested Your name to the men whom You have given Me out of the world. They were Yours, You gave them to Me, and they have kept Your word. I do not pray that You should take them out of the world, but that You should keep them from the evil one. They are not of the world, just as I am not of the world. Sanctify them by Your truth; Your word is truth. As You sent Me into the world, I also have sent them into the world. And for their sakes I sanctify Myself that they also may be sanctified by the truth. I do not pray for these alone, but also for those who will believe in Me through their word; that they all may be one, as You Father are in Me, and I in You; that they also may be one in Us, that the world may believe that You sent Me.

O righteous Father! The world has not known You, but I have known You; and these have known that You sent Me. And I have declared to them Your name, and will declare it, that the love with which You loved Me may be in them, and I in them." (Selected verses taken from John chapter 17)

It is not hard to understand that those without Christ are fearful about an uncertain future. However, it is regrettable so many believers in Christ live in fear, mainly because they are unable to enjoy intimacy with God. Without this strong foundation, Christians become vulnerable to all kinds of doom-sayers, whether secular or Christian. Thank God that the Bible is our source of comfort; and by resting in all the promises of our Lord and Savior Jesus Christ we can sleep peacefully.

I choose not to be lured into the trap of predicting a time-table for the End Time events. In the Holy Scriptures, God has revealed a plan which encompasses His entire creation from the beginning of time to all eternity. Those who believe in Him through His only begotten Son, the Lord Jesus Christ, will be joyful partakers of all His wonderful promises. Those who reject Him and His gift of salvation will end up in a place the Bible calls hell, which was prepared for Satan and his followers.

Of course, we are encouraged to humbly search the Scriptures in order to attain wisdom from our Creator and live righteously in the presence of God and men. We are also strongly encouraged to watch and pray so we will not fall into temptation, but always be ready when Christ calls us home into His presence. It displeases our Lord when we argue and create division among believers. We may disagree on secondary matters and still have loving relationships.

Jesus tells us that, when all these disturbing events begin to happen, to look up and lift our heads for our redemption draws near" (From Luke 21:28). I know, without any doubt, that I will be where Jesus is with all my friends, loved ones and millions who followed our Lord. There we will celebrate the Marriage Supper of the Lamb of God, when Jesus Christ, the Groom will be forever united to His Bride, the Universal Church.

Sometimes, when we share our excitement about our glorious future, while ministering to wounded people, we notice a sense of inner disconnectedness. After Jeanie and I establish a sense of mutual trust, we learn that, due to rejection early in life, they developed low self-esteem. Far too many have never experienced true, unconditional love and consequently become suspicious when someone gets too close to them, for fear of being hurt again. Only God's love can melt away those inner barriers.

On several occasions, after gaining access to their heart and while looking into their eyes, I asked them with a smile; "Has anyone ever told you, I love you?" The answer was usually; "never." Jeanie and I became convinced that our heavenly Father's love is the greatest healing power in the world.

Those who have been entrusted with the spreading of the Gospel of Jesus Christ, have an enormous responsibility to share the truth, permeated with the love of God, the fruit of the Holy Spirit, which is unique to the Christian faith. Unfortunately, the messengers of Jesus Christ are the ones least likely to receive healing for their own hearts; too many think they don't need it. Others do not dare to open their hearts for fear of losing respect and credibility in their community or church congregation.

I am aware that it is not easy to find an accountability partner. At times I believe that our friends in some of the traditional churches have an advantage over Evangelicals in that they confess their sins to one another (James 5:16). Others confess their sins to their priest or bishops and find absolution.

No matter how small your church group may be, and whether you meet in a home or in a church building, the promise of Jesus as recorded in Luke 12:32, applies to you, because God looks at the heart.

Chapter Fourteen

My Sheep Hear My Voice

Jesus said; "My sheep hear My voice and I know them, and they follow Me. And I give them eternal life, and they shall never perish; neither shall anyone snatch them out of My hand. My Father, who has given them to Me, is greater than all; and no one is able to snatch them out of My Father's hand. I and My Father are one" (John 10:27-30).

These words spoken by our Lord Jesus Christ constitute, to me, one of the most important and encouraging statements He has ever pronounced. His desire for us to be able to hear, understand and finally comprehend what Jesus, in agreement with His Father, conveys to us. Through my knowledge of the Spanish language, I think that the word "comprehend" goes beyond simply understanding, in that it expects an action on our part.

Hearing the voice of our Shepherd is neither inherited nor is it acquired by simply reading all kinds of books. I believe that Jesus speaks to every one of His followers, but truly hearing Him is a matter of the heart. At this point I must re-emphasize the need for our allegiance to our Lord who is our greatest teacher; and if we are willing to be still and know that He is our ALL, He will fine-tune our spiritual hearing and save us from unnecessary blunders. Perceiving our Shepherd's voice while not being ignorant of Satan's wicked devices, are essential in our walk with Christ.

Several weeks ago, we met a number of deeply wounded Christians who asked us for prayer ministry. Shortly before, I had a dream in regard to those who came for ministry. I saw them as small children holding on to Jesus' hand, and while the gentle Shepherd looked down to them, they looked up to Him with smiles on their faces. Suddenly, their smiles were gone as fear came over them. They had turned their faces away from Jesus and looked at a man with an open Bible in his hand, approaching them from the opposite direction. Confused by his unfriendly face and wildly gesticulating arms they looked up to Jesus and asked: "What does this man want, Lord?" "Just walk with Me and I will show you the way."

As mentioned earlier, I believe that our sanctification is unfolded through a three phase process; the pharisaic, brokenness, and the outflow of God's love. The timing and duration of each phase is determined by our obedience to our Master.

I am grateful for leaders and teachers that most powerfully influenced my walk with Jesus Christ. One of their greatest strengths was that they had humbled themselves under the mighty hand of God. By their "Christ-and others-centeredness" I could trust them because they exuded His love and compassion. The light they projected and their words spoken with grace and compassion provided the most fertile soil for the growth of my faith. When they looked at me, I knew they loved me and accepted me in spite of my idiosyncrasies; they exemplified Christ.

If the great apostle Paul, who after years of his dramatic encounter with the risen Christ, came to the conclusion that; "This is a faithful saying and worthy of all acceptance, that Christ Jesus came into the world to save sinners, of whom

I am chief" (1 Timothy 1:15), then I will add my name to the list and declare that God is not done with me! Praise the Lord that whatever remnant of the "Pharisee" within me is still alive, will be gone the instant I leave this "tent" to meet the King of Kings.

Praise God, that when we are home with our Lord Jesus Christ in Paradise, we will fully enjoy everything our heavenly Father has prepared for all who love Him. Only then will, "old things have passed away; behold all things have become new."